SEE SOMETHING SAY NOTHING

A HOMELAND SECURITY OFFICER EXPOSES THE GOVERNMENT'S SUBMISSION TO JIHAD

PHILIP HANEY & ART MOORE

RESOLUTE PRESS

SEE SOMETHING, SAY NOTHING

Book designed by Mark Karis

Paperback ISBN: 9781087913001

Library of Congress Cataloging-in-Publication Data: 2020946048

Printed in the United States of America

In loving memory of Philip Bruce Haney. A grateful nation salutes you, sir, for your relentless, costly, courageous pursuit of truth in fulfillment of your oath to support and defend the Constitution of the United States of America.

In loving memory of Francesca Maria Haney, Philip's faithful wife of forty-three years who stood with him through nine investigations.

Thank you, Geoffrey Stone and Mark Karis, for your excellent work on the hardcover edition and for helping launch the paperback edition. Thank you, Joseph Farah, for investing in the story.

TABLE OF CONTENTS

ACRONYMS USED IN *SEE SOMETHING, SAY NOTHING*

ACLU: American Civil Liberties Union

AMCLI: American Muslim Civic Leadership Institute

APHIS Animal and Plant Health Inspection Service

ATT: Advanced Targeting Team

ATU: Advanced Targeting Unit

CAIR: Council on American-Islamic Relations

CBP: Customs and Border Protection

CBPAS: Customs and Border Protection agricultural specialist

CBPO: Customs and Border Protection officer

CIA: Central Intelligence Agency

CIIG: Customs Intelligence Implementation Group

CRCL: Office of Civil Rights and Civil Liberties

CSCC: Center for Strategic Counterterrorism Communications

CTCC: Counter Terrorism Communications Center

CVE: Countering Violent Extremism

DDER: Deception Detection and Elicitation Response

DFO: District Field Office

DHS: Department of Homeland Security

DOD: Department of Defense

DOJ: Department of Justice

ECFR: European Council for Fatwa and Research

FBI: Federal Bureau of Investigation

FCNA: Fiqh Council of North America

FIS: Federal Inspection Station

FLETC: Federal Law Enforcement Training Center

FOIA: Freedom of Information Act

HLF: Holy Land Foundation

HSAC: Homeland Security Advisory Council

IAP: Islamic Association of Palestine

IAU: Islamic American University

ICE: Immigration and Customs Enforcement

ICSC: Islamic Center of Southern California

ICT: International Institute for Counter-Terrorism

IG: Inspector general

IIE: Institute for Islamic Education

IIIT: International Institute of Islamic Thought

IMMA: Institute of Muslim Minority Affairs

INS: Immigration and Naturalization Service

IRU: Intelligence Review Unit

IRW: Islamic Relief Worldwide

ISB: Islamic Society of Boston

ISNA: Islamic Society of North America

IUMS: International Union of Muslim Scholars

JTTF: Joint Terrorism Task Force

LEO: Law enforcement officer

LPR: Lawful permanent resident

MAS: Muslim American Society

MPAC: Muslim Public Affairs Council

MSA: Muslim Students Association

NAAE: National Association of Agricultural Employees

NAIT: North American Islamic Trust

NCTC: National Counterterrorism Center

NSCT: National Strategy for Counterterrorism

NTC: National Targeting Center

NTC-P: National Targeting Center-Passenger

NTEU: National Treasury Employees Union

ODNI: Office of the Director of National Intelligence

OFAB: One Face at the Border

OIC: Organization of the Islamic Conference

OIOC: Office of Intelligence and Operations Coordination

PAU: Passenger Analysis Unit

PPQ: Plant Protection and Quarantine

RAC: Resident agent in charge

SAC: Special agent in charge

SEFIU: Southeast Field Intelligence Unit

SME: Subject matter expert

TDY: temporary duty yonder

TECS: Treasury Enforcement Communications System

TJ: Tablighi Jamaat

TSA: Transportation Security Administration

UAE: United Arab Emirates

USCIS: U.S. Citizenship and Immigration Services

USDA: United States Department of Agriculture

PROLOGUE

As the shocking news spread of Philip Haney's death in February 2020, tributes flowed from across the nation. Whether from the halls of Congress, the national security community, or the grass roots of America, mourners regarded him not only as a "national treasure" but as a friend. He treated everyone the same.

That's why the label some critics ascribed to him, "anti-Muslim," clumsily missed the mark. He was in agreement with American Muslims who recognize the US Constitution as the supreme law of the land, affording them liberties they would not have in nations under Islamic law. And he took seriously the Muslim Brotherhood's stated ultimate aim of establishing a state ruled by Shariah.

Some mourners recalled that the soft-spoken, self-described "nerd"— who began as an entomologist—could easily be underestimated. Behind a disarming, playful demeanor was a focused, exceptionally brilliant, intrepid warrior for what is good, true and just. A man of deep faith, he saw himself first and foremost as a servant of God.

On the floor of the House of Representatives on February 26, 2020, Rep. Louie Gohmert, R-Texas, gave a lengthy tribute to Philip.

"He was one of the finest, most patriotic, competent people I've ever known in my life, a man of absolute honesty, complete integrity, who cared deeply about the future of this country," Gohmert said. "He also was a Christian brother, and that certainly affected so much of what he did."

The Texas lawmaker recalled that in June 2016, just weeks after the initial publication of *See Something*, Philip testified before a subcommittee of the Senate Judiciary Committee chaired by Sen. Ted Cruz, R-Texas. Titled "Willful Blindness: Consequences of Agency Efforts To Deemphasize Radical Islam in Combating Terrorism," the hearing probed the Obama administration's systematic "purge" of intelligence information. Two days later, Cruz confronted Department of Homeland Security Secretary Jeh Johnson with Philip's testimony, asking him if it was accurate.

"I have no idea," Johnson replied. "I don't know who Mr. Haney is. I wouldn't know him if he walked in the room."

"So, you have not investigated whether your department ordered documents to be modified?" Cruz followed up.

"No, I have not taken the time to investigate what Mr. Haney says. No." Johnson said.

However, six months earlier, Johnson had acknowledged at a gathering of Muslim university students that he was aware of Philip's claims. Responding to a question at the University of Michigan at Dearborn, Johnson said he had read an article Philip wrote in *The Hill*, the influential Capitol Hill newspaper. It was titled "DHS ordered me to scrub records of Muslims with terror ties."

So what *did* Jeh Johnson think about Philip Haney and his claims?

In May 2017, I flew to Los Angeles, where the American Freedom Alliance was to award Philip its American Freedom Award at its annual Conscience Awards Dinner.

At Los Angeles International Airport, I was walking down a long, virtually empty corridor when my eyes caught a gentleman to the right, slightly ahead of me. He looked awfully familiar. Could it be? I walked a little faster to come alongside him, and even then I wasn't sure.

I took a chance. "Mr. Johnson." He turned his head. It, indeed, was Jeh Johnson.

I introduced myself as the co-author of Philip Haney's book, noting

I was in town for an event to honor Philip for his service to the nation as a Homeland Security whistleblower.

"Do you remember Philip Haney?" I asked.

"Yes," he replied, pausing. "Did you see the exchange I had with Senator Cruz?"

"I did," I replied. "And, in fact, I'm still curious to hear what you thought about Mr. Haney's claims."

"Well, I'll put it this way," Johnson said, cordially. "I'm glad to be a private citizen."

Philip, who regarded himself as a "steward and a guardian" of his story until the day he died, regularly told audiences that he had not retired from the oath he took to support and defend the Constitution.

"I don't have any intention of stopping," he said at a December 2018 gathering. "I'm more focused now than ever."

In his speech accepting the AFA award in Los Angeles in May 2017, he said "the story is still in process."

"None of the cases I discuss in the book have been resolved to this very day," he said. "But it is my intention to remedy that. Those of you who believe in prayer, do pray for us, my wife, and me, because we intend to see this through to the end."

At the time of the publication of this edition, an investigation of Philip's death was underway by the Amador County Sheriff's Department in California with the assistance of the Federal Bureau of Investigation.

All of our questions may never be answered. What is clear is that the best way to honor Philip for his life and service is to become stewards of his story. Pass it on to others. Tell it to your representatives. Elect people to office who understand the problem. Run for office yourself.

Philip would point us to the inscription on one of the lesser known statues on the National Mall in Washington, where he made some fifty visits to members of Congress:

"Eternal vigilance is the price of liberty."

—ART MOORE, 2020

FOREWORD

As a member of the House Select Committee on Intelligence, I helped oversee the nation's clandestine services, focusing primarily on classified information related to the rise of terrorism through Islamic jihad. Ten years before I was appointed to the committee, America was attacked on September 11, 2001, by dedicated and trained young Muslim men. President George W. Bush and the US Congress responded by creating the Department of Homeland Security. Intended to thwart future terror attacks, airline security procedures were initiated at American airports together with security measures at nuclear power plants, water reservoirs, electrical power stations, and more.

Behind the scenes, our government hired men and women to create new security procedures to identify and to stop individuals who were terror risks from entering the United States. Other positions were created to look for patterns and links to terror organizations trying to bring down the United States both from within and without our borders.

The United States made a decision to go on offense to protect the American people, our property and our way of life against another 9/11. We now know that 9/11 was an attack by terrorists motivated by a literal belief in and active adherence to establishing Islamic sharia law in the US as the law of our land. But in the immediate aftermath of the 9/11 tragedy, our commander in chief, George W. Bush, and his administration publicly insisted Islam was a religion of peace.

To the American people, the "religion of peace" narrative sounded suspicious and didn't ring true to what the nation had just endured. They saw young, foreign-born Muslim men living in America on expired visas. Americans saw young men who intentionally trained for horrific attacks against our nation under the direction of the infamous terrorist that former President Bill Clinton chose to let get away in the 1990s—Osama bin Laden. Bin Laden was committed to acts of terrorism to advance the establishment of a global Islamic government, a caliphate ruled by Islamic sharia law. Bin Laden and his Muslim followers believed it was their duty to their god Allah to destroy America, which they regarded as a "friend of Satan."

Strangely, the US government willfully blinded itself to the Islamic terrorist motivation found in the guidebooks of Islam: the Quran and the Hadith. This motivation ignited violent terror against the United States and has only intensified around the world since. In other words, the official position of the US government regarding the origin of 9/11 was, "Don't believe your lyin' eyes!"

Enter Philip Haney. A founding member of the newly established Department of Homeland Security, Philip wasn't a guy looking to punch a clock until he could collect a pension check from the federal government. He dedicated himself, rather, to investigating the actual evidence of Islamic jihad as it really was, not as the forces of official bureaucratic political correctness deemed it should be.

As evidence of Philip's work ethic and value to DHS, he was granted numerous awards and certificates of commendation by his superiors. Living in post-9/11 America, citizens instinctively hoped and blindly trusted that our government had hired legions of Philip Haneys to diligently search for and uncover terror plots.

We wanted to believe our government was actively looking for clues and puzzle pieces to expose terror plots before another 9/11 unfolded. Philip did exactly that. He punched above his weight and amazingly uncovered networks and names of terrorists, and more. He went to his superiors with his information, but was actively undermined and shut down.

His work as an exemplary DHS employee was brought to my attention as a member of the United States Congress. After the 2010 elections, when I was appointed to serve on the House Select Committee on Intelligence, I learned and came to appreciate that the best intelligence information is grounded in truth: good, bad, or ugly.

I also learned that politically motivated interpretations of intelligence, whether shaded by political correctness, or by a desire not to embarrass a boss, or for other selfish reasons could get innocent people killed. Our intelligence analysts, like Philip at DHS, worked extremely hard to provide decision-makers like me with accurate, truthful information. Now, for the first time, readers will have the opportunity to learn the shocking truth of what Philip uncovered about terrorist networks operating in and outside the United States.

In *See Something, Say Nothing* you will learn how Philip Haney was not only shut down by his superiors at DHS but how he was silenced at a critical moment in the war on terror. These tragic, treasonous actions perhaps allowed the San Bernardino, California, shooters to enter the United States rather than be exposed and denied entry. If we had a sane administration, Philip's superiors would have listened to his pleas and would have rewarded rather than punished his service. Could Philip Haney's prescient warnings have saved innocent Americans from the San Bernardino tragedy? Read on and you decide.

For me, upon meeting Philip it was quickly apparent that he was legit and that the information he put together was profoundly important to protecting the safety of our nation. It was outrageously inexplicable that Philip was shut down by his superiors just as terror threats against the United States grew exponentially by the day, in light of President Obama's obviously failed foreign policy decisions.

I believed Philip and did everything I could within my power to introduce him to the decision-makers in DC who had the authority to see to it that his profound discoveries could be heard and heeded—before it was too late.

I thank God for this nation, and I thank God for patriots like Philip, a federal employee who risked much during his exemplary career to keep you and me safe from terrorists. Philip Haney is a national treasure. His discoveries deserve the thanks, respect, admiration, and appreciation of every American citizen. As a civilian and as a former member of the US Congress, I say, *Thank you Philip Haney for risking your all to keep our nation safe. You've demonstrated courage under fire.*

—US REP. MICHELE BACHMANN, FORMER MEMBER OF THE US CONGRESS
AND THE HOUSE SELECT COMMITTEE ON INTELLIGENCE

INTRODUCTION

At airports, train stations, sporting events, and just about anywhere Americans congregate in significant numbers, signs posted by the Department of Homeland Security urge, "If you see something, say something."

The campaign's stated aim is to "empower everyday citizens to protect their neighbors and the communities they call home by recognizing and reporting suspicious activity."[1]

"Tell the authorities who, when, and where you saw something, and specifically what you saw," the federal government asks of its citizens.[2]

When Philip Haney, a founding member of the DHS, saw something, he went above and beyond the call of duty to say something, according to his immediate superiors, who formally commended him numerous times for identifying direct and potential threats to the nation's security.

In his roles as an officer with the agency's Customs and Border Protection division, the nation's gatekeeper, and as a specialist at the National Targeting Center, the hub of intelligence for the CBP's counterterrorism efforts, he meticulously assembled actionable and background intelligence on hundreds of individuals and organizations.

But beginning with the later years of the George W. Bush administration and accelerating under the Obama administration, his efforts to report "suspicious activity" were met with punishing opposition.

Amid pressure from many of the very Muslim Brotherhood leaders he identified as threats to national security, a policy emerged that forbade mention of Islam in association with terrorism and downplayed supremacist Islam as just one among many violent ideological movements.

The policy, known as Countering Violent Extremism,[3] or CVE, forced Haney into a ten-year adversarial relationship with the agency's politically appointed officials and their subordinates.

While Haney was being commended by his colleagues and immediate superiors for identifying terrorist threats, his agency moved to push him out as it began exchanging the objective of enforcing the law with promoting civil liberties for Muslims.

He found himself at the center of many of his agency's most seminal events since its founding, including the Boston Marathon bombing, which exposed the deadly consequences of the policy and set in motion an apparent cover-up on behalf of a major ally that continues to this day.

He witnessed the federal government's development and execution of a "hands-off" policy specifically designed to protect Muslim leaders with known ties to Islamic supremacism and violent jihad, allowing them to freely enter and exit the United States.

He saw leaders of Muslim Brotherhood front groups invited into the highest chambers of power and given access to sensitive information to allow them to shape the nation's security policy.

When Philip Haney saw something and said something, some of his bosses—all the way up to the White House—responded not with gratefulness but with orders to sanitize or eliminate the information and launch investigations against *him* instead of the documented threats to the nation's security.

Newly retired, he's telling his story to the public for the first time in further fulfillment of his oath to "support and defend the Constitution of the United States against all enemies, foreign and domestic."

1

FROM JEDDAH TO SAN BERNARDINO

I stood at a tinted window on the second floor of the Customs and Border Protection agency's National Targeting Center (NTC) headquarters on March 27, 2012, on the outskirts of the nation's capital as a State Department van approached the entrance.

From the outside, the NTC building in Reston, Virginia, is a nondescript, dark-paned, office-park structure. On the inside, it looks like a scene from a Hollywood spy thriller: an intelligence nerve center of earnest and focused faces lit by the glow of giant TV screens and hundreds of computer monitors.

Established shortly after the 9/11 attacks, the NTC provides background and actionable intelligence in real time to frontline Department of Homeland Security (DHS) officers trying to stop people who pose a threat to the nation's security from entering through more than 350 air, land, and seaports across the country.

As a Customs and Border Protection officer from Atlanta since the formation of DHS in 2003, I was on a temporary-duty assignment at the NTC that had begun in November 2011. I was now working with the Advanced Targeting Team, the center's top unit.

The white State Department van pulled up to the curb, and seven men in black suits filed out. Up the stairs came an entourage of lawyers, along with three executive-level officials, who had come in a separate vehicle.

Assembled at a long oval table with my NTC colleagues, the officials wanted to talk about an initiative I helped launch, partly in response to a request by members of Congress to plug security holes in the Visa Waiver Program, which allows nearly 20 million people from thirty-eight friendly countries to enter the United States without a visa.

The officials apparently had "concerns" about our effort, which in government vernacular is never a good sign.

The project focused on vetting members of a worldwide Islamic group with more than 70 million members, known as Tablighi Jamaat.

Derived from the Deobandi movement in India, Tablighi Jamaat, or "the party of the promoters," trains and sends out Islamic missionaries in groups of two, three, or more who go door to door, visiting mosques and encouraging their Muslim brethren to live the strict, ascetic lifestyle of Islam's prophet, Muhammad.

The NTC's Tablighi Jamaat Initiative was a distinct investigative effort that connected members of the movement to terrorist organizing and financing at the highest levels, including Hamas and al-Qaeda. It had resulted in twelve hundred law-enforcement actions, including visa refusals, visa-waiver cancellations, and denial of entry. All of this happened in just the first nine months of the initiative, which had been approved by the DHS chief counsel in August 2011.

Observing from my seat in the far corner of the room, I never said a word during the entire meeting, but I listened carefully while taking notes in shorthand.

"We're here today because we just want to make sure we're all on the same page on this issue. We know that members of Tablighi Jamaat are fundamentalists, but they're not terrorists," a State Department official insisted.

"We look really closely at the Tablighi Jamaat people [who apply for visas], but we can't stereotype them," he explained. "Just because they belong to an Islamic group, it doesn't mean they are terrorists themselves."

He acknowledged "vetting them is a challenge" but concluded,

"We all know the group is way too big just to say that membership alone makes them ineligible for a visa." He then disclosed that "human rights," the State Department's Civil Rights Division, is working with Immigration and Customs Enforcement on the issue.

In a PowerPoint presentation we had prepared to make our case, a colleague of mine pointed out that US foreign consulates had approved only 25 percent of the requests for visas made by individuals affiliated with Tablighi Jamaat.

There was total silence in the room for some ten seconds.

It wasn't Customs and Border Protection that was rejecting Tablighi Jamaat visa applicants at a rate of 75 percent. Instead, as we showed them, it was their own consulate officers who didn't have confidence in these people.

One of the State Department lawyers raised his hand.

"How can we get that information in the PowerPoint to all of our consulate offices?"

At that moment, the scope of our initiative was about to go global. Or so we thought.

Despite the overwhelming evidence, not only did the State Department not spread the information and designate Tablighi Jamaat as a terrorist group, but the Obama administration effectively shut down our initiative, ordering that intelligence based on religious affiliation be disregarded on the basis of civil rights and civil liberties concerns.

By the time of that March 2012 visit from the State Department, I had watched the DHS, beginning with the George W. Bush administration, move from a law-enforcement-based approach to national security to a "civil rights"–based policy that became known as Countering Violent Extremism, or CVE.

Emphasizing "engagement and dialogue," CVE focuses on protecting civil rights and civil liberties. Not of American citizens in general, but particularly of Muslims, both citizens and foreigners, who in many instances are associated with a threat to the nation's security.

The new emphasis already had gained steam in 2009 when I was ordered to remove information from more than eight hundred records concerning individuals associated with Muslim Brotherhood front groups in the United States who had proven links to the Palestinian terrorist organization Hamas. The links had been verified in federal court in the 2008 Holy Land Foundation trial, the largest terror-financing trial in US history.

It was the keeper of the administration's CVE policy—the DHS Office of Civil Rights and Civil Liberties—that, together with the State Department, "moved" our Tablighi Jamaat Initiative "in other directions," as verified by Department of Homeland Security memos obtained through a Freedom of Information Act request.

Ultimately, interfering in the Tablighi Jamaat Initiative at NTC in 2012 prevented us from effectively intervening against individuals and organizations linked to this dangerous worldwide movement.

SAN BERNARDINO

Three years later, in December 2015, two figures linked to the Deobandi movement, Syed Rizwan Farook and his wife, Tashfeen Malik, fired automatic weapons at a holiday party in San Bernardino, California, killing fourteen people and wounding twenty-one after amassing a large stockpile of weapons, ammunition, and bomb-making equipment in their home.

Farook was described as a devout Muslim who showed up to pray every day at a Deobandi-affiliated mosque in the San Bernardino suburb of Muscoy, called the Dar Al Uloom al Islamiyah. Dar Al Uloom, which means "house of knowledge," is a brand name for all of the Deobandi schools in the world, including several in the United States.

Farook also had attained the status of *hafiz*, meaning he had been certified by Deobandi imams as having memorized the entire Quran. Consequently, he likely was well known within the community and had earned prestige and esteem for his pious devotion to the teachings and laws of Islam.

Two brothers who attended the Dar Al Uloom mosque with Farook described him as "a very nice person, very soft."[1] By the way, that is exactly how Anwar al-Awlaki was described before he became the world's leading English-speaking promoter of jihad against the West, particularly against America. It turned out that Farook, according to an FBI affidavit, listened to Awlaki's recorded sermons.

"We never saw him raise his voice. We never saw him curse at anyone, disrespect anyone. He was always a very nice guy, always very simple, very straightforward," Nizaam Ali, twenty-three, told NBC News of Farook. "He had a lot of manners."[2]

Of particular interest to me was the criminal complaint filed against suspected accomplice Enrique Marquez by FBI special agent Joel T. Anderson. It notes that in late 2005, Marquez and Farook "discussed the Tablighi Jamaat movement and MARQUEZ began to pray more frequently at Farook's residence."[3]

That short statement from paragraph 23 of the FBI affidavit offers insight into how members of Tablighi Jamaat operate. They are "promoters of Islam," or what we in the West would call "proselytizers" or "evangelists."

The FBI notation also counters a prevailing belief that "radicalization" largely takes place via the amorphous Internet rather than through direct, one-on-one interaction, as with most other human activity.

Farook's wife, Malik, appears to have been linked to the Deobandi movement either through her study at the Al-Huda girls school—another worldwide network of fundamentalist *Salafi* schools, with locations in the United States and Canada—or through her possible affiliation with the Lal Masjid, the "Red Mosque," in Islamabad, Pakistan. The Lal Masjid is well known in Pakistan and Afghanistan as a training center for jihadists who are in transit to the battlefield.

LAW ENFORCEMENT 101

The San Bernardino killer Farook fit the profile of the Tablighi Jamaat members I regularly interviewed when they came through Hartsfield–Jackson Atlanta International Airport, known as the world's busiest airport by passenger traffic.

My law enforcement colleagues and I would not necessarily have regarded Farook as a potential threat if he had been known to have "raised his voice" or "cursed" or "disrespected" someone.

Instead, it was specifically because of his overt adherence to a particular religious doctrine and global movement that attention should have been paid to him when he reentered the United States from his 2014 trip to Saudi Arabia, where he met the woman who became his fiancée.

A surveillance camera image that captured the couple July 27, 2014, standing in line at customs in Chicago showed Malik in a black *abaya*—a cloak typical of Saudi Arabia that covers a woman's hair and body—and Farook with an Islamic headdress and a beard.

Had I inspected the photograph in Farook's passport showing him with no beard or Islamic headdress, I would have been curious about what he had been doing in the meantime.

While dressing in traditional Muslim clothing is certainly not in itself a portent of a threat, when combined with other information a portrait could emerge of a young American citizen who had undergone a radical transformation and now posed a potential security risk.

Farook's relatively abrupt change in appearance and his association with the Tablighi Jamaat movement would have prompted me to ask him a few more questions, either while he was standing in line or at the counter as I processed his passport.

It's basic, commonsense Law Enforcement 101.

If the Tablighi Jamaat Initiative had not been shut down in 2012, it's plausible he would have been added to our database and possibly to the Terrorist Screening Center's no-fly list, because of his association with the San Bernardino mosque.

It is also just as plausible that Farook's intended fiancée would have been denied a K-1 visa, either because of his affiliation with the California mosque or because of her affiliation with the Al-Huda school. Both institutions were already part of the Tablighi Jamaat Initiative by mid-2012.

As it was, DHS relied, for example, on information she supplied on immigration Form I-485 in response to questions such as whether or not she had used or sold weapons or engaged in "terrorist activity."[4]

She, to no one's surprise, said no before amassing a huge stockpile of assault weapons, ammunition, and explosive devices in their Redlands, California, residence.

"ARMY OF DARKNESS"

The Deobandi school of Sunni Islam, which emerged in northern India in the late nineteenth century, was dubbed in the Urdu language *Tablighi Jamaat*, or proselytizing group. Later, in Arabic, it became known as *Dawah and Tabligh*, meaning "calling and proselytizing."

While relatively unknown in the United States, in Britain and elsewhere it is known as the "Army of Darkness" because of its secretive way of moving through the world's cities and towns, particularly in English-speaking countries that are not as familiar with the movement.

Mohammad Sidique Khan, who plotted the July 2005 terror attacks in London, prayed at a Dawah and Tabligh–affiliated mosque in northern England. John Walker Lindh, an American who fought for the Taliban, was also believed to have attended Dawah meetings in the United States.

The movement, with an estimated 70 million followers worldwide, is also connected to the "Portland Seven" group of Muslims in Oregon arrested in 2002 and convicted of attempting to join al-Qaeda forces fighting the United States, the six Yemeni-Americans in Buffalo convicted of aiding al-Qaeda, the 2006 transatlantic aircraft plot, the 2007 London car bombing attempt, and the 2007 Glasgow Airport attack.[5]

In Atlanta, I obtained valuable information from the foreign Tablighi Jamaat members I interviewed, including where they were going, what mosques they were visiting, the names of the imams, letters of invitation, phone numbers, and the names of their colleagues. All of this information eventually became part of the NTC's Tablighi Jamaat Initiative.

The TJ members would either be flagged before arrival by Customs and Border Protection (CBP) officers with expertise in analysis, or referred to me by an officer in "primary," the initial point of contact for passengers going through customs. If I saw one or more waiting in line, I would tell my colleagues who were assigned to work the line, "That's a Tablighi Jamaat member; when he comes through the line, send him over to my booth, and I'll interview him."

Even though I was never technically assigned to "secondary"—where passengers who merit further questioning are sent—I performed secondary duties by request. Whenever they would get a hard case, a supervisor would call me in my booth, or they would page me on the intercom.

After the interviews, I wrote a summary of what I found and posted it in the database, called TECS, the Treasury Enforcement Communications System.

Collecting this kind of relevant data over time is what enables law enforcement officers to "connect the dots" and determine whether or not a threat to the homeland exists. TECS is an archive database, meaning that anyone at any other port in the country can have instant access to information that other CBP officers enter into the system.

THE MADRASSA BOYS

At my post in Atlanta, I regularly encountered over several years a group of twenty-five to thirty young Deoband–Tablighi Jamaat members who traveled between their homes in the United States and an overseas madrassa. We got to know one another so well that I dubbed them the "Madrassa Boys," while they called me "the guy with the white hair."

I was watching the first generation of US citizens and lawful permanent residents to go through the seven-year program that prepared them to become imams.

It was fascinating to see them transform not only from boys to young men but also into pious, sharia-compliant candidates for positions of leadership within their communities.

Nearly all were the sons of immigrants who had been selected between the ages of ten and twelve by their parents and the Shura Council, the designated leadership of the local mosque, to train to become imams.

The boys were taken out of public school and put in a parallel madrassa system in the United States. Most never graduated high school or even received a GED. Instead, they concentrated on memorizing the Quran, and by the time they were of the age when students normally graduate from high school, they were qualified to leave America and go to the Darul Uloom Zakariyya madrassa in Johannesburg, South Africa.

Remarkably, the federal government already knew that the madrassa and others like it are centers of "radicalization." Nevertheless, these American citizens and permanent residents had been allowed to travel back and forth through US borders.

I still remember the names of some of the Madrassa Boys, and I fear that one day, one or more of them may turn up in the news as did Syed Farook, or Muhammad Abdulazeez, who opened fire on two military recruitment centers in Chattanooga, Tennessee, on July 16, 2015, killing four Marines and a Navy sailor, and wounding a police officer before he was finally killed by police in a gunfight.

DEVELOPING THE CASE

My colleagues and I interviewed the Madrassa Boys annually for four straight years when they returned to the United States from South Africa for the Islamic month of Ramadan.

It was almost funny, watching them spot me as they came through the customs line in Atlanta, then shake their heads with a look of, "Oh, no, it's him again, the guy with the white hair."

In the first year, I obtained an occasional address and the name of a mosque or two. By the second year, I was gathering considerably more biometric information, including names of family members and their imams.

In other words, we were connecting the dots.

Often, people who end up involved in terrorism are drawn in by someone in their own family. This linkage is well known within the intelligence community and is one of the most important "dots" when a case is being developed.

A good example of this was the close relationship between Syed Farook and Enrique Marquez Jr., who was suspected of supplying the rifles for the San Bernardino attack. Marquez was converted to Islam through Farook in 2005 and fraudulently married the sister of Farook's brother's wife.

HOW DID YOU KNOW?

One Sunday morning, June 19, 2011, William Ferri, assistant port director in charge of passengers at five airports in the metro New York area as well as the seaport of New York and New Jersey, placed a call to me on my personal line.

DHS policy forbids CBP officers from answering their personal phones on the line, so as soon as there was a pause in the flow of passengers, I went to the break room and returned his call.

"Haney," he said, "we've got these five guys at the port, and I don't know what to ask them."

What I didn't know at the time was that Ferri was at home and that the watch commander on duty at Newark had reached out to him.

I told him, "Don't let them go. They're Tablighi Jamaat, and they're going to Masjid Al-Falah in Corona-Queens, New York."

The New York mosque is the US headquarters of Tablighi Jamaat. In Arabic, Al-Falah means "success and well-being," especially with regard to conforming to the commands of Allah regarding daily living, such as not drinking alcohol.

So, Ferri called back the watch commander at Newark, telling him, "Don't let those guys go; they're Tablighi Jamaat, and they're going to Masjid Al-Falah in Corona-Queens, New York!"

The watch commander replied, "Okay, but how the hell did you know that? You're not even here at the port."

All five, traveling on the Visa Waiver Program, were denied entry.

The Newark Tablighi Jamaat case became one of the key components of the emerging Tablighi Jamaat Initiative.

Remarkably, Ferri had served as an Internal Affairs fact finder the first of nine times I was investigated during the course of my career. We met when he interviewed me in Atlanta on December 14, 2006, and four and a half years later, we broke a major case together.

GOING TO NTC

By late 2011, it was clear that my colleagues and I in Atlanta had put together a major case on Tablighi Jamaat, so I developed a PowerPoint presentation on my findings and presented it to our port director, Stephen Kremer, on October 26, 2011. CBP supervisors Frank Rodriguez and William Brannen also watched as I sat in Kremer's seat, and they took seats on the other side of his desk.

I told Kremer my goal was to "knock you off your chair in the first ten to fifteen seconds of this presentation."

I guess I did, because as soon as I was done, he looked right at me and said, "Haney, you're going to NTC."

I began my temporary duty yonder assignment, or TDY, at the NTC in late November 2011 with the intensive, three-week training program. Shortly after I was "released to the floor" and settled in to the high-speed pace of the NTC work routine, they transferred me over to the Advanced Targeting Team.

Now, I was working on my own case at NTC, building on what we had already learned in Atlanta and in a few other ports about Tablighi Jamaat. As we brought the case up to speed, it quickly grew in status from a collection of local events to a national "project" and soon a global "initiative," the highest-level designation at NTC.

It is important to note that the initiative had been authorized by the DHS chief counsel on August 30, 2011.

Along with the chief counsel's authorization and my port director's approval, I received an invitation letter from the NTC on November 7, 2011:

The intent of this memorandum is to solicit assistance in the operation and research associated to NTC-P Event [author's redaction] regarding research related to the Tablighi Jamaat (TJ) organization. I have been working extensively with CBPO P. B. Haney assigned to CBP-ATL and he has been instrumental in providing a background on TJ, as well as research dating back over two years of possible TJ member encounters and suspected destination addresses which have links to terrorism. CBPO Haney has been an essential part of this operation and his research is still being looked at for further links and possible Visa/ESTA denials and revocations. CBPO Haney continues to be a valuable asset in developing more names, addresses, and leads of TJ members.

The spreadsheet that formed the heart of the initiative became larger each day, soon expanding into hundreds of entries. We began to refuse admission to groups of three or four Tablighi Jamaat members at a time as they attempted to enter America at airports or land border stations.

Underscoring the importance of the case, we also found that about 25 percent of remaining detainees at the US prison at Guantánamo Bay, Cuba, were affiliated with Tablighi Jamaat.

COMMENDATION

At NTC, I continued to enter Tablighi Jamaat–affiliated subjects into the system, eventually expanding the entries to more than sixteen hundred, while also identifying more than three hundred individuals with potential ties to terrorism.

John Maulella, NTC's program manager for training, became one of my NTC friends, as well as a colleague who knew about my work with the TJ Initiative. One afternoon in February 2012, I took my wife, Dr. Francesca Maria, on a mini-tour of NTC, and we went and sat in his office.

He looked right at my wife, then pointed at me and said, "Your husband is a superstar."

She said, "I know."

Maulella told her, "We never send TDY'ers over to the Advanced Targeting Team. It's unprecedented. And not only is he on the team, but he's working on his own case. This has never happened before."

At the end of my six-month TDY assignment, June 8, 2012, I received a commendation letter from NTC director Donald Conroy, for my "outstanding contributions."

"Your display of dedication and effort in the fight against terrorism have been exemplary," he wrote, adding that my "expertise and experience have been invaluable while assigned to the Advanced Targeting Team (ATT).

"Your research on the 'Tablighi Jamaat Initiative' has assisted in the identification of over 300 persons with possible connections to terrorism," he said. "The NTC-P looks forward to your continuing support and assistance in the Program."

CASE DESTROYED

Before my tour of duty ended in June 2012, management at NTC offered to let me extend for another three-month tour. I tried to persuade my port director in writing and on the phone to let me stay, but my request was denied, and I had to return back home to the Port of Atlanta.

Almost immediately, Port Director Kremer assigned me to work with Supervisor Smith (not his real name), who was in charge of a newly formed special detail to analyze the statistics on the port's annual seizures of drugs, currency, and other contraband.

After we finished the initial assignment, we started working on other unsolved cases. One example was the theft of airport rental cars by a suspect with at least fifteen different names and ten different birthdates, who would rent the cars under a false ID and never bring them back.

Up to that point, no one could break the case, but I found the culprit. He was a naturalized citizen with a US passport who was originally from the West African country of Mauritania. And not only did we find the suspect; we also found his entire network of accomplices.

Breaking a case of that kind requires the same kind of intense database research and analysis that made our Tablighi Jamaat case so successful.

As Smith and I continued working together, I happened to come across an individual I recognized from an earlier case who was also linked to the Institute for Islamic Education. One of many US organizations in the Tablighi Jamaat network, the IIE was educating young American Muslim boys, just like the Madrassa Boys I interviewed, in the fine points of Islamic theology and sharia.

As I reviewed the IIE website, I noticed that it was offering these young students the option of memorizing the entire Quran, to become hafiz. The discovery was doubly important because I could see the IIE tied not only to the Madrassa Boys' case but also to the TJ Initiative. I brought this to the attention of Smith, and he immediately told me to go ahead and develop the case.

By the time I had finished researching and compiling all the links, I had found sixty-seven individuals or organizations that were linked to the IIE network, including some of the same Darul Uloom madrassas we had already included in the Madrassa Boys case and the TJ Initiative.

To make the case stronger, I sent all of the raw data up to a colleague at NTC. After he ran it through the "high side" and added relevant details to the spreadsheet for the case, I saw that virtually every single organization and individual in the IIE case had what we call "derogatory information."

It was a very solid case, verifying the same trends we were already tracking in the TJ Initiative. As some might say, it was a grand slam, a classic "connect the dots" law enforcement case.

So, we put the case report and all 67 linked records into the system on August 22, 2012. As soon as we downloaded it into TECS, we started getting hits back from our colleagues across the country, who were reading the report and cross-checking the information for possible links to individuals and organizations in their own regions.

Right after that, I took two weeks of annual leave and went to see my family in California.

Before I even got back from vacation, Smith called me.

"Haney, we've got a problem," he said. "They deleted all of your records out of the system. All 67 of them."

This time, I thought, they didn't just modify them, as happened in 2009 with 818 TECS records (more about that later). Instead, they completely obliterated the case by removing all 67 of the linked records from the system.

I know it happened, because my records were all tagged, so that whenever anyone else looked at them, I received an e-mail notification. The function was designed to help the original record owner keep track of how his or her case was developing in other ports.

Deleting TECS records requires hitting a precise series of keystrokes. Since all 67 records were removed from the system in fewer than forty-five minutes, they literally deleted them as fast as they could go from one record to the next.

But by the time they were finished, I had 67 e-mail notifications stacked in my in-box.

Smith and I had put together a strong law-enforcement case, with numerous solid ties to other ongoing cases. They completely destroyed the work we did, including all of the updated passport numbers, personal data, and background information I had entered on all of the individuals affiliated with the IIE network.

As my first-line supervisor, Smith had approved the records. When ordered by upper management to remove the records himself, he refused, he later told me.

Normally, refusing such a direct order would be a serious infraction, but he was never written up for what he did. Perhaps it was because upper management also knew that removing the records was wrong.

But deleting records was just the beginning. As soon as I returned from vacation on October 1, 2012, I was called into the port director's office, where members of management laid several papers on the table and told me to sign them.

"You are now being investigated for misuse of TECS."

The Madrassa Boys case, the Tablighi Jamaat Initiative, and the IIE case had all demonstrated the legitimacy of the concerns Congress expressed publicly about the "radicalization" of US citizens and the failure to connect the dots, particularly following the 2009 Christmas Day bombing attempt by Umar Farouk Abdulmutallab, the "Underwear Bomber."

But, now, here I was, being investigated once again by my own agency, for doing exactly what Congress had commissioned us to do.

Three years later, on December 10, 2015, as details of the San Bernardino shooting were still emerging, I appeared on Megyn Kelly's Fox News Channel program, *The Kelly File*, to talk about the Tablighi Jamaat case and its relationship to the massacre. The next morning, Smith called me, saying that all he could think about were the families of the people who were killed by Syed Farook and Tashfeen Malik.

2

FINDING THE TRAIL

On the morning of September 11, 2001, I was checking e-mails and reviewing the news headlines at my desk in the Department of Agriculture headquarters in downtown Atlanta. I was managing about twenty employees at the time in the department's nursery inspection program. From my window, I could see the sunrise reflecting off the gold dome of Georgia's capitol building.

At 8:46 a.m., American Airlines flight 11 flew into the North Tower of the World Trade Center at more than 460 miles per hour. Moments later, Yahoo! posted a photograph of black smoke billowing out of a huge hole near the top of the North Tower, and I knew the world would never be the same.

I stood up from my desk, walked into the hallway that led to the other offices in our group, and found my colleagues gathered there. "There's going to be a war," I told them.

A few days later, I met with Sen. Max Cleland, D-GA, and his staff in his Atlanta office, and offered my services to help protect our country.

Cleland was personally familiar with war. A triple amputee, he had received the Silver Star and the Bronze Star for his actions in combat in Vietnam.

In response to my offer, Cleland wrote a letter on my behalf to Tom Ridge, the assistant to President George W. Bush in the Office of

Homeland Security, which was created just eleven days after 9/11 and was still located in the White House.

In his December 17, 2001, letter, Cleland wrote:

> It is a pleasure to call your attention to the résumé of Mr. Philip Haney. Mr. Haney is interested in offering what services he can to our government. He is familiar with Middle Eastern culture, and feels he could be of value in our country's cause. I'm forwarding his information to you in hope that you will give him every consideration, for a position with the Office of Homeland Defense.

Yes, Cleland really did say *Office of Homeland Defense.* It was just the beginning of an unprecedented effort to unite disparate agencies tasked with protecting the nation's borders and keeping the peace.

A few days after the letter was sent, Ridge announced that the White House had settled on "substantial increases in spending" that would place the greatest emphasis on prevention of "renewed terrorism" and on bolstering the capacity of first responders and public health care agencies.[1]

On January 8, 2002, I sent a follow-up letter to Ridge, stating that I was "both encouraged and impressed by Senator Cleland's actions on my behalf, and look forward to what opportunities may develop from his kind endorsement."

A couple of months later, on March 26, 2002, Clay Johnson, assistant to the president for presidential personnel and deputy to the chief of staff, replied to Cleland:

> The outpouring of support nationwide has been exceptional as we continue to receive thousands of resumes from qualified candidates. Please be assured that your candidate will receive full consideration as we work to select those to serve the President and the country.

Cleland sent me a personal note assuring me I was still under consideration. But never one to sit idly by, I had also applied for a new position with the United States Department of Agriculture's Plant Protection and Quarantine (PPQ) division and was selected as a PPQ officer on

May 16, 2002. I was to be stationed at the Hartsfield–Jackson Atlanta International Airport.

It was to become just one of many remarkable confluences of events that led me into the Department of Homeland Security's Customs and Border Protection division, where I eventually became an armed law enforcement officer (LEO) and subject matter expert (SME) in counterterrorism, and in the strategy and tactics of the global Islamic movement, with an emphasis on Quranic Arabic.

On May 28, 2002, I submitted my letter of resignation from the Georgia Department of Agriculture to commissioner Tommy Irvin and reported for duty at my new position as a PPQ officer on June 3, 2002.

Later that year, Cleland lost his Senate seat to Republican Saxby Chambliss, and he wrote me a kind letter on December 19, 2002, suggesting who to contact if I wished to pursue an appointment to the Office of Homeland Security. He said it was "a particular honor that you allowed me to help you personally. Thank you for the privilege, and I wish you all the best."

I'm grateful to Max Cleland for his encouragement and support, which helped lead to the remarkable events that were to unfold in my life.

THE HALCYON YEARS

Meanwhile, as I was settling into my new job as a PPQ officer, the brand-new Department of Homeland Security was beginning to take shape.

The formal proposal to create the DHS, submitted in June 2002, characterized it as the "most significant transformation of the U.S. government in over a half-century" and "one more key step in the President's national strategy for homeland security."[2]

Next came the Homeland Security Act, a 187-page bill announced by President Bush on November 25, 2002.[3] Passed by the House July 25–26, 2002, it went through numerous revisions before it was considered and passed by the Senate on November 19, 2002, then reconsidered and passed in its final version by the House on November 22, 2002.

In January 2003, a list of the twenty-two federal agencies that would soon be consolidated into DHS was published,[4] followed by the March 1, 2003, announcement that DHS would become a "stand-alone, Cabinet-level department, to further coordinate and unify national homeland security efforts, opening its doors."[5]

As it turned out, one of the twenty-two federal agencies that would be blended into DHS was a relatively small USDA subagency called Animal and Plant Health Inspection Service (APHIS). Snuggled within APHIS was an even smaller subagency, called Plant Protection and Quarantine, which was precisely the agency that had just employed me.

I was now poised to become part of the agency for which Senator Cleland had recommended me, except that it would happen in a way that neither one of us had imagined.

A DIFFERENT ERA

In the process of becoming a stand-alone agency on March 1, 2003, about twelve hundred PPQ officers were enfolded into what became known as Customs and Border Protection. The new CBP brought under its umbrella career personnel from three formerly independent agencies: the Immigration and Naturalization Service, which was formerly part of the Department of Justice; the US Customs Service, previously part of the Department of the Treasury; and the selected officers from the PPQ.

The PPQ itself is still part of the Department of Agriculture. Since DHS never intended to absorb all of USDA-PPQ into CBP, those of us who were selected had to be given a new title and officially converted from GS-0401 federal agricultural officers to CBP agricultural specialists (CBPAS).

On February 19, 2003, we received a formal notification:

> The events of September 11, 2001, and others that have followed, demonstrated to all American that we are living in a different era with different threats. All Americans now realize that border security is no longer something to be taken for granted. Your position has been identified as one of the APHIS positions to be transferred; therefore, you will be transferred to the Department of Homeland Security on March 1, 2003.

To reinforce the seriousness of our mission, Secretary Ridge sent each new member of DHS an attractive signed and dated certificate that read:

> Be it known that Philip B. Haney is a Founding Member of the Department of Homeland Security, dedicated to preventing terrorist attacks within the United States, reducing America's vulnerability to terrorism, and minimizing the damage from potential attacks and natural disasters.

It was a simple, straightforward mandate, with a threefold emphasis on terrorism.

In addition, all of us—at ICE, Customs, and PPQ—retired our old uniforms and began wearing the now-familiar blue uniform and gold badge.

On March 21, 2003, my colleagues and I in "legacy agriculture" received a formal notification from PPQ deputy administrator Richard L. Dunkle:

> Your work and commitment to the [PPQ] mission honor that history. Now, you are part of another historic moment. In transferring to . . . DHS, you are part of the largest Government reorganization since the establishment of the Department of Defense. As part of DHS, you are playing a key role in a broader mission and the preservation of our way of life. I hope your career in DHS is rewarding, and I hope you continue to carry the proud history of PPQ with you.

As a student of history, in particular the history of the Middle East and of America's early encounters with the Muslim Barbary pirates, I recognized we were part of another historic moment.

My familiarity with the languages and religions of the Middle East was also why I took so seriously our new mandate to prevent terrorist attacks within the United States, reduce America's vulnerability to terrorism, and minimize the damage from potential attacks and natural disasters.

As a field entomologist, I worked in countries all over the world but was particularly focused on the Middle East. I traveled and interacted with mostly poor farmers in countries such as Egypt, Eritrea, Israel, Jordan, and Yemen. I was introduced to cultures that were unfamiliar to most of my colleagues in Customs and Border Protection, except for some of the younger military veterans who had served tours of duty in Afghanistan or Iraq.

Along with my twenty years of overseas experience, I brought an affinity for languages, cultures, and the meaning of names. From my father came a natural inclination to carefully observe the world around me.

ANT TRAILS

For more than twenty years prior to 9/11, I worked directly with farmers and their crops as an entomologist. I earned a bachelor of science degree from the University of California–Davis, and a master of science degree from the University of California–Riverside, with specialties in biological control of crop pests, agricultural economic analysis, and in particular, the behavior of ants.

There are two primary qualities a good entomologist must possess. The first is the ability to observe behavior. Animals, such as ants, for example, move around. But they have a nest, and if you can piece together their behavior and find the trail, it will always lead you to the nest.

That's counterterrorism in a few words. Find the trail; go to the nest. And then keep doing it, over and over again.

The other quality is attention to detail. There are more bugs in the world than any other kind of animal. If I, as an agricultural entomologist, mistakenly believe it's the bug with one hair rather than two hairs that is eating the potatoes and advise a farmer to spray accordingly, he can lose his crop and possibly even his farm. I can't make mistakes.

So, it wasn't such a stretch for me to transition to a subject matter expert in counterterrorism.

In 1984, I became the manager of the Fillmore Citrus Protective District, a self-contained, ten-thousand-acre area that in the 1920s became one of the first in the world to implement pest management based on biological control—"good" bugs eating "bad" bugs.

The job required an unusual combination of scientific knowledge and intuitive artistry that can't necessarily be taught. Along with a thorough knowledge of the crop's annual cycle, you have to discern when and how to apply the beneficial insects, the good bugs. The art and science of biological control also requires carefully rearing, collecting, and keeping healthy the good bugs until they can be released in the field.

One of the biggest problems Fillmore had was an ant imported from Argentina that thrived in California. A highly organized species, it ran in concentrated trails. Once I discovered the ants' secret—how they were exploiting low-hanging branches for nesting during the colder months—it revolutionized the whole district. Their productivity and quality went up, and their costs went down.

I published a paper on my major breakthrough in a journal and ended up presenting it at conferences in South America, where it was enthusiastically received.

Meanwhile, I got the idea to do a survey of ants and citrus worldwide.

From all over the world, I received boxes with wax seals and string containing ants from citrus orchards. Next I made a spreadsheet and categorized the ants, then published a paper titled *Identification, Ecology and Control of the Ants in Citrus: A World Survey,* which I presented four years later at the Sixth International Citrus Congress in Tel Aviv, Israel.[6] (I still have the collection of preserved ants from citrus orchards in more than thirty countries.)

My success led to a position at the University of California–Riverside, where I wrote a grant to the California Energy Commission to find ways of reducing energy consumption in the citrus-growing industry. My colleagues said, "Haney, you're nuts. You're not going to get this." But I was completely confident that if I turned it in, I would win the grant. And I did.

It became the Crown Butte Project in the three largest farming counties in California's San Joaquin Valley, which found ways to reduce energy and improve crop quality, and input costs, saving some $8 million.

ONE FACE

Before 9/11, our three legacy agencies in DHS were autonomous, with little interaction, even though we were working within the same, small enclosed areas of the nation's international entry ports.

Now, suddenly, we were all on the same team, wearing the same uniform, and learning a new motto, "One Face at the Border," or OFAB.[7]

Introduced by Secretary Ridge on September 3, 2003, the intent of OFAB was to "eliminate the previous separation of immigration, customs, and agriculture functions at US air, land, and seaports of entry, and institute a unified border inspection process."[8]

It wasn't nearly as easy to do as it was to say it, but we made progress and learned to work together, gradually adjusting to a new post-9/11 mission and to an entirely new management structure with many unfamiliar faces.

Apparently, my colleagues in legacy agriculture thought I was qualified to help lead us through this uncharted territory, so they elected me as president of our local union, known as the National Association of Agriculture Employees (NAAE).

I didn't run for the position and didn't even know that they were holding elections. But one afternoon in late December 2003, my colleagues came out to our work area in the Federal Inspection Services (FIS), known as "the Floor," and surprised me with the news that I was their brand-new union president.

I served as president for about a year, until the Atlanta branch of the NAAE was disbanded and we were all absorbed into the National Treasury Employees Union (NTEU). First organized by a few IRS employees in 1938, the NTEU currently represents more than 150,000 federal employees in thirty-one federal agencies and departments.

On September 15, 2004, my post-merger background clearance came through, which meant that I would now have access to the

Treasury Enforcement Communications System, or TECS. Before the merger, only US Customs officers could use TECS, but now personnel in all three legacy agencies would have access to the same law-enforcement information.

After the NAAE was disbanded in October 2004 and my term as union president came to an end, I was selected by management to serve as acting supervisor, where I remained through March 2005. During this time, I was given a commendation letter, a time-off award, and two cash awards from CBP management. I was commended for receiving a "superior" rating in my annual evaluation for fiscal year 2003–04; for my "outstanding performance," which was "vital in the agency's mission"; and for my "continued vigilance against terrorism."

"Your dedication to the mission is commendable and appreciated by the Port of Atlanta," the letter read.

We were now three years past the events of 9/11, and DHS had been operating as a stand-alone agency for less than two years. The language in the award letters reflected an agency still focused on terrorism as a mission, and I was commended by CBP management for being vigilant and dedicated to that objective.

CBP's vision statement is:

To serve as the premier law enforcement agency, enhancing the Nation's safety, security, and prosperity through collaboration, innovation, and integration.

Its core values are:

VIGILANCE is how we ensure the safety of all Americans. We are continuously watchful and alert to deter, detect and prevent threats to our nation. We demonstrate courage and valor in the protection of our nation.

SERVICE TO COUNTRY is embodied in the work we do. We are dedicated to defending and upholding the Constitution of the United States. The American people have entrusted us to protect the homeland and defend liberty.

INTEGRITY IS OUR CORNERSTONE. We are guided by the highest ethical and moral principles. Our actions bring honor to ourselves and our agency.[9]

I took our founding vision statement and all three of our core values very seriously.

"TO THE PEOPLE OF AMERICA"

After the end of my tour of duty as an acting supervisor in March 2005, I was appointed as the first CBPAS scheduling officer at the Port of Atlanta, where I served until October 2005. As part of our ongoing "One Face" effort, it would be the first time a legacy PPQ officer was pulled away from our core mission duties and reassigned to a team that was entirely separate from agriculture.

As it turned out, it was the first step toward my rapid transition into counterterrorism, and I never went back to agriculture.

Together with my colleagues, former customs officer Rickey Ferguson and former INS officer Sonia Lewis, we soon created the first unified work schedule, which helped synchronize the entire port. As schedulers, we became familiar with where everyone else was stationed in the floor on any given day.

Since we worked together on the same schedule, we became very efficient. Even though there were always a few changes to make before the next day's roster was sent up to management, we also had some downtime, which I began using to conduct research into current events in the "War on Terror" and to prepare intelligence briefings, which I would then send up the management chain of command.

The first briefing I sent to management was an analysis of Osama bin Laden's October 30, 2004, speech to the "people of America concerning the ideal way to prevent another Manhattan [9/11] and . . . the war and its causes and results."[10]

The five main points in the briefing were:

1. The historical and theological context of the passages from the Quran that bin Laden used have implications for our long-term fight against terrorism.

2. The speech is a clear, worldwide call for long-term action—years into the future—by a personality who has heroic standing and great influence in the Islamic world. This goal will be accomplished through *Jihad*.

3. The speech included an "Invitation" to the non-Islamic world (specifically, the United States and Israel) to repent and turn to Islam.

4. The speech appealed to an intense desire for the global Islamic community to return to its former time of dominance in the Middle East (and, ultimately, the world), and that this goal would be accomplished through *Jihad*.

5. The primary target for this message was not really the West—it was the Islamic world, as Osama called all Muslims to unify and return to the pure faith of Islam (*Salafi*).

Other briefings that I sent up to management in 2005 included one titled *Global Jihad & International Trends* and two others that analyzed the Council on American-Islamic Relations (CAIR), the Washington, DC, group that three years later was revealed in federal court to have been established as a front group for the Muslim Brotherhood.

I got a lot of positive feedback from the briefings, which culminated in a memo to top management on July 18, 2005, requesting that they meet with me regarding the information I had developed.

"WHAT ARE WE GOING TO DO WITH YOU?"
The invitation resulted in a meeting with several top managers at the district field office on July 28, 2005, in which we discussed how I could be of best use within the agency.

It had become clear to my superiors at that time that I had become an unclassified hybrid.

"Mr. Haney, what are we going to do with you?" asked Robert Gomez, the district field office director.

Officially, I was an agriculture officer, but I was also doing the intelligence work of an armed Customs and Border Protection officer.

For starters, they attached me to the newly formed CBP Intelligence Implementation Group (CIIG), and on August 2, 2005, I attended the inaugural CIIG meeting.

As we all listened to opening comments by Atlanta port director Stephen Kremer—which emphasized his intention for the port to focus on long-range analysis and antiterrorist-related activities—some of my colleagues noticed that I was taking notes in shorthand. They immediately designated me as the official notetaker for the CIIG meetings.

During the inaugural CIIG meeting, Kremer also said one of our goals was to make the focus on long-range analysis and antiterrorist activities a "lighthouse" for ports across the country, an aim that resonated with me.

Meanwhile, by early 2005, the war in Iraq was winding down, and events in Afghanistan were evolving rapidly. On February 4, 2005, Paul Wolfowitz, the deputy secretary of defense, announced that fifteen thousand US troops would leave Iraq within a month.[11]

In Afghanistan, riots that initially started over rumors that US personnel had desecrated a Quran turned into the biggest anti-American protests since 9/11. The same rioters also demanded that the Afghan government of President Hamid Karzai reject US intentions to establish a permanent military presence in the country.[12]

One of the reports I prepared during this period was titled "Green Tide Rising—Iraq Lost," which observed, "Despite the good that we have done in delivering the people of Iraq from the cruelty of Saddam Hussein, it is clear to me now that (in the end), we will ultimately . . . fail in our attempt to create a free, democratic government in Iraq."

I wrote:

The truth is the Shiite Jihadists have already taken over the southern region of the country (Basra). This is with the direct assistance of Iran. They are already imposing strict *sharia* law on the people, and are led by Muqtada Ali Sadr.

Their grip on the people will only tighten, and our own government cannot tell the difference between the Shiite *Jihadists* and those who support the democracy. They have infiltrated the police training program (managed by the British Army), and the local government at every level.

It is very likely that there will be civil strife (war) between the Shiite and Sunni factions, with larger countries (such as Iran on one side & Saudi Arabia and Syria on the other side) supporting them for their own advantage.

At the same time, I also followed reports that madrassas, or Quranic schools, in Pakistan were providing training and refuge for jihad fighters who were carrying out antigovernment attacks inside Afghanistan. Despite Pakistan's official denials, there were enough details leaking out for me to corroborate this emerging trend and to advise my colleagues during our weekly muster meetings to be on alert for individuals coming from that part of the world.

It was also one of the main reasons I started focusing on the global Deobandi movement and Salafi Islamic groups, such as Tablighi Jamaat, back in early 2005.

DEEP RESEARCH

Another outcome of our district field office meeting was to have me start focusing on "lookouts," meaning the evaluation of passengers before they arrive in the United States, and conducting secondary inspections, face-to-face interviews with passengers suspected of terrorist activity. To do this, I had to be reassigned again, this time to the Passenger Analysis Unit (PAU), where I remained from October 2005 through October 2006.

The PAU is a special CBP team within most of the ports around the country that focuses on prescreening and in-depth analysis of passengers seeking to enter America who may have a possible connection to terrorist activity.

During this same time period, I also cooperated with our Joint Terrorism Task Force (JTTF) liaison to put together weekly "muster topics," with titles such as "The Muslim Brotherhood & Global Jihad." These short briefings on specific topics were given to the entire port during our weekly muster meetings.

Apparently, I was so successful on the PAU team that on November 1, 2006, management established an entirely new specialty group called the Intelligence Review Unit (IRU), where, along with two other colleagues and CBP supervisor Joseph M. Rogers, we were authorized to conduct "deep research" into cases, based on interviews with passengers who had initially been referred for additional secondary screening and were found to have potential links to terrorism.

The IRU was a great success. Among the many difficult cases we worked on was a seven-month project that focused on the Hamas network in the United States. It led to nearly six hundred law-enforcement actions, along with many hundreds of responses from CBP colleagues in ports around the country.

Our comprehensive report on Hamas was also singled out by Aida M. Perez, director of the ICE Office of Intelligence for Southeast Field Intelligence Unit, and sent to every resident agent in charge (RAC) and special agent in charge (SAC) in the country.

This recognition also led to an offer from one of my colleagues in ICE for a temporary-duty assignment at the DHS Office of Intelligence and Operations Coordination (OIOC).

Management at my port, however, never even acknowledged the offer had been made.

In hindsight, it would be the first of many similar instances during my career with CBP, most without ever receiving the courtesy of a yes-or-no answer, or even a simple acknowledgment of the request.

Meanwhile, I also began to participate in secondary interviews with passengers coming from known hot spots in the Middle East or Asia. This early experience prepared me for the numerous interviews I would conduct in subsequent years.

All of the promotions, reassignments, and recognition from colleagues happened while I was still a CBP agricultural specialist. I had not yet converted to an 1895-series armed CBP officer. I mention it here simply because my hybrid status soon became a real problem.

3

SHADOW LINE

In his World War I–era novella, the great British-Polish author Joseph Conrad wrote of a "shadow line," a twilight threshold in which a major transformation takes place. Before reaching the shadow line, there are harbingers of what lies on the other side.

On June 21, 2006, members of a group that later was designated by the Justice Department as an unindicted coconspirator in a plot to fund the Palestinian terrorist group Hamas were invited to participate in a VIP behind-the-scenes tour of security at Chicago's O'Hare International Airport.

The representatives of the Council on American-Islamic Relations were shown the point of entry, customs stations, secondary screening rooms, and interview rooms. CBP agents described for the CAIR leaders specific features of the high-risk passenger lookout system.

According to an August 2006 news report, Brian Humphrey, Customs and Border Protection's executive director of field operations, "assured CAIR officials that agents do not single out Muslim passengers for special screening and that they must undergo a mandatory course in Muslim sensitivity training." Agents are taught in this course that Muslims consider jihad an "internal struggle against sin" and not holy warfare.[1]

But Customs agents assigned to the CAIR tour at O'Hare told a reporter they were outraged that headquarters would reveal sensitive counterterrorism procedures to an organization that had seen several of its own officials convicted of terror-related charges since 9/11.

A little more than a month later, in early August 2006, port director Anita Terry-McDonald asked me to help her arrange another VIP tour for CAIR, this time at our Atlanta airport. In response, I wrote her a memo on August 19, 2006, noting that I had been raising concerns about CAIR for some time. I reminded her that it was a Hamas front group—as FBI evidence in the 2008 Holy Land Foundation trial later confirmed—funded by Arab governments that actively support jihadist groups in Gaza, the West Bank, and elsewhere in the world.

"The more we know about CAIR, and its history, the less comfortable we should feel about having them looking over our shoulder," I wrote. "With the recent pledge from UAE of at least $74 million to support CAIR, and its new affiliation with the ACLU, we can expect an increase in high-profile obstructionist activities (i.e., PR campaigns and lawsuits) from CAIR in the near future.

"These activities will all have a direct bearing on our efforts here at CBP," I said.

As we can clearly see now, my warnings were legitimate, but they were not well received at the time.

McDonald responded by sending a copy of the memo directly to DHS headquarters, and I was soon banned from the presence of upper management.

To make matters worse, it turned out that Robert Gomez, our director of field operation, was acting port director at O'Hare when the VIP tour took place. I heard through third parties that I was accused of calling Gomez a terrorism supporter.

During my nearly fourteen-year career at DHS, I was investigated nine times. The first began October 15, 2006, after I attended a specialty class titled Deception Detection and Eliciting Responses, October 4–6, 2006, at the interagency Federal Law Enforcement Training Center in Glynco, Georgia. The class was taught by instructors and role players who were either active-duty or retired CIA officers.

Since the course centered on techniques for interviewing individuals with possible links to Islamic terrorism, I assumed that the DDER instructors and role players would be interested in an article I wrote, "Green Tide Rising." Based solely on my own expertise in Middle East affairs, with factual citations derived only from open-source documents, it had been published by the website *FrontPage Magazine* on March 16, 2006.[2]

However, less than two months after graduating from the DDER class—lightning speed in government time—I received an e-mail notifying me that CBP Internal Affairs had opened an investigation on the article. The e-mail also informed me that on December 14, 2006, a GS-13 Internal Affairs fact finder from Newark International Airport, named William Ferri, would be coming down to Atlanta to interview me.

I was accused of unethically accessing classified information to write the article and of violating prohibitions against the use of classified information by posting it on a public website.

After interviewing several of my colleagues and members of upper management, Ferri concluded his investigation and submitted the results up the chain of command.

During the several days that Ferri was in Atlanta, I also was interviewed on the telephone by another investigator from Internal Affairs. He asked me detailed questions about every place I had ever traveled, especially in the Middle East, as well as the websites I regularly queried. He wanted to know why I wrote "Green Tide Rising" and even asked how I "described myself."

In response, I provided the following answers in an Administrative Inquiry Affidavit, on December 14, 2006:

> All the information in the article in question is derived from open sources. Some examples include websites such as MEMRI (Middle East Media & Research Institute), Jihad Watch, and *FrontPage Magazine*.
>
> None of the information was derived from CBP electronic sources, or from information derived from any other CBP sources, or

from any Agencies associated with CBP. None of this type of information is available in the computer programs that we use.

This has been my field of study for 30 years, specifically, the Arab–Israeli Conflict, and the Theology of Islam. I began working in the Middle East in the 1980's; I have traveled and/or worked in Yemen in 1988 & 1989 and Egypt in 1991. I have been to the Middle East more than 15 times.

I began working in the Middle East as an Entomologist, in the field of Biological Control. This is what introduced me to the culture of Islam & the Middle East.

I submitted the article entitled "Green Tide Rising—Hamas Ascends" because the Internet is the modern forum for discussion.

In answer to your question about how I portray myself, I described myself as a professional observer of the Middle East with 30 years of experience. I wrote this byline in the original article, which still appears in versions that [are] posted on the Web.

To this day, I've often wondered, instead of reporting me to DHS headquarters, why didn't the DDER role player just ask me directly about the article?

In the end, the Green Tide Rising investigation yielded no evidence of wrongdoing, and I was finally cleared on August 2, 2007. Even so, there were serious consequences to face in the weeks, months, and years ahead.

As we moved into 2007, things started out well enough, as seen in this complimentary January 4, 2007, e-mail from Paul Conrad, my first-line supervisor in the Passenger Analysis Unit, where I had been working since November 15, 2005:

You're all doing great work. I am excited about what you're doing. You hit the ground running. The information from your reports is being forwarded up and out. This is great stuff. People are noticing, both locally, and in other agencies.

Conrad's support also is reflected in an August 8, 2006, status report that I sent him regarding my merger into PAU and my initial efforts to convert from a CBP agriculture specialist to a CBP officer:

> I'm not sure where this is all taking me. It does appear, however, that the prediction you made during one of our first meetings together in your office is coming true.
>
> You said that I would eventually end up working with NTC and/or HQ, and that it was just a matter of time before it happened. Nothing is official yet, but it does look like things are starting to move in that direction.

A July 20, 2006, memo from my PAU colleague, CBP officer Brown (not her real name), to another colleague in the CBP Office of Intelligence and Investigative Liaison, showed that I was valued by my colleagues:

> In Atlanta we have a legacy Agriculture officer, Philip Haney, who we have on our PAU team. He has not only worked in the Middle East (Afghanistan, Yemen) but has traveled extensively in many Middle East countries.
>
> In addition to his experiences, he has made it his personal mission (obsession) to study Islam and Islamic terrorism, on his own, for the past 20 years or so. On his own he compiles data, writes papers, essays, comparative studies, etc. . . . and he has a daily regimen of websites and open sources that he monitors and tracks.
>
> He is by far the most knowledgeable person on this subject that I have met or talked with including all the ICE, FBI, etc. . . . agents.
>
> He is on our team to pursue terrorism only. He is invaluable with research, background information, education, and in interviews.
>
> He knows some basic Arabic, can quote the Koran, and has an extensive knowledge of all aspects of Koranic learning and Islamic studies.

Nevertheless, on February 14, 2007, I was notified by our assistant port director that I would be removed from the IRU and reassigned back to PAU to do agricultural targeting, instead of targeting individuals and organizations with potential links to terrorism.

Assistant port director Robert Scholtens and chief Rickie Evans came to me that Valentine's Day morning.

"Mr. Haney, you've done a great job, taking the IRU from nothing to where it is now . . . and the database, *Jihad Groups in the World*, is really great," Scholtens said.

"But we're going to have to make a change. Since you're legacy Ag [Department of Agriculture], we're going to send you back to PAU."

When I told Scholtens and Evans that I didn't have any agricultural targeting experience, they looked at each other for a moment and both said, "We're shocked!"

To this day, I still don't know the real reason why the IRU team was shut down, but at that moment it seemed to me that a decision had been made without any regard for the importance of our work.

As the three of us looked at each other, I held up my hands in a "time out" sign.

"If the reason that I'm being stopped from doing this kind of work is because I'm a legacy agriculture officer, then I want to go to FLETC and convert to be a CBP officer," I said.

On February 23, 2007, I met with port director Michele James and expressed my concerns about shutting down the IRU, as well as my desire to convert from CBPAS to CBPO so I could continue doing counterterrorism work.

At the time, there was no formal protocol for making such a transition, but somehow James found a way to do it. On June 25, 2007, I received a formal "Conditional Offer of Employment" for the position of CBP officer GS 1895-11 with Customs and Border Protection in Atlanta.

Meanwhile, several of my colleagues who were upset about the decision to close down the IRU put their concerns in writing, including Joseph M. Rogers, my IRU supervisor.

In a February 20, 2007, memo that was sent up the chain of command, he argued that everyone knew that "no one in this Port and probably no one in CBP can replace Mr. Haney's scholarly knowledge on terrorism."

Last week when I learned that Mr. Haney was to be taken out of IRU, I requested a meeting with [Port Director Michele] James and Mr. Scholtens.

Not knowing the true nature of why this decision was made, it certainly leads to all kinds of speculation and rumors. I feel that Mr. Haney and I are owed an honest explanation of what is behind this decision and why management wants to disrupt the IRU at this point in time, especially at a time when I will be away at a detail.

Mr. Haney is working on a wonderful INTEL project, where he will be giving not only Atlanta, not only CBP, but perhaps many US government entities involved in the fight on terror, an in depth look at the HAMAS organization in the US and their proxies and how they are involved in a coordinated effort to disrupt the US government's fight on terror.

I've read the first 24 pages and it reads like a well-researched doctoral dissertation with virtually everything he says backed-up by references to other TECS records and Internet Articles. Mr. Haney estimates he has at least three full weeks of additional work to finish this assignment.

Once this MOIR [Memorandum of Information Received] is completed and approved, it will be sent out to all the Officers who currently have TECS Records that are associated to this group. This may assist them with their investigations, provide more leads and give the agents a better insight into the operations of HAMAS. Other INTEL entities will likely also find this MOIR very helpful.

If management is worried about the work Mr. Haney is doing, I can say that I have insisted and Mr. Haney has readily complied with documenting just about everything he has to say in his reports. Mr. Haney has been doing his work in WORD documents that are on the shared drive under IRU Muster Topics. I invite management or other INTEL persons to review his work and give us feedback. The information will not be downloaded into TECS until everyone feels we have a good product.

I appeal to management to put yourself in Mr. Haney's shoes, if only for a minute. Mr. Haney is a quiet, unassuming Officer who cares deeply about this country and the principles that guide CBP. Mr. Haney wants to put his knowledge and years of experience where it will do us the most good. To force him to go to PAU at this point in time will deeply wound his spirit and likely embitter him.

All of us as Supervisors, have an obligation to stand up and advocate for our employees, especially when decisions are being made that could and probably would have an adverse impact on our operations.

We all know that no one in this Port and probably no one in CBP can replace Mr. Haney's scholarly knowledge on terrorism. I ask you, to ask yourself the questions, where can Mr. Haney do the most for our mission? Where will he be the most effective in identifying and helping other officers identify possible terrorists? Who among us has the most understanding of "the big picture" when it comes to terrorism? Who at a glance can spot the name of a mosque or village or particular leader and say: "I think I found a piece of the puzzle we have been looking for"?

The IRU without Mr. Haney is just a post-analytical PAU Unit. They can maybe do more research on individuals, but identifying links and knowing where they fit will not be readily apparent and may often be missed. This HAMAS MOIR is likely only one of many great INTEL projects Mr. Haney will be working on, if we give him a chance. With Mr. Haney, we are on the cutting edge of INTEL and the fight against terrorism.

Do you want to drive a Mercedes or Ford Fiesta?
Regards,
Joseph M. Rogers, Supervisory Enforcement Officer

Six days before Rogers's memo, on February 14, 2007, my PAU colleague, Officer Brown, urged me to "fight like hell."

I heard . . . what is going on. Fight like hell. For [management] to act like they don't know what you have been doing this whole time is BS and a lie.

. . . If [management] doesn't back you then you know for sure what kind of people you are dealing with. They are scared of CBP not being politically correct and your level of research surpassing all of the JTTF and other agencies.

Propose to them that you need to be put on the JTTF directly. There is no reason to waste your skills. . . . But don't hang your hat on [management] completely. You can never totally trust anyone.

In the end, however, my request to remain on the IRU was denied. In fact, it was never discussed again. The IRU was disbanded simply because no one else at the port thought he or she could take my place.

Management did make one concession, and I was able to remain assigned to the IRU for three more weeks while my friend and colleague officer Martin (not his real name) and I finished compiling The Hamas Network in the United States report. This happened because Martin had the idea of printing a copy of the entire report and showing it to Chief Evans in his office.

Martin said, "They don't know what we really have here, so let's show them!"

As soon as Evans saw the Hamas report, he agreed that we should definitely finish what we had started. I'm thankful to Chief Evans for having the foresight and courage to allow us to finish this important project.

By early March, I was back in the Passenger Analysis Unit, but on March 13, 2007, my participation in the weekly CIIG intelligence briefings was abruptly terminated without explanation.

On May 21, 2007, the groundbreaking Hamas report was put into the TECS system, but only in the form of a three-page executive summary. Management apparently was concerned that some of the open-source information in the report was unreliable.

Meanwhile, I received positive feedback about another case I had worked on with our field analysis specialist and JTTF liaison.

In a June 15, 2007, e-mail, he praised the analysis I had prepared for the assistant US attorney:

> In addition, the Intel person for the AUSA [Assistant US Attorney's] Office requested his boss to send [the analysis] to the AUSA's. He said it should not be a problem. He also told me all the Intel people for the AUSA office were blown away by the paper. Good Work!!!!

Then, my colleague Holly Banks, stationed at the Southeast Field Intelligence Unit (SEFIU) in Miami, Florida, distributed the Hamas report on June 19, 2007, to the resident agents in charge (RACs) and special agents in charge (SACs) in Washington, DC; Atlanta; Baltimore; Norfolk, Virginia; Fort Lauderdale, Florida; Miami; and five other field offices in Florida. The cover letter stated that the SEFIU was "assisting CBP in attempts to disseminate this intelligence report to all ICE Office of Investigations, SACs and RACs whose areas of responsibility are specifically mentioned in this report."

On Monday, July 9, 2007, I met with Rep. Lynn A. Westmoreland, R-GA, and his aide, John Stacy, at the congressman's office in Newnan, Georgia. It was the first time I had reached out to a member of Congress, but there would be many more such efforts in the years to come.

After the meeting, I wrote a thank-you note to Westmoreland, which included the following remarks:

> Thank you both for meeting with me on Monday, July 09, 2007, at your office in Newnan. It was a pleasure to meet you in person. It is my hope that this will be the beginning of an alliance that will help make our country more secure from Jihad terrorism.

Meanwhile, on August 2, 2007, nine months after the Green Tide Rising investigation had started, I received an exoneration letter from Port Director James:

> This is to inform you, pursuant to Customs Directive 099 1520-010, dated November 05, 1993, that a Management Referral, OPR Case

No. [author's redaction], regarding alleged improper publication and dissemination of an internet article (*Green Tide Rising*) has been completed.

Based on the results of the investigation, I have determined that no action pertaining to the publication and dissemination of the above mentioned Internet article is warranted.

Despite the letter, the investigation wasn't actually over. On August 22, 2007, I was summoned to the DFO's office to give what became a twenty-one-page affidavit for a parallel investigation that was prompted by the original Green Tide Rising case. This time, I was accused of improperly querying my own name, home address, and travel records in what I understood to be the "training mode" of TECS, during a March 22–23, 2006, Advanced Targeting course at NTC.

The case was finally mitigated on October 16, 2007, from a possible two-day suspension without pay to a formal Letter of Reprimand from Director Gomez, which was placed in my personal file for one year.

Was what I wrote in Green Tide Rising correct? I believe that, read ten years later, it still rings true, especially the closing remarks, in which I wrote that "strategic attacks against the West will increase."

"These attacks will be planned and conducted in partnership with affiliated Jihadist groups," I wrote, "partly because the West is considered a distinct enemy of Islam itself, and partly to weaken Israel by alienating and isolating her from the West."[3]

But in 2006, my own agency and the CIA role players somehow found the subject so threatening that they investigated me twice for it, exonerating me in one case but finding me guilty of misconduct in the other.

While all this was happening, and despite the fact that it was not actually in TECS, the Hamas Network report continued to circulate internally within the federal law enforcement community.

One of the people who read it was José E. Meléndez-Pérez, the famous CBP officer who intercepted the twentieth 9/11 hijacker, Mohamed al-Kahtani, in Orlando.

Meléndez-Pérez was so impressed by the Hamas report that he nominated my colleague and me for the Diana Dean and José Meléndez-Pérez Anti-Terrorism Award, which is given to CBP officers who perform exemplary work in protecting the nation's borders.

On August 14, 2007, Meléndez-Pérez sent a letter to James M. Chaparro, deputy assistant secretary in the DHS Office of Intelligence and Analysis:

> It was a pleasure to meet you on August 9, 2007 at the Summer Hard Problem Program (SHARP) dinner in Orlando, Florida. I enjoyed the conversation we had and I would like to provide you some information regarding the two Customs and Border Protection Officers (CBPO) that we discussed at the dinner.
>
> I would like to recognize CBPO Philip B. Haney and CBPO [Martin] from the Atlanta, Georgia Passenger Analysis Unit who have gone above the call of duty to analyze, sort, and prepare intelligence reports and databases relating to Islamic terrorist groups and threats against the United States.
>
> The intelligence reports have been on topics relating to Global Jihad & Developing Trends. CBPO Haney has also created a database of approximately 185 Islamic Jihadist Groups operating in 81 countries. In addition to other reports, a report titled, Hamas Network in the United States has been created to provide the intelligence community with important information regarding terrorist groups.
>
> The documents they have prepared have been beneficial to local, state, and other federal agencies. We must recognize and keep motivating those that excel and go above the call of duty. Therefore, I feel that the initiative, determination and professionalism of these two officers should be commended.
>
> I will always be grateful to you for the opportunity to recognize these two Customs and Border Protection Officers. I believe this is the right thing to do for their service to the Department of Homeland Security and the United States of America.

Meléndez-Pérez never received a response from anyone in the agency regarding his recommendation.

Nevertheless, the Hamas Network report produced fruit.

RESPECTED COMMUNITY LEADER

On July 23, 2007, I was contacted by a US Citizen and Immigration Services officer in California regarding "respected community leader" Abdel Jabbar Hamdan, who had been arrested and detained by ICE on July 27, 2004, for a non-immigrant F-1 visa overstay.[4] He then was released from custody on July 28, 2006,[5] and was now pending deportation to his home country of Jordan.[6]

USCIS contacted me because the Hamas report included a TECS record on Hamdan, who had now filed a Petition for Employment Authorization, despite the fact that he was under an active court order to "voluntarily depart the U.S." by November 6, 2006.

Citing information in the report, I replied to my USCIS colleague that Hamdan was a "close affiliate of the Holy Land Foundation (HLF), which is currently on trial in Richardson, TX."

"Some of the people that Hamdan has been associated with are also on trial, and Mr. Hamdan himself has been named twice as an un-indicted co-conspirator in the trial," I wrote.

Two other colleagues in the e-mail string who had also created TECS records on Hamdan agreed with my assessment, with one replying "Ditto!" and the second adding:

> I totally concur with Mr. Haney's assessment and comments. We do not believe that Hamdan should not receive any benefits from the USG as SAC/Dallas proved in Immigration Court that he is defined as a "terrorist" for I&NA [Immigration and Nationality Act] purposes. The attached court order, which can be opened with MS Word, will give you more information.

On August 15, 2007, I received another word of thanks, in an e-mail from a CBP supervisor at the Port of Los Angeles/Long Beach:

Thanks to Atlanta for the great intelligence report on Hamas posted on DHS Fusion. And what a coincidence it was to find that our Port had also run across information on Hamas Network suspect [author's redaction] and the organization IslamiCity.[7]

Three weeks later, I was notified that I would be attending the Federal Law Enforcement Training Center (FLETC) program, October 30, 2007, through February 1, 2008, to prepare to become a Customs and Border Protection officer.

I got the news while I was in Herzliya, Israel, to attend the seventh annual International Conference on Global Terrorism, titled "Terrorism's Global Impact."

The conference is hosted by the International Institute for Counter-Terrorism, an Israel-based independent think tank providing expertise on national security that serves as a forum for international policymakers and scholars to share information.

The ICT sent me a formal invitation to speak at its 2007 conference, saying, "We believe that as an expert in this field, your participation in this debate, together with various other experts could be an important opportunity to examine terrorism trends and to reach operative conclusions to counter this phenomenon."

I was unable to speak at the 2007 conference, however, because my agency would not allow me to participate as a CBP officer. It was the second time I had requested CBP to sponsor my participation in the ICT conference, which included counterterrorism specialists from more than fifty countries. The port refused both times, so I paid my own way as a private citizen.

Over the years, I continued attending the ICT conferences, using the information I gathered to inform and enhance my work as a CBP officer.

In just one of many examples, in 2008, a South African political party leader informed me that jihadist training camps were forming all over his country.[8] Since Atlanta had a daily flight from Johannesburg at the time, I considered the information to be significant. However, I was never able to formally share any of the intelligence with port management.

4

WORDS MATTER

On October 30, 2007, I reported for duty at the Federal Law Enforcement Training Center, FLETC, for basic training with a class of fifty. I was fifty-four years old, well past the normal age when people consider putting themselves through such an ordeal. But I was determined to do whatever it took to continue working in counterterrorism as an 1895 CBP officer.

I mention my age here because about two or three weeks into the training program, our instructor announced that a change in policy had been made that would affect anyone who sought appointment to a position as a CBP officer from that point forward. CBP officers would now be eligible to retire after twenty years of service. That was good for the younger trainees coming in, but there was a catch for people my age.

According to the new official policy,[1] the "day before an individual's 37th birthday is the maximum age for original appointment to a position as a Customs and Border Protection Officer."[2]

Wow, *that* was a close one!

If, for some reason, my entrance into FLETC had been delayed for just a week or two, I would have been deemed ineligible to convert from agriculture to armed officer, and I would have been unable to continue working in the counterterrorism field at all.

I'm fairly sure that everyone who goes through basic training encounters difficulty in at least one part of the course, and I was no exception. I did well in the academic classes and even outperformed quite a few of my younger classmates in some of the physical training portions, such as running and training, defensive tactics, and search and arrest techniques (except for one remediation in the search and arrest qualification exam).

But what I had trouble with was qualifying with our H&K P-2000 .40 caliber pistol. In the first seven weeks of basic training, we went to the range about fifteen times to practice, but I never qualified. I got close a couple of times, but never shot over the minimum score of 240 out of 300 in the course of fire.

The problem was that if you didn't qualify in shooting, you failed the program and had to leave FLETC. Depending on the circumstances, some people come back to FLETC for a second chance, but I would be too old because of the new policy. If I failed shooting, I probably could never return.

By late December, I was getting concerned, and as I found out later, my classmates were also worried that I might not make it.

Fortunately, we were scheduled to go on Christmas break. On December 23, 2007, just before two of my friends from FLETC and I drove back to Atlanta for Christmas, I was practicing in my dorm room with a "red gun"—an exact replica made of hard plastic—when I suddenly realized I couldn't see the front sights correctly.

I decided to call my friend Rickey Ferguson, who was one of the firearms instructors at the Port of Atlanta. I told him I was having trouble qualifying.

"Meet me at the range in Henry County tomorrow about 1500," he said. "I'll bring a few boxes of ammo, and we'll just keep shooting until we figure out what's wrong.

"Don't worry; we'll get it figured out," he assured me.

The next day, on the way to the range, I stopped at a local pharmacy and bought full-frame reading glasses, which enabled me to see the front sights more clearly.

Right on time, Rickey met me at the range, and we did just what he said. We kept firing until we figured out that I was shooting low and down to the left. Now that I could see better, and now that I knew what I was doing wrong, I began to believe that I just might be able to qualify.

I didn't have to wait long to find out. Our class was scheduled for its qualifying session at the outdoor range on December 27 at 7:30 a.m. I remember how cold it was that morning, at least for southern Georgia.

We all lined up on the three-yard line, as we had done many times before.

With a snap, the targets flipped, and we went through the course of fire: three yards, seven yards, then back to the fifteen- and, finally, to the twenty-five-yard line.

We heard the final call, "The line is safe!"

We all stepped to the back of the range and waited for a few long minutes for the firearms instructors to score our targets.

Then came the announcement that we could go downrange to see how we did. Off to my right, at the far end of the line, I heard a female colleague shriek that she had passed, and then my target came into view.

There, written in black magic marker at the top of my target, in lane number seven, was the number 243.

Thank you, Lord, I passed!

Thank you, Rickey Ferguson.

Everyone was happy for me. "Mr. Haney passed!"

Standing there that cold morning on the firing range, looking around at my colleagues, is the moment when I *really* became a CBP officer. My life has never been the same since. (Just ask my wife!)

Then it gradually dawned on all of us that we had just gone through the last difficult pass-fail test we would have to face at FLETC. We were going to become certified federal law enforcement officers.

It was a great day.

Graduation was still a month away, but we had passed the last major obstacle together and would be able to help each other finish up the rest of our training.

DIRECTOR'S AWARD

We graduated on Friday, February 1, 2008, with friends and family from all over the country gathered in the FLETC chapel. My wife; granddaughter, Lydia; and sister, Diana, from California were there too.

To my great surprise, I won the Director's Award, the highest honor a trainee can be given at FLETC. It is awarded to the person, chosen by classmates, instructors, and staff, who most consistently exemplifies the core values of a federal law enforcement officer: integrity, fairness, respect, honesty, courage, and compassion.

One other amazing thing happened during the graduation ceremony that day. The commencement speaker was our director of field operations, Robert Gomez. He was the official who had led the CAIR VIP tour at Chicago O'Hare airport in June 2006, which I recounted in chapter 3.

When I went up to the stage to accept the Director's Award, Gomez was already there. As we stood side by side for photographs, he turned and said quietly, "This is one of the most significant things I have ever done as a DFO [director of field operations)."

During his commencement address a few moments later, in the presence of my family, FLETC friends, colleagues, and staff, Gomez mentioned me.

"When you go back to your home port, find yourself a mentor, someone you can follow as an example and learn from," he said. "For example, Mr. Haney here, one of your classmates, is one of the best-known counterterrorism specialists in the whole agency. Pick someone like him to mentor you, when you go back to your home ports."

It was a wonderful compliment, but it was put to the test many times in the years ahead.

I have often wondered: If my own management at the port and DFO level was already well aware that I was a gifted counterterrorism specialist, why didn't they back me up when higher management in Washington started pushing back against the work my colleagues and I were doing on the Muslim Brotherhood network in the United States and the Tablighi Jamaat Initiative?

But that aside, graduating from FLETC was a high point in my life.

After a couple of days of celebration and rest, I went back to the Port of Atlanta and reported for duty as a new CBP officer. There, I was assigned to primary, the most basic duty of CBP officers, to become familiar with the systems and procedures we use for processing passengers.

LETHAL DEFINITIONS

On January 28, 2008, just three days before I graduated from FLETC, the Federal Bureau of Investigation released an official policy document titled the *Counterterrorism Analytical Lexicon*.[3]

Fourteen pages in length, it mentions "violent extremism" four times and "religious" three times,[4] but never uses the words *Muslim, Islam,* or *jihad.*

The *Lexicon* contained a dizzying array of definitions, such as this one for "homegrown violent extremist":

> A "homegrown violent extremist" is a US person who was once assimilated into, but who has rejected, the cultural values, beliefs, and environment of the United States in favor of a violent extremist ideology. He or she is "US-radicalized" . . . and intends to commit terrorism inside the United States without direct support or direction from a foreign terrorist organization.[5]

For frontline officers who have taken an oath to "support and defend the Constitution of the United States" against "all enemies, foreign and domestic," these grammatically confusing, subjective definitions of the threat to America's security can be lethal.

In the real world, such abstract terms as "without direct support or direction from a foreign terrorist organization" muddy the waters and obscure the legal standard of probable cause, making it essentially impossible for law enforcement officers to conduct effective counterterrorism investigations and connect the dots.

On February 12, 2008, a colleague of mine with Immigrations

and Customs Enforcement (ICE) forwarded me an e-mail string that originated within the DHS Office of Civil Rights and Civil Liberties. It included the draft of a policy paper titled "Terminology to Define the Terrorists: Recommendations from American Muslims."[6] The document, which soon became known simply as the "Words Matter" memo, was being circulated for internal review among subject matter experts in the counterterrorism community.

The author of the original e-mail commended the document for adding "value to the ongoing discourse on terminology," noting it had been distributed to Michael Chertoff, the second Homeland Security secretary under President George W. Bush:

> Attached is a paper our Office [CRCL] recently produced, which summarizes the recommendations of a group of influential Muslim thinkers/commentators on the critical issue of terminology.
>
> Specifically, the paper addresses the terms USG officials should both use and avoid when describing terrorists and their ideology. Please note that this paper neither reflects DHS-wide policy, nor represents the final word on this topic.
>
> Nevertheless, we believe the opinions expressed in it add value to the ongoing discourse on terminology. You have seen earlier drafts of the paper; this version incorporates edits and thoughts from a wide range of people across government. We have shared the paper with Secretary Chertoff and other senior leaders in DHS, as well as officials from the UK and Canadian governments.

The message in the e-mail string from my colleague read:

> This was disseminated to all of ICE Intel. I value your experience and knowledge on this topic and would like to hear your opinion on the paper. My thoughts, I wonder who exactly contributed to the paper? Good question, don't you think?

I replied to my colleague with a few observations and questions. From my perspective, I wrote, the average person, having relatively little familiarity with the Quran or Islamic theology, "will probably be mystified by what the writers of this paper are really trying to say."

I also found the phrase "Recommendations from American Muslims" in the title to be problematic, because, from the standpoint of the global Islamic community, which Muslims call the *Ummah*, "American Muslims" aren't authorized to promote their own distinctive policy apart from a consensus of opinion derived from legal specialists within their branch of Islam.

In my response, I also wrote that their "policy may appear to be tailored for the current cultural/political sensitivities of the American audience, but in the end, it will always be based on the accepted and traditional policy of the historic global Ummah," meaning Islamic law, also known as sharia.

In addition, I noted there was no mention of the Hadith, a required source of reference for every theological and political policy in the Islamic world. In other words, it would be like trying to write new laws in America without referring to the US Constitution.

"No one, even 'American Muslims,' can create bona fide policy that excludes or contradicts the Hadith," I wrote.

> As a matter of fact, there is nothing in the position paper about the Quran itself. Who could blame someone reading this paper for getting the impression that the Quran is so inscrutable and sacred that it can't be discussed? However, the Quran, combined with the Hadith, form the Sharia, which is the foundation of Islam everywhere in the world, and has been since Muhammad died in 632. They are immutable and irrefutable—not subject to rational (secular) diplomacy or current political trends.

I noted that the early US ambassadors in Europe, including Thomas Jefferson, Benjamin Franklin, and John Adams, all knew this from firsthand experience. All three of them had encountered the *dey*—the Muslim leader—of the Barbary pirates, who was based in Tripoli.

In each of his encounters with the Americans, the dey plainly declared that he was leading a jihad against America and Europe. Ever the curious researcher, Ambassador Jefferson used a copy of the Quran to verify that what the dey had said aligned with Islamic theology and practice.

In response, the famous ship USS *Constitution*, better known as "Old Ironsides," was sent to Tripoli in the late 1790s to recover the crew and cargo of the freighter USS *Philadelphia*, which had been captured by the Barbary pirates and was being held for ransom, or *jizya*. In Islamic jurisprudence, the jizya, also translated "tax," is a tribute that conquered non-Muslims must pay as an act of submission to their Muslim overlords.

In the early years of the United States, the fledgling federal government paid up to 25 percent of its gross national product to ransom ships and crews held by the Mediterranean jihadi pirates.

Returning to the memo to my ICE colleague, I also wrote that it "follows, therefore, that any discussion of political policy, as per proposed 'Terminology to Define the Terrorists: Recommendations from American Muslims,' must be based on principles derived from sharia law," which is composed of both the Quran and the Hadith, as well as a large volume of theological and legal commentary, known as the *tafsir*.

"They are inseparable," I wrote. "Otherwise, we'll discover to our possible horror that we've been misled, and our naive misconceptions will be smashed to pieces by the powerful hammer of sharia."

I also argued that despite the obvious efforts of the writers of the "Words Matter" memo to diffuse the potency of the word *jihad*, all four of the most authoritative sources of the Hadith were saturated with teachings endorsing violent jihad against unbelievers—just as the dey of Tripoli had declared to America's early ambassadors.

"The legacy of Jihad is a fact of history, which cannot be diminished (or whitewashed) by a position paper prepared by 'American Muslims,'" I wrote.

In the memo, I also referenced the influential Islamic scholar Sayyid Qutb and his essay "Jihad in the Cause of God," which was first published in English by scholar Andrew Bostom on January 16, 2006. I referred to Qutb as the "Thomas Jefferson of modern jihad," for his carefully written declaration that gathered all of the thoughts and ideas of Islam's "founding fathers."

Continuing, I wrote that as a political theorist and recognized Islamic theologian, Qutb was very clear on what may be called the "four stages of Jihad."

In the United States, I said, we are now in stage one, which centers on the promotion of Islam through mostly nonviolent means, called *da'wah* in Arabic, which then lays the cornerstone and foundation for the remaining three stages. The "Terminology to Define the Terrorists" policy paper was a "classic example" of stage one jihad, as defined by Qutb.

I noted that no individual Muslim or Islamic organization anywhere in the world had ever accused Qutb of committing *takfir*, meaning the serious crime of doctrinal deviation from orthodox Islam.

In closing, I offered that if anyone higher up in the chain of command would like to discuss these concepts in further detail, I would be happy to do so.

I never received feedback from higher-ups, and to this day no one with DHS, CBP, or the administration has ever addressed any of my questions or concerns.

Most important, while the e-mail string noted that the "Words Matter" memo "neither reflects DHS-wide policy, nor represents the final word on this topic," it soon became obvious to subject matter experts like me that the recommendations would become official DHS policy.

"WORDS THAT WORK"

A little more than a month later, on March 14, 2008, another internal memo, "Words that Work and Words that Don't: A Guide for Counterterrorism Communication," began circulating around the administrative and law enforcement officer community.

Originally released by the Extremist Messaging Branch of the Counter-Terrorism Communications Center for "use in conversations with target audiences,"[7] the memo was also approved for diplomatic use by the US State Department, which planned to distribute it to all of its foreign consulates and embassies.

The State Department's Counter-Terrorism Communications Center was described in a November 1, 2007, dispatch as an office "staffed with experts from different agencies" that "develops culturally sensitive messages to undermine and discredit terrorists."[8]

A similar unit, the US State Department's Center for Strategic Counterterrorism Communications (CSCC), was established on September 9, 2011, "at the direction of the President and the Secretary of State to coordinate, orient, and inform government-wide foreign communications activities targeted against terrorism and violent extremism, particularly al-Qaida and its affiliates and adherents."[9]

Today, it appears that the CSCC is "guided by the National Strategy for Counterterrorism (NSCT) under the policy direction of the White House and interagency leadership." The CSCC coordinator "reports to the Under Secretary of State for Public Diplomacy and works closely with the Coordinator for Counterterrorism, other [Department of] State bureaus and many government agencies. CSCC liaises with agencies with domestic responsibilities to ensure coordination and consistency of message."[10]

The NSCT, which originated the frequently heard mantra "We are not at war with Islam; we are at war with al-Qaeda," narrowly defines the principal threat Americans face as al-Qaeda and its affiliates:

> This Strategy recognizes there are numerous nations and groups that support terrorism to oppose U.S. interests, including Iran, Syria, Hezbollah and HAMAS, and we will use the full range of our foreign policy tools to protect the United States against these threats.
>
> However, the principal focus of this counterterrorism strategy is the network that poses the most direct and significant threat to the United States—al-Qa'ida, its affiliates and its adherents.[11]

Remarkably, on February 8, 2015, the State Department appointed Rashad Hussain, a Muslim Brotherhood–linked leader who turns up later in my story, as the United States special envoy and coordinator of the Center for Strategic Counterterrorism Communications.[12]

Hussain—who declared in 2004 that the prosecution of University of South Florida professor Sami al-Arian on terrorism charges was "politically motivated persecution" to "squash dissent"[13]—now leads a staff drawn from a number of US departments and agencies to expand international engagement and partnerships to "counter violent extremism" and to "develop strategic counterterrorism communications around the world."[14]

Al-Arian later pleaded guilty to charges related to his leadership in the Palestinian Islamic Jihad terrorist group and was deported.

As with the "Words Matter" memo, my colleagues and I were assured that the "Words that Work" memo's "advice is not binding and is for use with our audiences." We were also informed that the memo "does not affect other areas such as policy papers, research analysis, scholarly writing, etc. The purpose of this paper," it said, "is to raise awareness among communicators of the language issues that may enhance or detract from successful engagement."[15]

Nevertheless, the memo included the following very specific "guidelines":

- Don't Invoke Islam: Although the al-Qaida network exploits religious sentiments and tries to use religion to justify its actions, we should treat it as an illegitimate political organization, both terrorist and criminal.[16]

- Use the terms "violent extremist" or "terrorist." Both are widely understood terms that define our enemies appropriately and simultaneously deny them any level of legitimacy.[17]

- When possible, avoid using terms drawn from Islamic theology in a conversation unless you are prepared to discuss their varying meanings over the centuries.

  Examples: salafi, wahhabist, caliphate, sufi, ummah. Do not use "ummah" to mean "the Muslim world." It is not a sociological term, rather, it is a theological construct not used in everyday life.[18]

It wasn't very long before we also told to stop using the word *terrorist* altogether, especially within the US government data systems, such as TECS. At the same time, the term *violent extremist* soon rose to prominence as the favored term in the emerging Countering Violent Extremism policy.

ADVANCED TARGETING

In September 2008, I traveled once again to Herzliya, Israel, to attend the ICT's annual World Summit on Counter-Terrorism, which focused on "Terrorism's Global Impact." As with every other ICT conference, I brought home valuable intelligence on developing terrorism trends around the world, but as I mentioned earlier, I was never able to share any of it with port management.

In early October 2008, I was assigned to the Advanced Targeting Unit (ATU), a specialty team that focuses on the movement of cargo instead of passengers. Robert Harer was our ATU supervisor, and we soon got to work developing new leads while continuing to follow up on cases that were already in progress.

I was also still receiving many e-mails every day from colleagues around the country who were looking at records related to the Hamas Network report or other linked reports, such as on the Deobandi-Tablighi Jamaat network in the United States.

I worked the night shift at the time, and late in the evening of November 23, 2008, I found an article reporting that officials with the Council on American-Islamic Relations (CAIR) had been served a summons and complaint for various civil and criminal offenses. I had already devoted more than two years of law enforcement–based research to CAIR, so I knew how closely the leaders of this organization were linked to Hamas and other supremacist groups.

It was no secret that in 1994, CAIR was incorporated by three leaders of the Islamic Association for Palestine: Omar Ahmad, Nihad Awad, and Rafeeq Jaber. An INS memo from 2001 documented at length the IAP's support for Hamas, while noting that the "facts strongly suggest" that IAP is "part of Hamas' propaganda apparatus."[19]

Nor was it a secret that Mousa Abu Marzook, a senior leader of Hamas to this day, once served on the IAP board of directors and provided the group with at least $490,000.[20]

A couple of days later, on November 25, 2008, I discovered an FBI story titled "No Cash for Terror: Convictions Returned in Holy Land Case," which informed us that the Department of Justice had convicted the Richardson, Texas–based Holy Land Foundation and 108 of its members and associates for funneling at least $12 million to the Muslim Brotherhood and Hamas.[21]

I have to admit that, as a federal law enforcement officer, I found it gratifying to realize that, two years earlier, I had put a detailed report on CAIR and the entire Hamas network in the United States into the system.

Now, my colleagues in the FBI and DOJ had just successfully convicted five top Holy Land Foundation leaders of conspiracy to provide material support and resources to a foreign terrorist organization; conspiracy to provide funds, goods, and services to a specially designated terrorist organization; and conspiracy to commit money laundering.

As soon as the HLF verdicts were announced, Mustafaa Carroll, director of the Council on American-Islamic Relations' branch in Dallas, held a press conference and warned that the verdicts could have a chilling effect on America's already traumatized Muslim community. "Muslims are concerned about how this is going to affect them," he said. "By criminalizing charity, it may even have an impact on American charities in general. People are really afraid."[22]

What Carroll didn't mention was that not only was CAIR named as an unindicted coconspirator in the HLF trial, but unlike the charities from other religions, Islamic charities, including CAIR, fund Islamic holy war. In fact, Islamic law requires that one-eighth of all the proceeds of Islamic charity—known as *zakat*—be designated for the support of jihad and/or jihad warriors, the mujahideen.[23]

However, as would become evident in the next few months, Carroll's complaint of possible infringement of civil rights and civil liberties was echoed by many other Muslim leaders in the United States and was soon given top priority by the Obama administration.

Perhaps even more important than the conviction for funding jihad was the evidence presented during the Holy Land Foundation trial of a plot to "destroy Western Civilization from within." This evidence implicated virtually every prominent Islamic institution in America, from the leading Islamic civil rights and political interest groups—including CAIR, the Islamic Society of North America, and the North American Islamic Trust—to the nationwide Muslim Student Association and the system for certifying military chaplaincies.

CAIR's parent organization, IAP, was named in the May 1991 Muslim Brotherhood document, "An Explanatory Memorandum on the General Strategic Goal for the Group in North America," as one of the Brotherhood's likeminded organizations that shared the aim of teaching Muslims that "that their work in America is a kind of grand Jihad in eliminating and destroying the Western civilization from within and 'sabotaging' its miserable house by their hands . . . so that . . . [Allah's] religion is made victorious over all other religions."[24]

The Holy Land Foundation trial should have been a turning point in America's counterterrorism efforts, allowing federal law enforcement officers to keep a sharp eye on individuals and organization who now had proven ties to terrorist groups such as Hamas.

But in fact, the exact opposite transpired.

5

INTEL SCRUB

On January 17, 2009, I wrote the first of a series of articles published in mass media under the pen name of Bruce Phillips. I used a pseudonym because I didn't want a repeat of what had happened in 2006, when I was investigated and endured an adverse action for publishing "Green Tide Rising."

Of course, even federal employees have a constitutional right to freedom of expression, but rather than belabor the point while I was still active duty, I simply chose to write under a different identity.

I wrote because I considered it my duty to inform my countrymen and to document some of the major historic events in the Middle East that were affecting the safety and security of America and the world.

The article, titled "The War Against Hamas: Why Does It Matter?" and published by WND, addressed a major military campaign called Operation Cast Lead, which began December 19, 2008, when Hamas operatives in Gaza began barraging Israel with rockets. Israel responded January 3, 2009, with a ground offensive into Gaza, which continued until January 18, when Israel unilaterally ended the conflict.

"The War Against Hamas" was published just one day before Operation Cast Lead was halted. At the time, I believed it was important to publish the article before the conflict ended, so I could not be accused of retroactive analysis.

As you can see in the concluding paragraphs of "The War Against Hamas," my underlying premise was shown to be correct:

> To conclude, if Hamas cannot be defeated in Gaza (when everyone in the world should know exactly who they are and what they stand for), then how can anyone else hope to defeat jihadists who are subtly diffused through the populations of nearly every other country in the world? Stated another way, if we can't defeat an enemy we can clearly see, then how will we ever defeat an enemy we cannot clearly see, who often enjoys the protection of governments operating under Islamic Shariah law, or at least cleverly and cynically hides behind the protections and benefits provided so generously by democratic, liberal Western governments?
>
> Or, if we lack the political will (and discernment) necessary to defeat an avowed, well-defined and unapologetic jihad group such as Hamas—concentrated as they are at this moment in space and time—then when and how will we ever find the will to engage the threat of jihad (in all of its myriad subtle expressions) against jihad groups and individuals that we can't even see, let alone define?
>
> What's more, in the immediate aftermath of Israel's failure to defeat Hamas, the leaders of every jihadist group in the world will come to a sudden (and thrilling) realization . . . that no power on earth can defeat them. Yes, they may suffer loss of life and property, and they may have to endure hardships and deprivations, but in the end, Islam will prevail. Of that, they will be resolute and certain.[1]

For much of January 2009, I also worked with my colleagues in other law enforcement agencies on a case involving a global-level Hamas leader, Salah Sultan (variously spelled Soltan).[2]

A onetime lawful permanent resident (LPR), Sultan is linked to several United States and European Muslim Brotherhood organizations, including the European Council for Fatwa and Research (ECFR), and the International Union of Muslim Scholars (IUMS), which is led by Youssef Qaradawi, another top Muslim Brotherhood leader.

While living in America, Sultan was also closely affiliated with the Fiqh Council of North America (FCNA), the Islamic American University (IAU), and the Muslim American Society (MAS).

In February 2005, Sultan spoke at the Islamic Society of Boston (ISB), the mosque attended by Boston Marathon bombers Dzhokhar and Tamerlan Tsarnaev.[3]

I was connected to the Sultan case because he was part of the Hamas Network investigation I had started in late 2006.

Sultan left the United States in October 2008 and has never returned. He made numerous media appearances during the Arab Spring but was arrested in Egypt in 2013, along with his son Mohamed Soltan, where he remains imprisoned under a death sentence.

Mohamed Soltan was released from prison in Egypt after a four-hundred-day hunger strike and returned to the United States on May 30, 2015.[4] If his father, Salah Sultan, somehow did try to return to America, his close association with Hamas and known terrorists makes him an inadmissible alien under INS code 237(4)(B), in accordance with 212(a)(3)(B), which is inadmissibility due to "terrorist activities."[5]

Two years after the Hamas report was finished, my continuing efforts to target individuals and organizations tied to the network led to another invitation. On January 29, 2009, Brooke McCoy, a colleague and friend of mine in the Operational Analysis Branch, Office of Intelligence and Operations Coordination (OIOC), e-mailed my port director, asking that he release me to work for an extended time on a "new joint FBI/ICE/JTTF/FinCEN [Financial Crimes Enforcement Network] project" initiated by my research on Hamas:

> Initial project discussions indicate that we will be targeting individuals associated with Hamas through PNR [passenger name record] for outbound examinations for currency and potentially other extremist material.
>
> Upon notification by our group, FBI will coordinate the physical examinations of these individuals. Potentially, this could expand to include Phil's research on Tablighi Jamaat, and could open additional

avenues within Intel for someone with his insight, research, and writing skills.

Please let us know if he is available for this detail. I'm very pleased that he has the opportunity to be a part of something initiated by his diligence and creative thought.

As happened so many times during my career in CBP, no reply was ever given regarding this important temporary-duty assignment opportunity with the Office of Intelligence and Operations Coordination.

The memo also indicates I was already working on the Tablighi Jamaat case in January 2009, which eventually evolved into the initiative that was shut down by the NTC in June 2012 and came to national attention following the San Bernardino shootings December 2, 2015.

Who can say what law enforcement actions may have been taken to help protect the country if we had all been allowed to work together on a case such as this?

Less than a month after the invitation, February 24, 2009, I received a copy of a commendation letter from FBI Special Agent in Charge Gregory Jones to Port Director Stephen Kremer:

> It is with great appreciation that I write this letter to thank your agency, specifically Officer Philip Haney for his assistance in support of the joint CBP/FBI IOIL program.
>
> The success of this program . . . relies significantly on the conscientious efforts of dedicated CBP Officers. Through 2007 and 2008 Officer Haney consistently conducted thorough and insightful interviews, and provided detailed IOIL information, upon which the FBI Joint Terrorism Task Force places great value.
>
> In this new age of information sharing, Officer Haney's efforts, professionalism and dedication to this program reflect great credit upon himself and Customs and Border Protection.

On March 10, 2009, I met with Supervisor Harer to review the status of seven active cases related either to the Hamas network or the Tablighi Jamaat Initiative. In the six months since I joined the ATU team to that day, there had been 914 inquiries or requests for information from law-enforcement colleagues around the country.

I also asked Harer to check into the status of the OIOC TDY opportunity, but we were never given the courtesy of a response.

PROTECTING MUSLIMS

On June 4, 2009, we arrived at what I considered a significant turning point in history, when President Obama addressed the entire Muslim world in his speech "A New Beginning," in Cairo, Egypt, at Al-Azhar University, regarded as the center of the Sunni Islamic world.

With specially invited Muslim Brotherhood leaders seated at the front of the audience, the speech made it clear to those of us in the counterterrorism community that a civil rights–based counterterrorism policy, known as Countering Violent Extremism (CVE), had completely overtaken the initial post-9/11 law enforcement–based counterterrorism policy.

To reinforce the point, attorney general Eric Holder released a statement timed to coincide with President Obama's speech in Cairo:

> The President's pledge for a new beginning between the United States and the Muslim community takes root here in the Justice Department, where we are committed to using criminal and civil rights laws to protect Muslim Americans. A top priority of this Justice Department is a return to robust civil rights enforcement and outreach in defending religious freedoms and other fundamental rights of all of our fellow citizens in the workplace, in the housing market, in our schools and in the voting booth.
>
> There are those who will continue to want to divide by fear—to pit our national security against our civil liberties—but that is a false choice. We have a solemn responsibility to protect our people while we also protect our principles.[6]

The president's speech came just six months after the Dallas jury in the Holy Land Foundation trial had returned 108 guilty verdicts against five individuals for material support of terrorism.

As I considered the intent of President Obama's speech to the Islamic world, combined with the timing of Holder's announcement that the DOJ would now pursue a policy of "robust civil rights enforcement and outreach," I realized that the DOJ would probably not proceed to a "phase two" of the Holy Land Foundation case and pursue the US-based groups in the Hamas network on which I had been reporting.

Meanwhile, on July 19, 2009, I wrote a memo to Harer, alerting him to a disturbing trend of Muslim passengers creating a scene—cussing, screaming, and exhibiting other disruptive behavior—after they were referred either to the baggage inspection or secondary inspection area for questioning.

My colleagues in other ports filed graphic, verbatim incident reports that described how, right in front of everyone, these well-known Muslim passengers would shout, for example, "I'm a US citizen. You don't have the f***ing right to do this, to treat me like this! I'm going to call my senator!"

In the memo to Harer, I observed:

> I have a feeling we're being set up, i.e., that incidents like these are deliberate, and will be used in an attempt to deflect attention from people who are affiliated with known Muslim Brotherhood front groups, etc.
>
> These passengers are deliberately provoking CBP officers so that they can build a case of harassment and discrimination against the agency.
>
> They're setting this up like a Sunday potluck; eventually, they will bring all of their complaints to the table, and then someone like CAIR will file a macro suit.
>
> I'll keep you informed of any other incidents I find.

A few months later, on October 27, 2009, a lawsuit brought by six Muslim clerics—the "flying imams"—who claimed religious discrimination for being removed from a flight was settled out of court for an unknown amount. A CAIR-affiliated lawyer represented the imams, who were removed before takeoff from a November 20, 2006, US Airways Minneapolis-to-Phoenix flight after their behavior alarmed passengers and crew.

The imams refused to sit in their assigned seats and moved out in pairs to occupy front, middle, and rear exit seats. They were observed praying loudly in Arabic, ordered seat-belt extenders they didn't need, criticized the Iraq War and President Bush, and talked about al-Qaeda and Osama bin Laden. The lawsuit was filed against US Airways, the airport authority, and even the passengers who reported the suspicious activity. Congress later passed a law to protect citizens who report suspicious behavior or activity.

A few months before the "flying imams" settlement, July 24, 2009, seven members of Congress requested that Attorney General Holder meet with the leaders of at least nine major US Muslim groups to discuss a "decline in relations" between Muslims and the Justice Department. Virtually every one of the nine groups mentioned in the letter are known Muslim Brotherhood front groups. Worse, at least two of them had just been named as unindicted coconspirators in the Holy Land Foundation trial, CAIR and ISNA.

The Congress members wrote:

> We are writing to request that you host a meeting with leaders of the American Muslim community to discuss the decline in relations between the American Muslim community and the Department of Justice, as well as ways to repair it.
>
> These concerns raise legitimate questions about due process, justice, and equal treatment under the law. We hope that you will meet with American Muslim leaders to ensure that core American values are respected for all Americans, regardless of race, ethnicity, or faith. For your convenience, we have attached a contact list of American Muslim leaders.
>
> Thank you for your attention to this important matter.

The letter was signed by Democratic Reps. Lois Capps, Mike Honda, and Loretta Sanchez of California; Adam Schiff, Mary Jo Kilroy, and Dennis Kucinich of Ohio; and James Moran of Virginia.[7]

The Islamic groups named in the letter also included the Islamic Circle of North America (ICNA), which adheres to a similar ideology as Jamaat-i-Islami, a Pakistani organization that calls for Islamic revolution and the creation of an Islamist state in Pakistan. Also listed was the Muslim Public Affairs Council (MPAC), which has argued that Hezbollah should not be designated as a terrorist organization, and the nationwide Muslim Brotherhood–founded university campus organization, the Muslim Students Association (MSA).[8]

It would have been prudent for these seven members of Congress to do some basic vetting before they signed a letter on behalf of American Muslim groups with proven ties to terrorist organizations.

On the very same day, July 24, 2009, we also learned that despite strenuous objections from personnel within the intelligence and law enforcement communities, the FBI formally designated ISNA as its official point of contact with the American Muslim community.[9]

The FBI already had presented intelligence at the Holy Land Foundation trial showing that ISNA conferences "provided opportunities for the extreme fundamentalist Muslims to meet with their supporters."

"The annual conferences are used for both religious and political purposes," the FBI said. "The political purpose is to further the Islamic Revolution, which includes the providing of anti-U.S. and Israel publications, and publications that support the war effort of Iran in the Iran–Iraq war."[10]

NO MORE "WAR ON TERRORISM"
Another policy tsunami hit August 6, 2009, when we were informed the White House had insisted on a "new way of seeing" the nation's biggest threat, declaring that the United States was no longer in a "war on terrorism" and was not fighting "jihadists."

John Brennan, assistant to the president for homeland security and counterterrorism and deputy national security adviser, explained that President Obama "does not describe this as a 'war on terrorism.'"

"We are at war with al-Qaeda," he said. "We are at war with its violent extremist allies who seek to carry out al-Qaeda's murderous agenda."

By now, I was so concerned about the emerging threat and the Obama administration's tightening restrictions on the ability of law enforcement officers to do our job that I made a second appointment with a member of Congress.

This time, I met with Thomas Price, my representative from Georgia's Sixth Congressional District.

Speaking as a private citizen, with my wife sitting beside me, I met with Price in his office on the afternoon of September 1, 2009. I shared the following prepared remarks with him:

> This is an extraordinary time in American history—nothing quite like it has come before. As a 35-year analyst of events in the Middle East, I am convinced that the U.S. and her allies face a hazardous global crisis. This crisis has arrived in the form of terrorism, and in a concurrent rise in radical Islam.
>
> The road we face is fraught with potential dangers. It is imperative that we correctly understand the nature of this world-wide conflict— any major mistake in judgment could be catastrophic.
>
> I believe that America's intelligence agencies must make full and creative use of every human resource available. I also believe that I have something valuable to offer in this new national mandate.
>
> To borrow from Shakespeare's play, *Julius Caesar* (Act 4, Scene 3) –
> *The enemy increases every day;*
> *We, at the height, are ready to decline.*
> *There is a tide in the affairs of men,*
> *Which, taken at the flood, leads on to fortune;*
> *Omitted, all the voyage of their life*
> *Is bound in shallows and in miseries.*
> *On such a full sea are we now afloat;*

And we must take the current when it serves,
Or lose our ventures.

I believe that we are now at the turning of that tide. I would like to help America continue her "voyage of life."

I'm grateful to Representative Price for his cordial reception that day and for listening to what I had to say.

QURANIC PRISM

By late September 2009 at my home Port of Atlanta, I had served on the ATU team for a full year, with Robert Harer as my direct supervisor the entire time.

On September 26, 2009, I opened the first case at the Port of Atlanta that linked the movement of cargo to possible terrorism. My motto in ATU was, "Boxes don't move without people."

The case focused on the importation of school textbooks titled *Quranic Prism: Subject Index of the Holy Quran*.[11] In a status memo to management summarizing the case, I wrote:

On page 1221 of the most recent edition (2007) of the *Quranic Prism*, the Prologue states that "In the current critical times of Islam-bashing, the present publication will go a long way in helping to remove the mischievous myths, naïve misunderstandings about Islam and mistrust between Muslims and the West. This 'PRISM' is designed to benefit the readers not well versed with Arabic and the Muslim community living under overwhelming Western influence, especially the younger generations lured by the spell of Secular Westernization."

In light of these facts, i.e. that [1] the *Quranic Prism* would like to "remove the mischievous myths, naïve misunderstandings about Islam and mistrust between Muslims and the West," and [2] that it has been openly endorsed by the ICNA, ISNA and Al-Azhar University (i.e., organizations that usually go out of their way to avoid being openly associated with jihad), it is "surprising" to find that the *Quranic Prism* is so explicitly pro-jihadist in content.

The first indication of this may be found on pages 99–100 of the *Quranic Prism*, which provide a summary of the *Fundamentals of Faith— Foundations of Islam*. These eight "Fundamentals" (better known as the "Pillars of Islam") specifically include jihad, also known as "Holy War."

The *Quranic Prism*'s open declaration that jihad is one of the main "*Pillars of Islam*" is also surprising, because most US-based Islamic organizations will never publicly admit that jihad ("holy war") is a central part of orthodox Islam.

Another example of the pro-jihad teachings in the *Quranic Prism* may be found on page 660, under the heading "Hypocrites Who Stir Up Sedition Shall Be Seized and Slain": "Accursed, they will be seized wherever found, and slain with a (fierce) slaughter. That was the way of Allah in the case of those who passed away of old; you will not find any change in Allah's practice" (Quran 33.61–62).

In fact, a total of 289 verses (found in 47 of the 114 chapters in the Qur'an) are cited a total 324 times in pages 642–669 of the *Quranic Prism*. In addition, 14 of the Quran's 16 major chapters on jihad that are cited in the *Quranic Prism* are also included in the *Quranic Concept of War*, a well-known book on orthodox, historical jihad-based military strategy and tactics that was written in 1986 by the Pakistani author S. K. Malik.

I concluded the memo:

Much more could be said about the complex nature of this case, but this memo is really meant to be a basic overview of the case for those who may have an interest in pursuing it further.

One thing I am sure of—we will never find a more explicit example of materials that can be used to radicalize people, either child or adult, new believers in Islam or old, than the teachings that are found in the *Quranic Prism*.

I also believe that this case warrants further involvement with colleagues in other agencies, especially in light of the apparent increase in radicalized Muslims who live right here in the USA.

On October 6, 2009, I notified NTC in writing about the case, and our JTTF liaison informed me that details of the investigation would be forwarded to the appropriate colleagues in Texas for follow-up.

By October 24, I had spent 116 hours on the case, linking numerous individuals and organizations with known terrorist ties to the network of schools and businesses that were importing Quranic Prism into American schools.

But that very day, October 24, 2009, everything came to a screeching halt.

One of the first casualties was the Quranic Prism case, which I never worked on again.

"A LEARNING OPPORTUNITY"

To go back just slightly, on October 15, 2009, I had a meeting with Port Director Kremer. At the time, my perception of the meeting was that I would be giving him a status report on the new Quranic Prism case, as well an update on the seven active cases that I had reviewed with Supervisor Harer on March 10, 2009. Since there had been several hundred more law enforcement actions attributed to these cases since March, I was looking forward to the meeting, which was scheduled for 9 a.m.

As I always did, I brought along an outline of my proposed talking points and gave a copy to Kremer. Then I went through my points, summarized under the headings "Past," "Present," and "Future." In particular, I talked about the Quranic Prism case, mentioning that according to my JTTF colleague, along with additional NTC confirmation, it appeared to be the first case in Atlanta that linked potential terrorism to shipments of cargo.

After a half hour or so, we had covered all the talking points in the outline, and everything seemed to be okay, until just before the meeting was about to end.

Suddenly, Kremer asked, "How's your case with Ingrid Mattson, Mr. Haney?"

I was surprised, but said, "It's watertight, sir."

At the time, Mattson was president of the Islamic Society of America

(ISNA), the largest Muslim organization in America. But it also was a known Muslim Brotherhood front group that recently had been designated an unindicted coconspirator in the Holy Land Foundation case.

And that was it. Or so I thought, until a week or so later, when I was working on an outbound inspection detail with ATU team members and Harer handed me his duty phone.

"It's Mr. Kremer," Harer said. "He wants to talk with you."

"We have a new project for you," Kremer told me. "We're going to use it as a learning opportunity.

"We're going to reassign you back to PAU, and you're going to start modifying all of your TECS records. We've been directed from headquarters that we can't have any information in TECS that has to do with terrorism, so you're going to have to go in and change all of your records.

"This comes right from the top," he emphasized.

REMOVE THE DOTS

I was stunned. By order of DHS headquarters, I was about to remove valuable intelligence information—the "dots"—from every one of the records I had ever put into TECS.

There were hundreds of these records, which had taken years of painstaking research and careful attention to detail. Most of the records were linked to the Hamas Network investigation, but some of them were part of the Tablighi Jamaat case, which was not yet as well developed as the Hamas report but still was a solid case.

For three years now, I had been targeting the leaders of all the major Muslim Brotherhood front groups in the United States, some of whom were becoming closely affiliated with the administration, the DOJ, and with law enforcement agencies such as the FBI. Eventually, I documented more than fifty meetings between 1998 and 2009 between leaders of Muslim Brotherhood front groups and members of the executive or legislative branches of the US government.

Now, we had come to the point where DHS and the State Department, with influence from the DOJ, had to make a moral decision about how to deal with the information that officers like me had put into the system.

The choice they faced was either to respond to the information in a law-enforcement manner and begin to prosecute these Muslim Brotherhood–linked individuals and organizations, disregard it, or eliminate it.

In this instance, they chose the last option, elimination.

TRAUMATIZED

By this time, late in October 2009, it had been only a year since US attorneys in federal court had proven beyond reasonable doubt that American Muslim organizations such as CAIR, ISNA, and the North American Islamic Trust (NAIT) were not only operating as front groups for the Muslim Brotherhood but had direct ties to Designated Foreign Terrorist Organizations such as Hamas.

However, it was also obvious that a discernible shift in attitude was taking place within DHS and in other law enforcement agencies, such as the FBI.

Instead of a counterterrorism policy built on a facts-based analysis of the threat that follows through with strong, law-enforcement actions, the emerging civil rights and civil liberties–based approach essentially afforded foreign nationals—including members of known violent Islamic groups—the same constitutional rights as US citizens.

I was now faced with another great moral crisis. It was not the first one since joining CBP and certainly would not be the last.

I was also badly traumatized, both professionally and personally, to the point that sometimes I had to remind myself to take the next breath.

How could I remove years of work on groups like Hamas and Tablighi Jamaat that clearly posed a threat to national security? On the other hand, how could I refuse to comply with a direct order?

So, I decided to do two things. First, inside the agency, I would begin documenting all of my concerns in writing, and second, I would seek legal advice and help outside of Customs and Border Protection.

On Thursday, November 5, 2009, I took some annual leave from work and drove from Atlanta to the nation's capital to meet the following day with my colleague Stephen C. Coughlin in his office in Crystal City, Virginia. This was the same day that Nidal Malik Hasan shot forty-three people at Fort Hood, Texas, killing thirteen. In light of what I had just been ordered to do back at the port, imagine my sense of urgency during that twelve-hour drive as I listened to news reports on the radio about a person named Hasan who shouted, "*Allahu Akbar!*" as he killed his own colleagues and countrymen.

The meeting was arranged by Jeffrey M. Epstein, a counterterrorism activist who produced a number of symposiums drawing experts in the field. None of us had ever met in person. Coughlin is a former Joint Chiefs of Staff intelligence analyst who was fired by the Pentagon at the request of Hesham H. Islam, who has since been suspected of being an Islamic terrorist sympathizer.[12] Coughlin's warnings that ISNA was a Muslim Brotherhood front group led Mr. Islam to call Coughlin "a Christian zealot with a pen."[13]

Subsequently, the Joint Chiefs of Staff did not renew Coughlin's contract as an intelligence analyst.

Our meeting went well. Coughlin is a consummate professional, and we had both suffered professional and personal damage for speaking the truth about the nature of the threat we face.

At the end of the day, I was encouraged and believed that we possibly had found an avenue to safely go outside the agency but still remain within the chain of command. In other words I was advised not to go public, as Edward Snowden had done, but to follow the process and stay within the structure of the US government.

The meeting also started the process of finding legal counsel. I'll address this issue in more detail as the story unfolds, but for now, let's just say that finding a good lawyer for a whistle-blower could easily be an entire book in itself.

Back at work, I had already started putting my concerns in writing, producing what became a series of twelve memos to management. The most important memo was the tenth, dated November 18, 2009, in which I expressed concern about the impact of "modifying" records:

> The questions arising from the Ft. Hood shooting incident have direct bearing on our [Modification] Project, because, for the last five years, I have been working hard to (1) "connect the dots" regarding Individuals & Organizations affiliated with the Muslim Brotherhood network here in the US, and (2) describe the strategy and tactics of the Muslim Brotherhood in the US, as based specifically on Sharia law.
>
> This "connect the dot" approach has been borne out by the successful conclusion of the Holy Land Foundation trial in 2008, which led to the conviction of five Individuals on 108 counts of providing at least $12 million in material support to Hamas, a Specially Designated Global Terrorist Organization ("SDGTO").
>
> In fact, the legal team for the Holy Land Foundation was provided with all of the information contained in "The Hamas Network in the United States," as per JTTF.
>
> … Thus, my concern at the present time is that the process of modifying my records will undo thousands of hours (years) of work, specifically designed to "connect the dots," and/or to describe the Sharia-based strategy and tactics of Muslim Brotherhood front-groups operating in the US.
>
> In addition, the information in these records is based on careful, detailed analysis that is not otherwise available in the TECS system.

The same day, I was called in for a meeting with my immediate supervisor, Bill Green (not his real name). As we sat down and began the meeting, he laid a copy of my tenth memo on the table between us and underlined the portion that read, "Thus, my concern at the present time is that the process of modifying my records will undo thousands of hours (years) of work, specifically designed to 'connect the dots.'"

I know shorthand, having taken it in high school on the advice of my father, and as we sat at the table, I began writing down every word Supervisor Green said.

He looked at me and said, "What are you writing, Mr. Haney?"

I replied, "Everything you're saying."

But he didn't stop talking, and I kept writing.

In response to my concerns, not only as expressed in that memo, but also in the previous one, I was told, according to my notes:

> No CBP Officer was ever supposed to be creating these [kinds of TECS] records in the first place; people who do this kind of work are not CBPOs at [ports of entry].
>
> We're not really undoing years of your work . . . It is a procedural issue . . . No one is saying you haven't done good work . . . We like what you are doing . . . You just did it wrong . . . You can still nominate the records for B10 status [known affiliation with terrorism].
>
> This agency has established channels for doing this kind of work, but you have been creating your own individual channel. You seem to believe that no one can do this job as well as you do, and you don't trust that others are as capable of doing it as you.
>
> You have no statutory authority to do the work you have done.

Green closed the meeting by reiterating that no CBP officer is allowed to create TECS records that are related to terrorism, while adding that my career in research and creating reports was over and that the agency would no longer be giving me any "special consideration."

AS SEEN ON TV

After the meeting, I went back to work on the modification project, which took until March 2010 to finish.

On December 10, 2009, I received my ten-year pin and certificate for "recognition of service in the Government of the United States of America." With a decade of government service now officially in the books, I recall wondering where I might be ten years later and where our country might be in the year 2019.

A couple of weeks later, on December 25, Umar Farouk Abdulmutallab attempted to detonate plastic explosives hidden in his underwear while on board Northwest Airlines Flight 253, en route from Amsterdam to Detroit.

Within moments, I ran some queries and discovered that Abdulmutallab was not only linked to Anwar al-Awlaki, the senior al-Qaeda recruiter, but was also president of the University College London's Islamic Society.[14] He was the fourth president of a London student Islamic society to face terrorist charges in the three years prior to 2009.

I also found that some of the individuals and organizations linked to Abdulmutallab were already part of the Hamas Network case, or would subsequently be linked to either the Tablighi Jamaat Initiative, or to the sixty-seven records in the Islamic Institute of Education report that were deleted in September 2012.

Additionally, I discovered that Abdulmutallab had received a multiple-entry visa from the American embassy in London, valid from June 12, 2008, to June 11, 2010, which he used to visit the Al-Maghrib Institute in Houston, Texas.

The Al-Maghrib Institute already had ties to other organizations in the Hamas network, and an Al-Maghrib leader would later be linked to the Dar Al Uloom al Islamiyah of America mosque in San Bernardino, California, attended by San Bernardino killer Syed Rizwan Farook.

The small office where I worked on the modification project had a TV, and I followed the Abdulmutallab case from the original news reports to the congressional hearings on C-SPAN.

As one member of Congress after another expressed concern about the radicalization of American citizens and permanent residents, and the failure to connect the dots,[15] I was literally removing those very dots from TECS, the system we all used to track the activities of individuals and organizations with known or suspected ties to terrorism.

6

A NEW RELATIONSHIP

On January 20, 2010, Secretary of State Hillary Clinton signed a special order allowing Tariq Ramadan—the grandson of Muslim Brotherhood founder Hassan al-Banna—and Adam Habib, both previously suspected supporters of Islamic jihadists, reentry into the United States. In fact, after consulting with DHS secretary Janet Napolitano, Clinton invited them to apply for a visa.

While publicly claiming she was simply exercising her exemption authority, it appears that Clinton's highly visible move was actually designed to draw attention to President Obama's 2009 Cairo pledge to pursue "a new relationship with Muslim communities based on mutual interest and mutual respect."[1]

The visas were granted in spite of major opposition from the law enforcement community and with total disregard to the fact that since 2004, the State Department had repeatedly denied previous visa requests from Ramadan and Habib, arguing they both presented a national security threat.

The Clinton–Napolitano special order read:

INA§212(a)(3)(B)(iv)(VI)(dd)[2] shall not apply, for purposes of any application for nonimmigrant visa or for admission as a non-immigrant, to Mr. Tariq Ramadan, relative to donations made to the

Comite de Bienfaisance et de Secours aux Palestiniens and the *Association de Secours Palestinien* prior to 2003.[3]

The two groups named in the special order, the Comite de Bienfaisance et de Secours aux Palestiniens and the Association de Secours Palestinien, not only remain affiliates of Hamas to this day, but were named as unindicted coconspirators in the Holy Land Foundation case.

Then, on January 27–28, 2010, the Office of Civil Rights and Civil Liberties hosted a controversial "inaugural meeting" between American Muslim leaders and DHS Secretary Napolitano. Held two years after the release of the "Words Matter" memo and just over a year after the November 2008 Holy Land Foundation verdicts, the invitation-only, two-day conference in Washington, DC, included known affiliates of two of the Muslim Brotherhood front groups named as unindicted coconspirators in the HLF trial. A third invited group, the Muslim American Society (MAS), was also a known Muslim Brotherhood affiliate.

The documents related to the meeting became public on July 29, 2010, but only because a Freedom of Information Act (FOIA) request had been filed by Judicial Watch.

We learned from the FOIA documents that one of the front groups invited was the Islamic Society of North America (ISNA), which was founded in 1981 by students at the University of Illinois at Urbana–Champaign who were members of the Muslim Students Association (MSA).

ISNA was listed in the 1991 Muslim Brotherhood "Explanatory Memorandum" as among the "members of the US Muslim Brotherhood."[4] The MSA was the first Muslim Brotherhood front group founded in America, in January 1963.

Another front group invited to the meeting was the Muslim Public Affairs Council (MPAC), founded in 1988 as an offshoot of the Islamic Center of Southern California (ICSC) by brothers Maher and Hassan Hathout, both well-known, self-declared Muslim Brotherhood members who were heavily influenced by the teachings of founder Hassan al-Banna.

One prominent invitee to the meeting was Hassan Al-Jabri (aka

Hossam AlJabri and Hossam Jabri),[5] former executive national director of MAS. Al-Jabri was both the imam and one of three original leaders of the Islamic Society of Boston, which is closely linked to several front groups, including ISNA, the North American Islamic Trust (NAIT), and the International Institute of Islamic Thought (IIIT), as well as the Holy Land Foundation and the five defendants in the HLF case.

Other invitees included Salam Al-Marayati, president of MPAC; Mohamed Elibiary, president of the Freedom and Justice Foundation; Mohamed Magid, past president of ISNA and imam of All Dulles Area Muslim Society; Ingrid Mattson past president of ISNA; and Dalia Mogahed of the Gallup Center for Muslim Studies.[6]

In essence, DHS-CRCL actively recruited and "vetted" prominent leaders of at least three well-known North American affiliates of the international Muslim Brotherhood organization—which maintains a clearly stated strategy of promoting the supremacy of Islam in America—to attend the meeting and help develop the nation's counterterrorism policy.

On January 28, 2010, Napolitano and her senior staff had met privately with a select group of Muslim, Arab, and Sikh organizations, including three directly associated with Hamas, an outlawed terrorist entity.[7] PJ Media reported that Napolitano briefed the leaders on DHS counter-radicalization and antiterrorist programs. The story also quoted Walid Phares, then director of the Future Terrorism Project at the Foundation for Defense of Democracies, who criticized the partnership concept.

"Through the so-called 'partnership' between the jihadi-sympathizer networks and US bureaucracies, the US government is invaded by militant groups," he said. He further stated that this Obama-embraced policy is "how American national security policy has been influenced" by Muslim groups, who, he warned, are duping administration officials.[8]

Finally, the DHS-CRCL meeting, which was convened to "ask for their help with membership in the upcoming DHS faith-based information sharing task force," led to the formation of the Countering Violent Extremism Working Group in the spring of 2010.[9]

Meanwhile, on the weekend of March 12–14, 2010, I took some R & R and met with some friends in the beautiful Blue Ridge Mountains of Virginia.

After more than three months, I was still working on the "modification" project. As I left my friends and drove south toward Atlanta that pleasant Sunday afternoon, I was doing a lot of talking out loud and praying as I searched for the right thing to do.

I knew something bad would happen, sooner or later, and that the information I was deleting would eventually connect in one way or another to individuals with known or potential ties to terrorist activity.

THE WORD IS OUT

The next day was Monday, March 15, 2010. I went back to work, and, after getting settled in, checked my e-mail.

At the top of the in-box was an e-mail string dated March 12, 2010, that originated with our assistant port director and was forwarded by my immediate supervisor, who added, "I had hoped to tell you in person but the word is out."

At the bottom of the string, the assistant port director wrote, "Effective immediately, please place Haney back in the [Federal Inspection Station] rotation—he is no longer needed in CTRT and we can certainly use him on primary."

CTRT is the Counter Terrorism Response Team. Aside from the fact that I wasn't even assigned to the CTRT, the point of the memo was that I would no longer be working as a subject matter expert in counterterrorism.

For a few moments, I just stared at the screen. The e-mail was not only incomprehensible, but incredibly disrespectful.

First, I'm not a "Subject." I'm Officer Haney, or Philip Haney, not just "Haney," like some kind of object or inconvenience.

Second, I had just spent the last four-plus months removing the dots from hundreds of TECS records and was still only half finished, at least in terms of how management had originally defined the project.

I say half finished because the eight-hundred-plus records I had worked on since November 2009 were only for individuals; there were still at least 850 more records linked to their affiliated organizations that had not been touched.

But there was no mention in the e-mail of the status of the modification project. In fact, there was no mention of the project at all, as if it had never happened. No explanation, no follow-up, no minimal professional courtesy; just a sterile mischaracterization that I was "no longer needed in CTRT."

Moreover, not a single one of the fifteen nomination packages—the recommendation of names for inclusion in the Terrorist Screening Database—that I had already prepared and redone three times had been forwarded to the National Targeting Center.

The most important lesson to take away from the whole modification project fiasco is that we had now come to a point in our counterterrorism policy where putting information into the system on individuals with known or potential ties to terrorism was officially prohibited.

From late 2009 into early 2010, there were murky official explanations offered, but in the next few years, the real reasons for such a policy would become much clearer.

For example, as DHS spokeswoman Marsha Catron explained to MSNBC on December 17, 2015, officials must ensure that any vetting follows "current law and appropriately takes into account civil rights and civil liberties and privacy protections."[10]

The key word in this statement is "appropriately."

From the very beginning, the Obama administration made the deliberate policy decision that it was more "appropriate" to take into account the civil rights and civil liberties of foreign nationals than to consider the nation's security.

As we'll see in chapter 10, the danger of this policy would become tragically apparent at 2:49 p.m. on April 15, 2013, when two bombs exploded near the finish line of the Boston Marathon.

Just one day after learning I was being moved back to primary, I received an e-mail from a colleague in the FBI, inviting me to work on a project with his agency and the Joint Terrorism Task Force.

"I just wanted to reach out to you via my FBI e-mail," he wrote, "so that we could establish communication. I will be working with my partner here at Washington Field and our boss to find out if there is a way we can get you on board some of the things we are working here in our office. . . . Given your analytical background and experience, I think you can offer some much needed assistance."

He then had a couple of questions for me: "What would you be willing to accept for work situations, i.e. if you are willing to travel to DC, how long would you be willing to stay?" And "What level clearances do you hold?"

He went on to say that some of the agency's information was at the "Secret" level, and I would need to be authorized to see it if I were to be of help with their project.

I passed the initial exchange up the chain of command, then waited to hear back. In the meantime, I went ahead and filled out the paperwork for secret clearance and continued preparing for the opportunity to work with my FBI colleagues.

Two weeks later, on April 2, 2010, I was cc'ed on a follow-up e-mail from my FBI contact:

> Below is an e-mail contact I had with an excellent analyst, Philip Haney, from CBP. In the last few years he has put together very informative analytical pieces on much of the MB front here in the US, solely for DHS use. In subsequent conversations with him, he would very much enjoy continuing to work [on] the MB.
>
> My question is how can we facilitate that? In response to my questions below, he has a confidential clearance pending and has requested that be upgraded to a Secret level (working with us could be part of the justification for that).
>
> He works out of the Atlanta CBP office. Is there a way to provide access at the Atlanta office and/or request something akin to a JTTF TDY for a CBP analyst?

I've spoken to him a lot about the MB, and his knowledge on the subject matter, and can tell you that he possesses a very deep level of knowledge even without access to our material.

Please let me know your thoughts.

That was the last official exchange I had with my FBI colleague, who was obviously making every effort he could to find a creative way for us to work together on a national security-level case.

However, as I had already seen several times since 2006, port management never followed through with his request and never bothered to notify me of their decision to deny this TDY opportunity to work on the Muslim Brotherhood case with the FBI in Washington, DC.

"RIGHT OFF THE FLOOR"

That same week, we had a morning muster on the floor of the Federal Inspection Station. We did this often, for a few minutes just before the first flights of the day arrived, to talk things over and to make sure we were all on the same page.

On this particular morning, we gathered around the central command area as usual, and Port Director Kremer spoke to the staff.

"For a while now, Mr. Haney and I have been having this ongoing discussion about where the best place for him to be is," Kremer said. "I think the best place for him to be is right out here, where he can pull live cases right off the floor.

"We don't need him to be in the back, out of sight, working with old information, but out here, where he can develop new cases, and get new information," he said. "Don't you agree, Mr. Haney?"

I didn't answer him. Instead, I just sighed and gave him a half smile. What else could I say? I certainly wasn't about to disagree with him in front of all my colleagues.

At the time, it was anything but a funny moment. Kremer had turned our private, professional conversation into a public discussion.

However, a few months later, something "funny" did come of it.

By December 2010, I had put together twenty-eight solid cases from "right off the floor," including many individuals who were US citizens returning from Deobandi madrassas in South Africa.

From my booth in primary, I came in a little early and did all the targeting before the flights landed. I then put the lookouts into the TECS system and made sure each person was referred for a secondary inspection.

In most of the cases, I also went to secondary to conduct the interviews and wrote up the final report for each case in a standardized format, which I had created.

I used a standardized format to ensure that every passenger I interviewed was asked exactly the same questions. That way, no one could say that I discriminated, or asked random or arbitrary questions.

After these final reports were downloaded into TECS and approved by the duty supervisor in secondary, I would close up shop in secondary and go back out to the floor and finish up my shift on primary.

Exhausting, yes, but rewarding.

I received support and encouragement from my two direct supervisors at the time, William Brannen and Frank Rodriguez, who worked closely with me and made it possible for this important case to come to life.

Ironically, these "off the floor" interviews formed the core of what became the Tablighi Jamaat Initiative at NTC. I worked on the case for another year and a half, and by November 2011, I was sent to NTC for a six-month TDY in which I was assigned to manage the Tablighi Jamaat Initiative.

WORKING WITH "COMMUNITIES"

Meanwhile, the Countering Violent Extremism Working Group was in full swing.

On May 26, 2010, the DHS Homeland Security Advisory Council (HSAC) released a document stating its intent to work with "communities":

Recognizing that there have been many successful cases of local law enforcement working with communities to fight violent crime, at the February 2010 HSAC Meeting Secretary Napolitano tasked the HSAC to ". . . work with state and local law enforcement as well as relevant community groups to develop and provide to me recommendations regarding how the Department can better support community-based efforts to combat violent extremism domestically, focusing in particular on the issues of training, information sharing, and the adoption of community-oriented law enforcement approaches to this issue.[11]

One of the CVE Working Group recommendations was a precursor to the implementation of civil rights and civil liberties policies in the law-enforcement and immigration-enforcement arenas:

Recognizing that policies implemented by DHS can affect local community partnerships, DHS Civil Rights Civil Liberties (CRCL) and other relevant DHS offices should continue and expand their engagement and grievance resolution efforts at DHS.[12]

It is important to recall that all of the individuals appointed to the 2010 Working Group were selected by DHS-HSAC after the Holy Land Foundation trial in 2008 and the surfacing of its list of unindicted coconspirators.

Apparently, the DHS-CRCL selection committee did not consider direct affiliation with organizations that were known financial supporters of Hamas to be a factor worth considering when it vetted the candidates for the Working Group.

This proved to be true on February 5, 2014, when a public notice was posted in the *Federal Register* that softened the standards for refusing to admit a foreigner on terrorism-related grounds:[13]

Following consultations with the Attorney General [DOJ], the Secretary of Homeland Security [DHS] and the Secretary of State [USSD] have determined that the grounds of inadmissibility at section

212(a)(3)(B) of the Immigration and Nationality Act (INA), 8 U.S.C. 1182(a)(3)(B), bar certain aliens who do not pose a national security or public safety risk from admission to the United States and from obtaining immigration benefits or other status. Accordingly, consistent with prior exercises of the exemption authority, the Secretary of Homeland Security and the Secretary of State, in consultation with the Attorney General, hereby conclude, as a matter of discretion in accordance with the authority granted by INA section 212(d)(3)(B)(i), 8 U.S.C. 1182 (d)(3)(B)(i),[14] as amended, as well as the foreign policy and national security interests deemed relevant in these consultations, that paragraphs 212(a)(3)(B)(iv)(VI)(bb) and (dd) of the INA, 8 U.S.C. 1182(a)(3)(B)(iv)(VI)(bb) and (dd), *shall not apply with respect to an alien who provided limited material support to an organization* [emphasis added] described in section 212(a)(3)(B)(vi)(III) of the INA, 8 U.S.C. 1182(a)(3)(B)(vi)(III), or to a member of such an organization, or to an individual described in section 212(a)(3)(B)((iv)(VI)(bb) of the INA, 8 U.S.C. 1182(a)(3)(B)(iv)(VI)(bb), that involves (1) certain routine commercial transactions or certain routine social transactions (i.e., in the satisfaction of certain well-established or verifiable family, social, or cultural obligations), (2) certain humanitarian assistance, or (3) substantial pressure that does not rise to the level of duress, provided, however, that the alien satisfies the relevant agency authority that the alien . . . [several exclusion clauses follow].[15]

In simpler language, the use here of the legal term "discretion" meant that the federal government would henceforth begin issuing entry and immigration visas (i.e., a path to citizenship) to individuals who had only provided "limited material support" to a known terrorist organization or to a known member of that organization if it was given as part of a "routine transaction" or in the satisfaction of certain "well-established . . . cultural obligations."

Let's turn now to a review of the Working Group appointees with close affiliations to known Muslim Brotherhood front organizations.

The first two were Omar Alomari, affiliated with the Muslim

American Society and several other Muslim Brotherhood front groups, and Mohamed Magid (ISNA), who was mentioned earlier in this chapter.

A third Muslim Brotherhood–affiliated member of the Working Group was Mohamed Elibiary, who was closely associated with Shukri Abu Baker, one of the five defendants in the Holy Land Foundation trial, as well as with CAIR, an HLF unindicted coconspirator. Elibiary also was appointed to President Obama's Homeland Security Advisory Council on October 18, 2010, but resigned on September 3, 2014, after a controversial series of tweets.

In one, he wrote that, as he had said before, it is inevitable that the "caliphate," the Islamic empire government by sharia, will return. And he said he considered the United States to be an "Islamic country with an Islamically compliant Constitution."[16]

His resignation was also due to his alleged role in the "inappropriate disclosure of sensitive law enforcement documents," as described in a letter from DHS.[17]

A fourth Working Group appointee was Dalia Mogahed, a member of the 2008 Leadership Group on US-Muslim Engagement. She maintained close relationships with CAIR, ISNA, MAS, and MPAC after her April 6, 2009, appointment to the White House Office of Faith-Based and Neighborhood Partnerships.

A fifth member of the Working Group was Nadia Roumani. From the time of her appointment to the Working Group to the present day, she has served as either director or contributing fellow at the American Muslim Civic Leadership Institute (AMCLI). Although the AMCLI was not designated as a Muslim Brotherhood front group in the HLF trial, the list of its alumni is a who's who of individuals affiliated with these known coconspirators.

Another member of the Working Group was former Los Angeles deputy mayor Arif Alikhan, who was appointed as assistant secretary for policy development by Napolitano on April 24, 2009. Alikhan is also a close associate of MPAC and the Islamic Shura Council of Southern California (ISCSC), yet another adversarial Muslim Brotherhood umbrella organization for Islamic organizations, including CAIR's Southern California branch, MPAC, and Islamic Relief, which was led in past years by the Hathout brothers.

In turn, the ISCSC is directly linked to still other individuals and organizations with known ties to Muslim Brotherhood front groups, such as ISNA, MAS, and MSA. Many of these individuals and the Islamic organizations they represent have been engaged in a years-long adversarial relationship with the federal government over its counter-terrorism and law-enforcement policies. Often, this has been in close collaboration with the DHS Office of Civil Rights and Civil Liberties. In fact, according to a June 11, 2013, federal court order in a case discussed in chapter 9, CAIR and other Islamic groups attempted to use their close association with the US government to immunize themselves from law-enforcement scrutiny.

Arguing for allowing a claim that the government violated the Fifth Amendment with discriminatory questioning of Muslims based on religious beliefs at ports of entry, the US District Court for the Eastern District of Michigan Southern Division cited a May 3, 2011, letter from a DHS Civil Rights and Civil Liberties officer, who wrote:

> We thank you for your complaint; inquiries like yours help the Department of Homeland Security meet its obligation to protect civil rights and civil liberties. You can expect to receive a letter from us informing you how we have concluded this matter.[18]

The tactic was also evident when the government intervened on behalf of CAIR and MAS after the UAE had designated them as terrorist organizations on November 15, 2014, along with groups such as al-Qaeda and ISIS.

Today, despite all the evidence to the contrary, these American-based front groups are allowed to use the civil rights and civil liberties–based CVE policy as a protective shield, while refusing to acknowledge any connection between the Islamic supremacy they promote and the steady rise in jihad attacks in the United States and around the world.

At the same, the Obama administration continues to make overtures and concessions to them in both domestic and foreign policy.

Meanwhile, on August 10, 2010, Brian Lamkin, the FBI's special agent in charge in Atlanta, recognized ten of my colleagues and me for a "proactive interagency initiative" that had "supported 98 FBI investigations conducted throughout the U.S. the identification of suspicious activity on behalf of 67 persons previously unknown to the JTTF, and the identification of 24 persons of interest through a program called Operation Good Neighbor." Operation Good Neighbor was a very successful IDSO, or Intelligence Driven Special Operation, based on specific targeting rules, combined with some very precise analytical criteria.

The operation continued for several more years and was the trigger for many of the interviews I conducted in secondary between 2010 and 2012. My experience and insights, gained from studying the Quran and working in the Middle East, proved very valuable in this operation and helped the team refine and improve our counterterrorism efforts.

In other words, things worked just like they're supposed to.

INFORMANT

On August 13, 2010, I became involved in one of the oddest investigations in my entire CBP career. This time it had to do with possible improper targeting of an alleged informant operating inside ISNA.

Two investigators from the inspector general's office in downtown Atlanta sat with me in a side office and asked why I had included this alleged informant in one of the reports I had created. According to the investigators, the alleged informant accused me of being impolite and abusive, and claimed that I had "threatened" to send him to secondary.

I call the investigation odd for two reasons: first, because I had never talked to the person. Second, it was no secret that US personnel were attending ISNA meetings, despite the fact that the federal government was right in the middle of the Holy Land Foundation trial and despite the well-established fact that it was a Muslim Brotherhood front group.

The *Washington Times* reported on August 7, 2007, that the

Department of Justice cosponsored the annual ISNA convention in an effort to educate Muslims about their civil rights. As in previous years, the DOJ's Civil Rights Division had a table at the ISNA convention—which is said to attract more than thirty thousand American Muslims—to hand out literature and answer questions about the division's work.[19]

I also regarded the investigation as odd because if I were an informant, I would consider being "sent to secondary" a pretty good way to maintain my cover.

Apparently, someone must have thought I had access to a highly classified database, so the IG investigators were ordered to come and interview me. When I showed them the actual spreadsheet for the case involving the alleged informer, they were both quite impressed and realized that this particular individual was just one small part of a much bigger case.

Two and a half years later, on February 5, 2013, I finally received a letter of exoneration, in which I was told that "based on the facts of the investigation, there was insufficient evidence to support an administrative action which has been taken. Therefore," the letter concluded, "this case has been closed."

To this day, however, I still don't know what the phrase "there was insufficient evidence to support an administrative action which has been taken" actually means.

Meanwhile, on August 18, 2010, the men and women of CBP were notified via an e-mail from Commissioner Alan Bersin that the journeyman grade for CBP officers would be raised to GS 12, effective August 29, 2010, because, since the 9/11 attacks, the work has become "increasingly dangerous and complex" as the agency "confronts all threats to our national security."

A couple of months later, on October 28, 2010, I received a copy of an e-mail from my colleague Holly Banks, a program manager and senior intelligence officer in the Forensic Document Laboratory division of Homeland Security Investigations, asking the port's upper management to release me to assist in an investigation:

Good afternoon,

In May 2010, as the FDL [Fraud Document Laboratory] Program Manager for Operation [author's redaction], we requested the opportunity to provide refresher training to CBP Officers participating in Operation [author's redaction] [passport and document fraud] at the ECCF's and IMF's nationwide.

We received a positive response via DFO Robert Gomez. Our training in Memphis was very successful and the officers and supervisors were very attentive and dedicated.

As a result of completing this nationwide training we have been receiving an increase in referrals and they all deserve our recognition. The FDL is submitting this request for the assistance of CBP Officer Philip Haney's subject matter expertise, which will be explained hereafter.

Recently, the FDL received an OWC referral from CBP containing 55 passports and other documents. I conducted a preliminary review of the information received at which time I noticed certain suspicious indicators and subjects that may be of potential national security interest.

Based on some of the suspicious indicators I observed, I contacted Officer Philip Haney, who I consider a highly knowledgeable expert on many issues and most importantly Counterterrorism issues, to consult on my observations and theories.

During our conversation, he was able to confirm that I was on the right path, but after this discussion, I realized that I cannot reiterate all the knowledge and expertise that he can provide during the research and analysis of this sensitive and urgent referral.

One day later, management sent a negative response to Banks:

Ms. Banks,

Unfortunately, Officer Haney is assigned to CBP Atlanta's core mission of passenger processing, and will not be able to provide the dedicated time for document / investigative support.

In the interest of providing support for the request, CBP Atlanta can provide assistance through the use of its FAS staff if needed.

Another lost opportunity, but at least in this case, I knew right away that the answer would be no.

As the season changed and 2010 drew to a close, I took some time to review the major events and global trends that I had observed during the year. Chief among them was the buildup of violent protests in North Africa and the Middle East that soon became known as the "Arab Spring."

I put these observations into a November 1, 2010, memo, and sent it to port management, asking if they would like to meet to discuss the issues and offering suggestions for training:

> In all these years, I have never seen such a rapid, aggressive expansion of the Strategy & Tactics of the Global Islamic Movement (GIM) as I am seeing now. Briefly, the Strategy of the global Islamic movement is to establish Islamic Sharia Law in the entire world, while the Tactics of the global Islamic movement—including several distinct types of *Jihad*—are designed to first ensure that Sharia is established in the world, and then to protect and support it from that time forward.
>
> At this time, the GIM in the West is using two simultaneous aggressive tactics; [1] unifying the social/political narrative vis-à-vis the West (i.e., the OIC [Organization of Islamic Cooperation] & "Islamophobia"), and [2] putting America into tactical check(mate).
>
> These two tactical methods are essential components of MB Supreme Guide Mohamed Badi's September 30, 2010 call to global *Jihad*, citing the doctrine of Tumult & Oppression.[20]
>
> Recognizing that these are complex subjects that can't be adequately covered in a memo, I would like to request an opportunity to meet with Management, to discuss these subjects in more detail, and to offer suggestions (e.g., more training in CT and in Strategy & Tactics) that could be helpful to Officers here in our Port.

For an example of a possible training course, please see my PowerPoint presentation entitled *Strategy & Tactics II*, which is saved on the Share Drive. For additional historical background, also see my 2006 article entitled "Green Tide Rising."

By the way, the Muslim Brotherhood leader Badie, mentioned in the memo, called for global jihad based on the principle of *fitna*, which is commonly translated as "oppression." But it also means "opposition," "tumult," or "resistance" to the global advancement of Islam and the implementation of Islamic law.

I never received any feedback from management regarding the memo.

On December 29, 2010, I closed out the year in a meeting with one of my chiefs to discuss a couple of promising TDY opportunities.

The first was an offer to work with William Ferri—the Green Tide Rising fact finder from Newark Airport I'd met in 2006—who invited me to come up to his port for a week or two and help teach CBP officers about counterterrorism, targeting, and the strategy and tactics of the global Islamic movement, with a focus on Tablighi Jamaat and the Muslim Brotherhood network in the United States.

The other pending opportunity was to liaison in Washington, DC, as a supervisory intelligence analyst with the FBI's Threat Review Unit in the Counterterrorism Division.

I'm sure it will come as no great surprise by now that neither one of these proposals ever saw the light of day.

7

THE GREAT PURGE

On December 21, 2010, US Attorney General Eric Holder went before a television audience to warn the nation that the threat of terrorism had evolved, and that Americans should be aware that fellow citizens within their borders could pose a danger.

"What I am trying to do in this interview is to make people aware of the fact that the threat is real, the threat is different, the threat is constant," Holder said in an interview on ABC's *Good Morning America*.

"The threat has changed from simply worrying about foreigners coming here, to worrying about people in the United States, American citizens—raised here, born here, and who for whatever reason, have decided that they are going to become radicalized and take up arms against the nation in which they were born."[1]

One month later, on January 31, 2011, the Obama administration declared for the first time that it supported a role for the Muslim Brotherhood in a reformed government in Egypt, where the organization had been banned.[2]

In a February 10, 2011, hearing before the House Intelligence Committee, Rep. Sue Myrick, R-NC, questioned James Clapper, the director of national intelligence, about the threat posed by the Muslim Brotherhood.

Clapper described the Muslim Brotherhood as "a very heterogeneous group, largely secular, which has eschewed violence and has decried al-Qaida as a perversion of Islam . . . They have pursued social ends, a betterment of the political order in Egypt," he said. "In other countries, there are also chapters or franchises of the Muslim Brotherhood, but there is no overarching agenda, particularly in pursuit of violence, at least internationally."[3]

While the Brotherhood renounced violence in the 1970s in response to brutal crackdowns by autocratic regimes in the Middle East, including Nasser's Egypt, it hasn't changed its motto: "Allah is our objective. The Prophet is our leader. The Qur'an is our law. Jihad is our way. Dying in the way of Allah is our highest hope. Allahu akbar!"[4]

As the Arab Spring arose in 2011, the uprising was characterized by the Obama administration and the media as a popular, secular movement, empowered by the noble goals of liberty, freedom, and democracy.

But analysts who thoroughly studied the Muslim Brotherhood knew from the very beginning that the real forces behind the Arab Spring were ominous and malevolent.

For example, on February 18, 2011, an immense crowd numbering in the hundreds of thousands gathered in Tahrir Square in Cairo to welcome leading Muslim Brotherhood theologian Yusuf al-Qaradawi, who is banned from entry into the United States.

At his first public speech in Egypt since 1981, the crowd chanted and roared in approval as Qaradawi spoke.

"Don't let anyone steal this revolution from you—those hypocrites who will put on a new face that suits them. The revolution isn't over. It has just started to build Egypt. Guard your revolution," he said.[5]

While Qaradawi was speaking, the crowd chanted, "Al-Quds, Ra'ahin, Shahadin, Al-Mil'yoneen," or, "To Jerusalem we will march, as jihad martyrs by the millions."[6]

The imperious declaration was echoed in 2012 by prominent Egyptian Muslim cleric Safwat Hagazy, who said to an enthusiastic crowd at a rally for Muslim Brotherhood candidate Mohamed Morsi that Jerusalem will become Egypt's capital, and "Our chants shall be:

'millions of martyrs will march towards Jerusalem.'"[7]

In the crowd at Tahrir was Shadi Hamid, a research director at the Brookings Institute's Doha Center in Qatar, who explained to the *Christian Science Monitor* that Qaradawi "is very much in the mainstream of Egyptian society, he's in the religious mainstream, he's not offering something that's particularly distinctive or radical in the context of Egypt. He's an Islamist and he's part of the Brotherhood school of thought, but his appeal goes beyond the Islamist spectrum, and in that sense he's not just an Islamist figure, he's an Egyptian figure with a national profile," Hamid said.[8]

Another example of the true Islamic nature of the Arab Spring was seen on May 21, 2011, when the well-known Muslim Brotherhood leader Rashid Ghannouchi returned to Tunisia after a long exile in the United Kingdom to become the leader of the Tunisian Islamist Movement, also known as Ennahda.

From the beginning, Ennahda was directly tied to the global Muslim Brotherhood network though Ghannouchi's affiliation with the European Council for Fatwa and Research, and the International Union of Muslim Scholars. Both of these organizations are still led today by Qaradawi.

According to Ghannouchi, the Arab Spring wasn't really about democracy. Instead, it was about the dawning of a new age of Islam that would lead not only to the destruction of Israel, Islam's greatest enemy, but also to the fall of the West:

> Altogether, the Arab revolutions are positive for the Palestinians, and threaten to bring Israel to an end. The Palestinian problem lies at the heart of the [Islamic] Nation [umma], and . . . all the land between the mosque in Mecca and Jerusalem represents the heart of the Islamic Nation, and any [foreign] control over part of this heart is a stamp on the umma's illness. There is no doubt . . . that the revolutions open a new age, in which the regimes which support the West and Israel will fall—Egypt, Tunis and soon Libya, Yemen and Syria. The foundations of Western interests in the Arab countries are shaking.[9]

So, what to do?

How does any active duty federal officer, who has sworn an oath to protect the country from threats, both foreign and domestic, navigate through such treacherous water and avoid crashing into the rocks of an overtly hostile administration?

For me, the answer was to communicate and document.

Sometimes, being direct and right out in the open is the best defense.

On January 29, 2011, I had the opportunity to give a PowerPoint presentation to the entire port, titled *Strategy & Tactics of the Global Islamic Movement—"Going to the Source."* In it, I highlighted three major fatwas calling for global jihad against America and Israel that were issued amid the chaotic Arab Spring.

On July 19, 2010, Anwar al-Awlaki issued a fatwa calling on Muslims everywhere—including those living in San Diego and Washington, DC—to wage continuous jihad against the West. In this case, Awlaki called for *al jihad bi-al-mal,* or jihad against the West's financial system.

The declaration was followed by an October 6, 2010, fatwa by Muslim Brotherhood supreme guide Mohamed Badie, titled "How Islam Confronts the Oppression and Tyranny," which explicitly called for a never-ending global jihad against the "Zio-American arrogance and tyranny."[10]

The third fatwa was issued January 8, 2011, by Imad Mustafa, professor of *fiqh* at Al-Azhar University in Cairo, declaring that engaging in a continuous global jihad against non-Muslims everywhere, especially Israel and the West, was legitimate.

Yes, that's the same Al-Azhar where President Obama gave his "A New Beginning" speech just a year and a half earlier with the top leaders of the Muslim Brotherhood in Egypt in the audience.

Moreover, at least two of these fatwa authors were public leaders of the same so-called moderate Muslim Brotherhood organization with which the Obama administration had just formed a public alliance.

The third fatwa author, Awlaki, may or may not have been an "official" Muslim Brotherhood member, but it is known that Brotherhood affiliates in Yemen sheltered him before he was killed by a drone strike in October 2011.

With all of these developments in mind, I requested an informal meeting with CBP Chief Evans to review and discuss the three fatwas, the Hamas network in America, and the rapid Islamization of the Arab Spring. At Evans's request, I had another informal follow-up meeting with him on May 12, 2011. In both cases, he expressed alarm about what I was reporting and appreciation that I was keeping management abreast of current events. In every meeting we ever had, Evans was always courteous and professional.

In April 2011, my colleague asked me to help teach a portion of the counterterrorism class that was part of our port-level, post-FLETC training program for new CBP officers. Technically, I had been an NTC-certified counterterrorism instructor since 2006, so I was qualified to teach the course and did so on several occasions in the next three years. It was one of the most enjoyable collateral duties of my career, and I appreciate my colleague's enthusiasm and willingness to let me participate in these classes.

These opportunities, especially the positive feedback from our new CBP officers, encouraged me to keep moving forward during some of the difficult challenges I faced.

On April 6, 2011, BBC News published an article titled "Salafist Groups Find Footing in Egypt After Revolution," which confirmed the shift from a secular, political protest movement toward Islamism that some Middle East specialists were already seeing:

The Salafists have a strict interpretation of the Koran and believe in creating an Islamic state governed by Sharia law as it was practised by the Prophet Muhammad, and enforced by his companions in the 7th Century.

They argue that the Muslim Brotherhood has become too focused on politics at the expense of religion.

"An Islamic government is a government that is based on Sharia law," said Abdel Moneem Al-Shahat, a rising star of the Salafist satellite TV circuit. "Sharia can't be changed because it comes from the days of Prophet Mohammed."[11]

It's true: sharia cannot be changed, not for democracy, and not even for America. The constitution of the Muslim Brotherhood, and Islam, is the Quran (or, Koran, as it is variously spelled). It is not compatible with our political system, which is based on the self-evident truths of life, liberty, and the pursuit of happiness, not the rigid statutes of Islamic law.

As the year progressed, much of our attention was focused on Arab Spring events, which pertained mainly to the Muslim Brotherhood network case, but there was also a lot activity in the Tablighi Jamaat case.

On July 11, 2011, with the trend of visa waiver abuse having been confirmed, NTC prepared a draft operations plan for establishing criteria to deny entry to suspected members of Tablighi Jamaat.

Back on the ground in Atlanta, on July 31, 2011, I provided management with a status report on the Madrassa Boys project, which included "information from a series of 33 interviews in 2010 & 2011 with (mostly) USC's returning from Zakariyya Madrassa in RSA."

I continued:

This project is derived from long-term observations on the emerging influence of two closely related groups: [1] Darul Uloom-Deoband & [2] Tablighi Jamaat. It is also reinforced by at least two [author's redaction] rules, with an added sense of urgency derived from the [administration's] growing recognition of an emerging "homegrown threat."

For more on the emerging (evolving) nature of this domestic (i.e., "homegrown") threat, please see the newly released DHS report entitled *Implementing 9/11 Commission Recommendations*, which can be accessed at http://www.dhs.gov/xlibrary/assets/implementing-9-11-commission-report-progress-2011.pdf.

Thank you all for your support during the difficult process of gathering all of this information, which I believe will help shed light on what I call a "[author's redaction] Network" of Individuals & Organizations. This network is already having a significant influence on a carefully chosen group of young men, who are in the process of becoming *Alims* (teachers) & *Imams* (leaders) in *Masjids* [mosques] here in the United States.

The remainder of the status report summarized a trend in Atlanta that had also been observed in several other ports and was now being addressed at the NTC.

The status memo also set in motion a rapid sequence of events, starting with folding the entire Madrassa Boys case into what was now being called the Tablighi Jamaat Project.

After the TJ Project was approved by the DHS chief counsel on August 30, 2011, I presented a follow-up PowerPoint presentation on the case to Port Director Kremer and my two first-line supervisors, William Brannen and Frank Rodriguez.

On September 30, 2011, I prepared a detailed walk-through of the entire case, from our first encounter with a Tablighi Jamaat member in January 2006, through more than seventy-five cases we had initiated in Atlanta.

On November 7, 2011, a CBP colleague sent a formal letter to port management in Atlanta inviting me to work with NTC:

> The intent of this memorandum is to solicit assistance in the operation and research associated to NTC-P [National Targeting Center-Passenger] Event [author's redaction] regarding research related to the Tablighi Jamaat (TJ) organization.
>
> I have been working extensively with CBPO Haney [who is] assigned to CBP-ATL, and he has been instrumental in providing a background on TJ, as well as research dating back over two years of possible TJ member encounters and suspected destination addresses which have links to terrorism.
>
> CBPO Haney has been an essential part of this operation and his research is still being looked at for further links and possible Visa/ESTA denials and revocations. CBPO Haney continues to be a valuable asset in developing more names, addresses, and leads of TJ members.

I would like to make a formal request to have the assistance of CBPO Haney in the furtherance of this operation until all targeting rules have been set, subjects identified, and development of further field contacts across CBP to continue the research on this potentially dangerous group.

This assistance would preferably be in the form of a TDY to NTC-P for a period of 60–120 days for assignment to the NTC-P ATT to get up to full speed with functions within the TF and ATS-P for future targeting efforts.

A second option would be to send an officer from NTC-P to ATL for 2–3 days for a briefing of operations with CBP-ATL and to get CBPO Haney set up with proper TF functions and access to develop further Intel and to document that information into the TF.

CBPO Haney is currently assigned to passenger operations with CBP-ATL and he would be a great asset to this operation either working here at NTC-P or being designated to work on this operation from ATL at the request of NTC-P.

Finally, on November 21, 2011, I received my TDY selection letter from NTC:

On November 3, 2011, I distributed a memorandum soliciting volunteers for temporary duty assignments (TDY) to the National Targeting Center-Passenger (NTC-P).

With your concurrence, I am selecting Customs and Border Protection Officer (CBPO) Philip Haney (Atlanta) for participation in this TDY opportunity. If you concur with this TDY participation, please ensure that the attached travel details are forwarded to CBPO Haney.

A few days after the receiving the confirmation letter, I entered my travel voucher into the system and set off to the NTC, near the nation's capital, where I reported for duty the first week of December 2011.

"OFFENSIVE MATERIAL"

Meanwhile, some of my colleagues within other federal government agencies were also experiencing opposition and personal attack from officials within the Obama administration.

In August 2011, DHS and the CIA abruptly canceled a conference on homegrown radical extremism that was to be held at CIA headquarters in McLean, Virginia. The conference would have been cohosted by the CIA's Threat Management Unit and the Intelligence Subcommittee of the Metropolitan Washington Council of Governments.

In an e-mail announcing the postponement, CIA police officer Lt. Joshua Fielder said, "The conference topic is a critical one for domestic law enforcement, and the sponsors—in partnership with the Department of Homeland Security—have decided to delay the conference so it can include insights from among other sources, [and] the new National Strategy for Counterterrorism in an updated agenda."[12]

It turned out, according to another official, that the conference was stopped because Muslim advocacy groups contacted DHS and the White House about the scheduled speakers, who included two counterterrorism colleagues, Stephen Coughlin, the former consultant on Islamic law for the Joint Chiefs of Staff, and Steven Emerson, a well-known researcher and investigative reporter.

However, cancelling the conference wasn't enough. The same official said that to prevent Coughlin and Emerson from taking part in future conferences, the Obama administration was drafting new guidelines designed to prohibit any "non-authorized" US government personnel from teaching classes on Islamic history or doctrine.

The new rules also would seek to prohibit the use of federal funds to pay contractors for such training.

Less than a month later, on September 15, 2011, FBI spokesman Christopher Allen announced his agency had also discovered "offensive material" in its counterterrorism training courses and that policy changes "had been underway to better ensure that all training is consistent with FBI standards."

He disingenuously reasoned that the offensive training "was largely derived from a variety of open source publications and includes the opinion of the analyst that developed the lesson block."

Allen's announcement also highlighted a PowerPoint presentation from a March 21, 2011, FBI training course titled "Strategic Themes and Drivers in Islamic Law," which included supposedly inflammatory statements such as: "There may not be a 'radical' threat as much as it is simply a normal assertion of orthodox ideology" and the "strategic themes animating these Islamic values are not fringe, they are main stream."[13]

About three weeks later, on October 5, 2011, the Muslim Public Affairs Council posted a statement on its home page titled "MPAC Co-Signs Letter to FBI Demanding Reformation in Flawed, Anti-Muslim Training."

Representing a coalition of progressive, left-wing and Muslim Brotherhood–linked organizations—including CAIR, ISNA, and MSA—MPAC said it had "signed on to a letter authored by the ACLU requesting the FBI withdraw documents and reports published by the bureau with biased and flawed information about Islam and Muslims."

> Since the rise of the post-9/11 Islamophobic era, the FBI has explicitly stated numerous times "strong religious beliefs should never be confused with violent extremism." However, the ACLU found numerous documents, such as the FBI intelligence assessment "The Radicalization Process: From Conversion to Jihad" published in March 2006 that lists the supposed "steps" and "indicators" of "homegrown Islamic extremists" as those who practice Islam. . . .
>
> In the letter, several organizations ask the FBI to conduct a comprehensive review of intelligence and "issue new guidance clearly stating that religious practices and political advocacy are protected activities under the First Amendment, and are not indicators of future violence."[14]

Next, DHS joined the purge when the Office for Civil Rights and Civil Liberties, in partnership with the National Counterterrorism

Center, issued an October 7, 2011, two-page handout titled "Countering Violent Extremism (CVE) Training Guidance & Best Practices."[15]

On December 14, 2011, the publication was supplemented with a virtually identical DHS CRCL document called "Countering Violent Extremism Training: Do's and Don'ts." Its introduction reads:

> In recent years, the United States has seen a number of individuals in the U.S. become involved in violent extremist activities, with particular activity by American residents and citizens inspired by al Qaeda and its ideology. We know that violent extremism is not confined to any single ideology, but we also know that the threat posed by al Qaeda and its adherents is the preeminent threat we face in the homeland, targeting Muslim American communities for recruitment. Accordingly, it is urgent for law enforcement personnel to be appropriately trained in understanding and detecting ideologically motivated criminal behavior, and in working with communities and local law enforcement to counter domestic violent extremism. Training must be based on current intelligence and an accurate understanding of how people are radicalized to violence, and must include cultural competency training so that our personnel do not mistake, for example, various types of religious observance as a sign of terrorist inclination. Misinformation about the threat and dynamics of violent radicalization can harm our security by sending us in the wrong direction and unnecessarily creating tensions with potential community partners.[16]

In the fine print at the bottom of page 2 of this training document is a citation for MPAC's August 11, 2010, publication, *Building Bridges to Strengthen America: Forging an Effective Counterterrorism Enterprise between Muslim Americans and Law Enforcement.*

The *Building Bridges* document itself discusses an array of intriguingly abstract sociopolitical topics, in sections with titles such as "Current Theories of Radicalization and Terrorist Recruitment" and "Community-Oriented Policing Toward Counterterrorism."[17] It then tries to reassure:

Conservative groups like the Muslim Brotherhood pose long-term strategic threats to violent extremists by siphoning Muslims away from violent radicalism into peaceful political activism. . . .

[Building Bridges cites a Combating Terrorism Center report that says]: Hard-line Jihadist organizations like Al-Qai'da both fear and despise the Islamist political movement called the Muslim Brotherhood, in large part because the Brotherhood effectively garners support from the same constituencies that Jihadists are desperate to court. Because the Muslim Brotherhood and Jihadists share a similar ideological lineage, Jihadists tends [sic] to focus their criticism on the Brotherhood's willingness to participate in secular politics as a vehicle for attacking their Islamic credentials.[18]

The "Countering Violent Extremism Training" document warns against using "training with a political agenda. This is not the time to try to persuade audiences, for example, on views about the Israeli/Palestinian conflict, reformation within Islam, or the proper role of Islam in majority Muslim nations," it cautions. It also says that trainers "who equate the desire for Sharia law with criminal activity violate basic tenets of the First Amendment."[19]

Significantly, one of the training "Don'ts" is relevant to the case of San Bernardino shooter Syed Farook, whose change in apparel and growth of facial hair in adherence to the Tablighi Jamaat movement coincided with his efforts to carry out violent attacks, including a plot against his community college in Riverside, California. The handout instructs: "Don't use training that reasons broadly from anecdotal evidence; e.g., Omar Hammami started to wear more religious clothing, therefore starting to wear religious garb is an indicator of terrorism."[20]

It also warns against "training that relies on fear or conspiracies to motivate law enforcement":

Don't use training premised on theories with little or no evidence to support them. Examples (from the report "Manufacturing the Muslim Menace") of unsubstantiated theories include:

A. Many mainstream Muslim organizations have terrorist ties

B. Mainstream Muslim organizations are fronts for Islamic political organizations whose true desire is to establish Sharia law in America. Muslim Americans are using democratic processes, like litigation and free speech, to subvert democracy and install Sharia law.[21]

"PURGE ALL MATERIALS"

But even after all the public apologies and promises for improvement, the purging efforts of the CIA, DHS, DOD, and FBI still weren't good enough for US Muslim groups.

On October 19, 2011, fifty-seven Muslim organizations wrote a letter to CIA director John Brennan, complaining of "the federal government's use of biased, false and highly offensive training materials about Muslims and Islam." Their chief demand was, "Purge *all* federal government training materials of biased materials."[22]

"The seriousness of this issue cannot be overstated," the Muslim leaders said, "and we request that the White House immediately create an interagency task force to address this problem, with a fair and transparent mechanism for input from the Muslim, Arab, and South Asian communities, including civil rights lawyers, religious leaders, and law enforcement experts."

Among the groups that put their names on the letter were unindicted coconspirators in the Holy Land Foundation trial, the Council on American-Islamic Relations, the Islamic Society of North America, the Islamic Circle of North America, Islamic Relief, and the Muslim Public Affairs Council.

Islamic Relief, another signatory to the ACLU–Brennan letter, also has a long history of affiliations with individuals and organizations with known links to terrorism.

Later, on December 25, 2013, Egypt designated the Muslim Brotherhood as a terrorist organization. It was followed months later by Saudi Arabia and the UAE. In addition, on November 15, 2014, the UAE designated CAIR, IRW, and MAS as terrorist organizations, specifically labeling IRW as a part of the global Muslim Brotherhood network.

In their letter, the Islamic groups took particular offense at statements in federal government training materials such as: "Islamic doctrine is based upon the establishment of its culture in dominance of all others. In essence, all other cultures must not only accept, but convert or submit, to Islam." They also highlighted the PowerPoint presentation titled "Strategic Themes and Drivers in Islamic Law," mentioned earlier in this chapter, used in FBI training. And they specifically criticized Coughlin for saying in January 2011 that Islamic law is not compatible with the US Constitution.[23]

The organizations demanded: "Implement a mandatory re-training program for FBI agents, U.S. Army officers, and all federal, state and local law enforcement who have been subjected to biased training." They also called for the issuance of "guidance clearly stating that religious practice and political advocacy are protected activities under the First Amendment, not indicators of violence, and shall not be the basis for surveillance or investigation."[24]

Remarkably, the Brennan letter also included several specific demands for discipline of law enforcement personnel, which were carried out during my career.

"Ensure that personnel reviews are conducted and all trainers and other government employees who promoted biased trainers and training materials are effectively disciplined," the Muslim leaders insisted. They also called for "quality control processes to ensure that bigoted trainers and biased materials are not developed or utilized in the future."[25]

October 19, 2011, was indeed a dark day for the American law enforcement and counterterrorism community. On the same day the letter to Brennan was issued, we received word that Attorney General Eric Holder was "firmly committed" to removing anti-Muslim material from law-enforcement training.[26]

Former US attorney for the District of Oregon Dwight C. Holton said he had spoken with Holder about the "egregiously false" FBI training: "I want to be perfectly clear about this: training materials that portray Islam as a religion of violence or with a tendency towards violence are wrong, they are offensive, and they are contrary to everything that this resident, this attorney general and the Department of Justice stands for," Holton said. "They will not be tolerated." He further stated that the materials "pose a significant threat to national security, because they play into the false narrative propagated by terrorists that the United States is at war with Islam."[27]

SEE NOTHING

Meanwhile, spokesmen for the well-known Muslim Brotherhood front groups were now complaining about the DHS signature campaign, "If You See Something, Say Something."

It seemed that even the reporting of "suspicious activity" by the general public was intolerably Islamophobic and that they should be the only ones with the authority to report on possible domestic Islamic radicalization.

On October 24, 2011, CAIR and MPAC were among Muslim organizations who wrote to Margo Schlanger, officer for the Office of Civil Rights and Civil Liberties:

> We are writing to follow up on a meeting request made at the last CRCL Committee meeting on September 26, 2011 to discuss the DHS "If You See Something, Say Something" campaign. As civil liberties, civil rights, human rights, immigrant rights, national security and privacy organizations, we are deeply concerned about how suspicious activity reporting programs, such as the DHS See Something, Say Something program lead to racial and religious profiling and impact Arab, Middle Eastern, Muslim, Sikh, and South Asian communities. . . .
>
> We would . . . like to learn what policies DHS has employed to collect, retain, and purge data obtained through the campaign. . . .
>
> We would like to discuss what measures your office is taking to ensure accountability, transparency and oversight related to civil rights and civil liberties protections as DHS expands its work against domestic radicalization and "homegrown" terrorism.[28]

The DHS website describes "See Something" as "a national campaign that raises public awareness of the indicators of terrorism and terrorism-related crime, as well as the importance of reporting suspicious activity to state and local law enforcement":

> Informed, alert communities play a critical role in keeping our nation safe. The U.S. Department of Homeland Security (DHS) is committed to strengthening hometown security by creating partnerships with state, local, tribal, and territorial (SLTT) governments and the private sector, as well as the communities they serve. These partners help us reach the public across the nation by aligning their messaging with the campaign's messages and distributing outreach materials, including Public Service Announcements (PSA's).[29]

In fact, the "See Something" campaign was doomed to failure from the start, simply because the "something"—the indicators of terrorism and terrorism-related crime—we were supposed to be looking for were never adequately explained, nor were any clear guidelines ever provided for what we were supposed to "say."

GOING GLOBAL

While the "Great Purge" came about amid pressure from Muslim Brotherhood front groups, President Obama's speech to the Muslim world in Cairo, Egypt, on June 4, 2009, was the inaugural public announcement that the United States was going to reset its relationship with the Muslim world.

Now, we were going to redefine the threat to exclude its originators. We would no longer publicly acknowledge that Islam has anything to do with the mayhem and violence seen around the world. Instead, we would have to find a new explanation for why things are happening. It wouldn't be Islam. It would be lack of jobs, colonialism, anger at past policies, the Internet.

At the United Nations on March 24, 2011, non-binding Resolution 16/18 was adopted, titled "Combating intolerance, negative stereotyping and stigmatization of, and discrimination, incitement to violence and violence against, persons based on religion or belief." Point 5(f) calls for "adopting measures to criminalize incitement to imminent violence based on religion or belief."[30] This language is distressingly similar to the Pakistan Penal Code, which includes death penalties for a variety of draconian blasphemy charges, including any form of verbal defamation of Muhammad or the religion of Islam.[31]

On July 15, 2011, Secretary of State Hillary Clinton appeared at the inaugural Organization of the Islamic Conference (OIC) High-Level Meeting on Combating Religious Intolerance in Istanbul, Pakistan, where she welcomed the resolution:

> I want to applaud the Organization of Islamic Conference and the European Union for helping pass Resolution 16/18 at the Human Rights Council. I was complimenting the secretary general on the OIC team in Geneva. I had a great team there as well. So many of you were part of that effort. And together we have begun to overcome the false divide that pits religious sensitivities against freedom of expression, and we are pursuing a new approach based on concrete steps to fight intolerance wherever it occurs. Under this resolution, the international community is taking a strong stand for freedom of expression and worship, and against discrimination and violence based upon religion or belief. . . .
>
> The Human Rights Council has given us a comprehensive framework [i.e., Resolution 16/18] for addressing this issue on the international level. But at the same time, we each have to work to do more to promote respect for religious differences in our own countries. In the United States, I will admit, there are people who still feel vulnerable or marginalized as a result of their religious beliefs. And we have seen how the incendiary actions of just a very few people, a handful in a country of nearly 300 million, can create wide ripples of intolerance. We also understand that, for 235 years, freedom of expression has been a universal right at the core of our democracy. So we are focused on promoting interfaith education and collaboration,

enforcing antidiscrimination laws, protecting the rights of all people to worship as they choose, and to use some old-fashioned techniques of peer pressure and shaming, so that people don't feel that they have the support to do what we abhor.[32]

Five months later, on December 12, 2011, the State Department hosted a series of closed-door follow-up meetings to augment the inaugural "Istanbul Process" on Islamophobia, only this time the proceedings were held in Washington, DC.

According to Rizwan Saeed Sheikh, director of cultural affairs at the OIC general secretariat and spokesman for the OIC secretary general:

OIC Secretary-General Ekmeleddin Mehmet İhsanoğlu launched a process, known as the Istanbul Process, in July 2011, together with the then US Secretary of State Hillary Clinton and EU Foreign Policy Chief Catherine Ashton, as well as with leaders of OIC and non-OIC member states, to build consensus on confronting Islamophobia.

Similar meetings were held later in Washington and London as part of the Istanbul Process, and now the US, UK, the African Union, the Arab League and the OIC are moving in a circle, subscribing the process and taking it forward to discuss the issue specifically. The OIC is going to hold the next event focusing squarely on the issue of criminalizing denigration and deciding on whatever actions need to be taken on the basis of Article 20 of the [December 16, 1966] International Covenant on Civil and Political Rights (ICCPR).[33]

Since countries within the OIC already have blasphemy laws in place, it appears that Clinton willingly submitted to the Istanbul Process, in partnership with the OIC, to implement measures in the West against speech or expression that negatively stereotypes Islam and Muslims.

The proceedings continue to this day. The Second Session of the Istanbul Process, which opened December 3, 2012, was hosted by the UK and Canada at the Canada House in London. The third was hosted by the OIC in Geneva, Switzerland, on June 21, 2013. The fourth took place March 24–25, 2014, in Doha, Qatar, and the fifth in Jeddah,

Saudi Arabia, June 3–4, 2015.

Meanwhile, on October 5, 2012, the Office of the UN High Commissioner for Human Rights convened in Rabat, Morocco, and released a document titled "Rabat Plan of Action on the Prohibition of Advocacy of National, Racial or Religious Hatred that Constitutes Incitement to Discrimination, Hostility or Violence." Known today as the Rabat Plan of Action, its recommendations included:

- Being alert to the danger of discrimination or negative stereotypes of individuals and groups being furthered by the media.

- Avoiding unnecessary references to race, religion, gender and other group characteristics that may promote intolerance.

- Raising awareness of the harm caused by discrimination and negative stereotyping. . . .

  At the same time, international human rights standards on the prohibition of incitement to national, racial or religious hatred still need to be integrated in domestic legislation and policies in many parts of the world.[34]

The Istanbul Process culminated a thirteen-year-long process that began in 1998, when the fifty-seven-member OIC won a majority approval in the UN Human Rights Council in Geneva as well as the UN General Assembly in New York, for annual resolutions on "combating defamation of religions."

During the entire arduous process, critics continued voicing their concerns, warning that the defamation-of-religion concept was not only contrary to international law and free speech, but also left the way open for draconian, sharia-based blasphemy laws, such as those in Pakistan, which are frequently invoked to justify killing journalists and moderate politicians.

However, both the White House and the State Department disregarded these concerns, choosing instead to submit to the demands of the OIC to criminalize "Islamophobia" and defamation of religion.

It was the culmination of seven years of effort within the Obama administration to extend American-style civil rights and civil liberties to foreign nationals who do not have America's best interests in mind, conducted in blatant disregard for the Constitution and the self-evident freedoms and liberties endowed by our Creator.

8

PRIMARY ACCESS

In the summer of 2012, five members of Congress wrote to the acting inspector general of DHS, raising the provocative claim that the Muslim Brotherhood was infiltrating Washington.

The Congress members—Michele Bachmann of Minnesota, Louie Gohmert of Texas, Trent Franks of Arizona, Thomas Rooney of Florida, and Lynn Westmoreland of Georgia—were widely ridiculed by angry and indignant members of Congress, both Republican and Democrat, as well as the establishment media and major Muslim Brotherhood front groups, such as CAIR and the Muslim Public Affairs Council.

I had a front-row seat, because I knew the Congress members, with the exception of Rooney, and because I was an active-duty DHS CBP officer with a specialty in the subject that caused so much controversy.

It was an opportunity, similar to the Holy Land Foundation convictions, for our nation's leaders to evaluate the effectiveness of our counterterrorism policies, and, in both cases, they failed to seize the moment.

On June 13, 2012, the five Congress members sent signed letters to the inspectors general of five major agencies, charging that Muslim leaders from groups intent on "destroying Western Civilization from within" were being invited into the highest chambers of power to shape and enforce national security policy.[1]

The recipients were Charles Edwards of the Department of

Homeland Security, Lynne M. Halbrooks of the Department of Defense, Michael E. Horowitz of the Department of Justice, Harold W. Geisel of the State Department, and I. Charles McCullough III of the Office of the Director of National Intelligence.

The lawmakers pointed to Secretary of State Hillary Clinton's top aide, Huma Abedin, as a possible Muslim Brotherhood influence on US policy. They asked the inspectors general at the Departments of Homeland Security, Justice and State to investigate, prompting Democrats and Republicans to rush to Abedin's defense.

Washington Post columnist Dana Milbank suggested the researchers and lawmakers who presented evidence of the Muslim Brotherhood ties of Abedin and her family were motivated by racism. He commented in a column that it's "hard to escape the suspicion" that the charges have "something to do with the way she looks and how she worships."[2]

Sen. John McCain, R-AZ, called the request for an investigation of Abedin and her family "sinister" and "nothing less than an unwarranted and unfounded attack on an honorable woman, a dedicated American and a loyal public servant."[3]

Democratic Rep. Keith Ellison, the first Muslim to serve in Congress, accused fellow Minnesota lawmaker Bachmann of failing to provide evidence to support what Muslim Brotherhood front groups were calling a "witch hunt" against Muslims in the US government.[4]

On July 19, 2012, Republican Speaker of the House John Boehner denounced Bachmann's accusations. "From everything that I do know of [Abedin], she has a sterling character and I think accusations like this being thrown around are pretty dangerous," Boehner told reporters during a briefing.[5]

CAIR joined the fray. On July 24, 2012, CAIR national executive director Nihad Awad sent a letter to Bachmann, saying, "We remain eternally grateful that, like Sen. Joseph McCarthy before you, your power is limited, enumerated and constrained by our nation's constitution. Your letters challenging the loyalty of patriotic American Muslims based on discredited anti-Muslim conspiracy theories can only be described as devoid of a sense of decency."[6]

Two days later, Bachmann was scolded by Republican House Intelligence Committee chairman Mike Rogers, who was described by Politico as "incredibly angry."[7]

The Muslim Public Affairs Council held a press conference August 6, 2012, in front of the Republican National Committee's headquarters in Washington, DC, calling on Republican presidential candidate Mitt Romney to rebuke Bachmann.[8]

But did these five members of Congress have a reason to be concerned?

The Muslim Brotherhood's internal Explanatory Memorandum, entered into evidence at the Holy Land Foundation trial, said its members "must understand that their work in America is a kind of grand jihad in eliminating and destroying the Western civilization from within and 'sabotaging' its miserable house by their hands and by the hands of the believers so that it is eliminated and Allah's religion is made victorious over all other religions."[9]

Should we at least take them at their word and examine whether or not they might be trying to implement such a plan?

Regarding Abedin, she worked for an organization founded by her family, the Institute of Muslim Minority Affairs (IMMA), established in 1979 by a Saudi citizen named Abdullah Omar Naseef. In 1988, Naseef also founded the Rabita Trust, a known financier of al-Qaeda. About one month after the 9/11 attacks, the US Treasury Department identified Rabita Trust as a terrorist organization and froze its assets.

In 1996, Abedin joined IMMA's editorial board, where she remained as an assistant editor until 2008. She also was a member of the executive board of the Muslim Brotherhood's Muslim Student Association.

The five Republican lawmakers were simply pointing out that security clearance guidelines for federal employees state that a "security risk may exist when an individual's immediate family, including cohabitants and other persons to whom he or she may be bound by affection, influence, or obligation are not citizens of the United States or may be subject to duress."[10]

The guidelines also express concern for any "association or sympathy with persons or organizations that advocate the overthrow of the United States Government, or any state or subdivision, by force or violence or by other unconstitutional means."[11]

These few facts alone should be enough for any of our elected officials to be concerned. At the very least, they are entitled to straight-forward, honest answers to their simple questions.

As an aside, all federal employees must go through a background clearance. Part of the process includes a very detailed set of questions about family background, travels to foreign countries, and business dealings with foreign nationals. Failure to disclose this information can disqualify an applicant from federal employment.

In 2009, the WND Books best-seller *Muslim Mafia: Inside the Secret Underworld That's Conspiring to Islamize America* featured an internal CAIR memo written in 2007 that called for infiltrating the "judiciary, intelligence and homeland security committees" by, among other things, "placing Muslim interns" in Capitol Hill offices. The book also uncovered new evidence that CAIR directly funded Hamas and al-Qaeda terrorist fronts.[12]

When the book was released, Rep. Sue Myrick, R-NC, cofounder of the bipartisan House Anti-Terrorism/Jihad Caucus and a member of the House Permanent Select Committee on Intelligence, pointed out at a press conference in Washington that groups such as CAIR and the Islamic Society of North America "have a proven record of senior officials being indicted and either imprisoned or deported from the United States."[13]

Myrick also exposed the absence of a formal vetting process by Congress for screening radical Muslims invited to work, pray, or speak at the Capitol.

Al-Qaeda leader Awlaki, for example, participated in weekly prayer sessions at the Capitol after 9/11.[14] He also was a lunch guest of military leaders at the Pentagon within months of his assisting the 9/11 hijackers.[15]

NO CONCERN

As the firestorm spread across Capitol Hill and into the media, with the Muslim Brotherhood groups cheering on the sidelines, imagine what it must have been like from the perspective of a federal law enforcement officer with subject matter expertise in the Muslim Brotherhood network in America.

During more than forty-five meetings with members of the House and Senate and their staff, I have provided information to many lawmakers, including Bachmann and Gohmert, who took their oaths of office very seriously and were willing to risk their careers by making an unpopular stand. Through the summer of 2012, I watched with amazement as they faced open, public criticism, rejection, abandonment, and betrayal from their own colleagues, from misinformed media people, and from the cynical leaders of Muslim organizations with well-established ties to Islamic supremacist groups. It was painful watching leaders in Congress, such as John Boehner and John McCain, humiliate themselves in public, making one misguided pronouncement after another, but never actually addressing the concerns that were raised in the letters. I recall thinking, *If I could just set them down in front of a computer terminal and show them how to access information in our law-enforcement databases, it would take less than two minutes for them to confirm everything the five members of Congress were alleging.*

For some, probably much less two minutes.

Watching the media circus on TV also made me wonder how I had managed to survive almost ten years inside one of the agencies that had received the lawmakers' letter. If my own elected officials, with higher access to classified material than I have, couldn't seem to tell their right hand from their left, then what chance did I have?

Nonetheless, I remained undeterred and vowed to continue seeking a way to alert my countrymen to the threat, within the structure provided by our constitutional republic.

A few months later, a prominent Egyptian weekly political magazine essentially affirmed the claims outlined in the letters, reporting that six American Muslim leaders with significant influence on US policy were Muslim Brotherhood operatives working inside the Obama administration.

Egypt's *Rose El-Youssef,* in a December 22, 2012, article asked whether "these six characters" in the Obama administration had turned the White House "from a position hostile to Islamic groups and organizations in the world, to the largest and most important supporter of the Muslim Brotherhood."[16]

The Egyptian article was translated and reported by Steven Emerson's Investigative Project on Terrorism, which said that, while the story was largely unsourced, it was significant because it raised the issue to Egyptian readers, to the Muslim world in general, and to analysts in America.

The individuals named or suggested in the *Rose El-Youssef* article were Arif Alikhan (or Ali Khan), assistant secretary of Homeland Security for policy development; Mohamed Elibiary, a member of the Homeland Security Advisory Council; Rashad Hussain, the US special envoy to the Organization of the Islamic Conference; Salam Al-Marayati, cofounder of the Muslim Public Affairs Council; Imam Mohamed Magid, president of the Islamic Society of North America; and Eboo Patel (Abu), a member of President Obama's Advisory Council on Faith-Based Neighborhood Partnerships.

Alikhan, former Los Angeles deputy mayor, was appointed as assistant secretary for policy development by DHS Secretary Napolitano on April 24, 2009. He is a close affiliate of MPAC, as well as the Islamic Shura Council of Southern California, yet another adversarial Muslim Brotherhood umbrella organization. In turn, the Islamic Shura Council of Southern California is directly linked to still other individuals and organizations with known ties to Muslim Brotherhood front groups such as ISNA, MAS, and MSA.

The *Rose El-Youssef* article also pointed out that Alikhan may have been one of the main catalysts for the meeting of the American administration leaders with the Muslim Brotherhood since the events of

September 11, 2001, and that he appears to have been the link between them during and after the Arab Spring revolutions in 2011.

Elibiary, as I have mentioned, was appointed to President Obama's Homeland Security Advisory Council on October 18, 2010, but resigned on September 3, 2014, after a controversial series of tweets and "inappropriate disclosure of sensitive law enforcement documents," as a letter from DHS framed it.[17] (See chapter 6.)

The disclosure was brought to light after Gohmert singled out Elibiary at a House hearing in November 2011. The congressman confronted Napolitano with a charge that Elibiary, who had a security clearance as a member of the DHS advisory council, had "accessed a federal database and shopped sensitive reports to a left-leaning media outlet to publicize his claim that the department is promoting 'Islamophobia.'"[18]

Former assistant US attorney Andrew McCarthy documented that the DHS working group helped devise the new Obama counterterrorism strategy. McCarthy, who prosecuted the perpetrators of the 1993 World Trade Center bombing, said the strategy envisions having "law-enforcement pare back their intelligence-gathering activities and take their marching orders from 'community partners.'"[19]

Elibiary has been known as a strong supporter of Islamic theologian Sayyid Qutb, whose teachings inspired and continue to govern the Muslim Brotherhood, al-Qaeda, and numerous other Islamic jihadist organizations worldwide. He has also criticized the US government's prosecution and conviction of the five former Holy Land Foundation officials, characterizing the case as a defeat for the United States. He was closely affiliated with Shukri Abu Baker, one of the "Holy Land Five" defendants, as well as with CAIR. And in 2004, Elibiary spoke at a conference that honored the founder of the Iranian Islamic revolution, Ayatollah Khomeini.[20]

The Egyptian magazine also said that Rashad Hussain maintained close ties with people and groups in the Muslim Brotherhood network in America and that he participated in the June 2002 annual conference of the American Muslim Council, formerly headed by convicted terrorist financier Abdul Rahman Al Amoudi (aka Abdurahman Alamoudi).[21]

Hussain advised the National Security Council in the development of President Obama's "A New Beginning" speech. He has also served as Obama's deputy associate counsel (2009), special envoy to the Organization of Islamic Cooperation (2010), and special envoy for Strategic Counterterrorism Communications (2015).

MPAC's Marayati has been among the most influential Muslim American leaders in recent years. The Egyptian magazine showed the links between MPAC and the international Muslim Brotherhood infrastructure. Marayati has met numerous times with government and law enforcement officials in the last fifteen years.

Obama appointed Magid (aka Mohamed Magid Ali), former president of the Muslim Brotherhood–founded ISNA, as an adviser to the Department of Homeland Security and to a seat on the Countering Violent Extremism Steering Committee in 2010. Beginning in 2003, Magid also has served as a board member of MPAC's Washington, DC, branch.

According to *Rose El-Youssef,* he has also given speeches and participated at conferences on American Middle East policy at the State Department and offered advice to the FBI.

Patel maintains a close relationship with Tariq Ramadan, the grandson of Muslim Brotherhood founder Hasan al-Banna, *Rose El-Youssef* reported. He was also a member of the Muslim Students Association.

WND reported on July 5, 2011, that Patel spoke at the main event of a three-day convention held by the Muslim Students Association and appeared on a panel alongside Tariq Ramadan and Siraj Wahhaj, who was named as a possible coconspirator in the 1993 World Trade Center bombing. Wahhaj has also defended the convicted WTC bomb plotters and has urged the Islamic takeover of America. The convention was arranged by HLF coconspirator ISNA.[22]

ASTONISHING COOPERATION

To add some additional context, the Muslim Brotherhood, founded in Egypt in 1928, has had a complex and often violent relationship with the Egyptian government and people.

It's why Egyptians were astonished to see the Obama administration's cooperation with the Brotherhood during the Arab Spring.

The trend surfaced in early 2008 with policy documents such as the "Words Matter" memo, but everyone in Egypt saw it up close and personal on June 4, 2009, when Obama came to Al-Azhar University and delivered his policy speech.

Through some of my friends and contacts who were native Arabic speakers, I heard that little children were running through the streets of Cairo, shouting that the "American president quoted the Quran during his speech!" They were referring to a passage from Quran 5.32–33, which Obama paraphrased:

> Indeed, none of us should tolerate these extremists. They have killed in many countries. They have killed people of different faiths—but more than any other, they have killed Muslims. Their actions are irreconcilable with the rights of human beings, the progress of nations, and with Islam. The Holy Koran teaches that *whoever kills an innocent . . . it is as if he has killed all mankind . . . [and] whoever saves a person, it is as if he has saved all mankind . . .* The enduring faith of over a billion people is so much bigger than the narrow hatred of a few. Islam is not part of the problem in combating violent extremism—it is an important part of promoting peace.[23]

On the surface, this paraphrased Quranic passage sounds reasonable, perhaps even biblical.

However, the entire un-paraphrased passage is much more ominous:

> 5.32: Because of that, We decreed upon the Children of Israel that whoever kills a soul unless for a soul or for corruption [done] in the land—it is as if he had slain mankind entirely. And whoever saves one—it is as if he had saved mankind entirely. And our messengers

had certainly come to them with clear proofs. Then indeed many of them, [even] after that, throughout the land, were transgressors.

5.33: Indeed, the penalty for those who wage war against Allah and His Messenger and strive upon earth [to cause] corruption is none but that they be killed or crucified or that their hands and feet be cut off from opposite sides or that they be exiled from the land. That is for them a disgrace in this world; and for them in the Hereafter is a great punishment [emphasis added].[24]

As the Christian world is familiar with John 3:16, so the people of Egypt and Muslims around the world are familiar with the Quranic passage paraphrased in Obama's speech. Some probably could not help but wonder that an American president would actually quote from a section that explicitly calls for violence and killing.

Meanwhile, during the summer of 2012, Gohmert continued pushing for an investigation of the Muslim Brotherhood's influence on the federal government, contending a probe was necessary, partly because of the Obama administration's "horrendous decisions" in backing the Arab Spring revolutions.[25]

Incidentally, there is a double meaning in the phrase "Arab Spring." In English, the term connotes political renewal, growth, and vibrancy.

In Arabic, however, the term is a play on words. Ar-Rabi Al-Arabi (الربيع العربي) means the "Arab Revival," with a connotation of Islamic supremacy and Arab global domination, so that the entire world would ultimately submit to Islamic law, sharia.

This is exactly the stated purpose of the Muslim Brotherhood, which was formed in response to the demise of the Ottoman Empire to help establish Islamic rule worldwide.

Here in North America, its stated goal, according to the Explanatory Memorandum, is that "Allah's religion is made victorious over all other religions,"[26] which comes directly from Quran 2.193:

And fight with them [unbelievers] until there is no more *fitna*, and the religion is only for Allah. But if they cease fighting [i.e., submit to Islam], then there should be no more hostility, except against the unjust polytheists and wrong-doers.

In other words, Muslims are to keep fighting against anyone and everyone who does not embrace Islam—including you and me—until all of us finally submit.

Then, there will be peace on the earth.

THE FIVE

By now, it should be abundantly clear that Muslim Brotherhood front groups like CAIR, ISNA, and NAIT should have no access to the American political process.

And now that we've had more than three and a half years to consider the changes in the Middle East and the world, let's go back and address the simple question that I posed at the beginning of this chapter.

Did the five outspoken members of Congress have a valid reason to be concerned about the influence of the Muslim Brotherhood, not only within the American political system but in the world at large? Were those "five Jeremiahs" right, or was the scorn of their impassioned detractors in Congress and the media, and in the Muslim Brotherhood front groups such as CAIR and MPAC, justified?

Since the summer of 2012, the entire Middle East has devolved into chaos and violence, and the ubiquitous Muslim Brotherhood has been right there in the middle.

In Egypt, the Arab Spring quickly turned into an attempt by the Muslim Brotherhood to impose Islamic law on the entire country, prompting a second, 30-million-strong popular uprising and the overthrow of the Mohamed Morsi's Muslim Brotherhood–led government by the Egyptian army. Egypt today is on daily alert for attacks by any one of several jihad groups operating within the country and in the Sinai Peninsula.

Libya, meanwhile, has descended into anarchy due to militias and Muslim Brotherhood–linked groups such as Ansar al-Sharia and the Libyan Islamic Fighting Group, many with ties to similar groups fighting in Syria.

In Syria, there are several groups affiliated with the Muslim Brotherhood of Syria fighting to overthrow Bashar al-Assad.

Meanwhile, back here at home, not a single one of the groups named as unindicted coconspirators in the Holy Land Foundation trial has been brought to trial or even sanctioned. Instead, the leaders of these groups continue exerting influence on our political process and our immigration, law enforcement, domestic, and foreign counterterrorism policies.

What happened in the summer of 2012 was about much more than a single individual named Huma Abedin and the specific ties she may or may not have had to the Muslim Brotherhood. Rather, it was an opportunity to come to terms with what we really believe as a nation and our responsibility to work together to help preserve and protect the constitutional liberties on which our great country was founded.

My hope and prayer is that we will not miss the next opportunity. Either way, we will eventually have to confront the forces that seek to impose their own definitions of "life, liberty, and the pursuit of happiness" upon us.

9

HANDS OFF

By March 2012, I had been at the National Targeting Center for about four months, assigned to the Advanced Targeting Team (ATT), where I worked mainly on the Tablighi Jamaat Initiative.

As I recounted in the first chapter, we were paid a visit on March 27, 2012, by State Department officials who had expressed "concerns" about our focus on individuals affiliated with Tablighi Jamaat, because it was not a designated terrorist group and because of possible violations of its members' civil rights and civil liberties.

A day later, March 28, 2012, I happened to be off duty and had the first opportunity to meet with a member of Congress in the nation's capital. The previous meetings, with Reps. Lynn Westmoreland in 2007 and Tom Price in 2009, had been in their district offices. This time, I met with Rep. Michele Bachmann, R-MN, and her personal assistant, Tera Dahl, at noon in their office at 103 Cannon Building, across the street from the US Capitol.

My purpose for meeting with Bachmann was to alert her—and Congress, hopefully—to the difficulties law enforcement officers like me were facing inside the federal government. I provided her with a brief review of the concerns I had raised as early as 2007, then filled her in on more recent events, including the extraordinary meeting I had just attended at NTC with State Department officials.

This initial meeting with Bachmann in the Cannon Building led to a series of more than forty-five briefings and presentations to various members of both the House and the Senate, which have continued to the present day. In every case, these elected officials were disturbed by what I shared with them, and whenever they asked me to come back, I would add something new to the story.

It was Congress, not my own agency, that first called me a whistle-blower, which is not a term I used. As far as my own agency was concerned, I was subject to the same potential legal action, criminal charges, social stigma, or termination from my position that whistle-blowers have always faced.

I recall one meeting with several Senate staff members.

"You know, there's one thing I've learned about this whole [whistle-blower] process," I declared.

They all waited for a moment; then someone said, "What's that?"

"Well, what I've learned from this whole process is that . . . there is no process!"

There is no magic "Room 248" that a whistle-blower can go to in DC or anywhere else where a smiling, helpful person hands you a package of forms, then calls you back a few days later for a follow-up appointment. Neither is there any real rhyme or reason to how someone becomes a whistle-blower, or who officially designates that individual as worthy of protection, or who will pay for his or her legal fees.

In fact, legal protection of whistle-blowers is subject to a dizzying array of contradictory stipulations. And even though there are hundreds of state and federal laws that grant protection to whistle-blowers, there are so many blank spots, holes, gray areas, and exceptions to the rules, that we remain an endangered species, highly vulnerable to retaliation and reprisal.

Not to mention the traumatizing effect on our families and our friendships (*Is this guy even safe to be friends with?*).

Reprisal, which is never *called* reprisal, often comes at the hand of the very same organization that we accuse, or sometimes from a related agency, such as the Department of Justice, and other times under the subtle guise of legal actions.

In my case, all three types of reprisal—internal, external, and legal— happened at the same time, which I will discuss later.

ORDERED FROM THE TOP

Along with keeping track of the Tablighi Jamaat Initiative, I continued monitoring the activities of the individuals and organizations who were part of the Hamas Network case, which was started in 2006.

In early May 2012, as the original author of the Hamas report and the "owner" of hundreds of linked sub-records, I was copied on a string of interoffice e-mails concerning a well-known Muslim Brotherhood leader named Jamal Badawi, who sought to enter the United States from Canada.[1] A close affiliate of the International Institute of Islamic Thought (IIIT[2]) and cofounder of the Boston-area mosque attended by the Tsarnaev brothers, the Egyptian-born Badawi is one of the Muslim Brotherhood's top leaders in North America.

Badawi is also a close associate of Khaled Meshal, the current leader of Hamas, as well as Salah Sultan, a former US permanent resident who is now imprisoned under a death sentence in Egypt. He also is associated with Yusuf al-Qaradawi, currently a resident of Qatar who supports Hamas, Hezbollah, and Palestinian Islamic Jihad.

Badawi also has been a member of the Council on American-Islamic Relations, the Fiqh Council of North America, European Council of Fatwa and Research, and International Union of Islamic Scholars. The latter two organizations are also led by Qaradawi.

In 2004, the International Union of Islamic Scholars issued a fatwa stating that it was a religious duty for all able-bodied Muslims inside and outside of Iraq to wage jihad against the American military.

In an Islam Online forum in June 2006, Badawi justified Muslim suicide bombings as a legitimate tactic of jihad. In 2007 he visited Sudan, ruled by an authoritarian Islamic regime, to attend a conference with Qaradawi, who has been banned from traveling to certain countries.

Badawi was also named as an unindicted coconspirator in the Holy Land Foundation case.

In the May 2012 e-mail string between US Immigration and Customs Enforcement officers and US Customs and Border Protection (CBP) officers, an astonishing policy was revealed: ordered from the very top of the administration, according to the e-mails, a so-called hands-off policy allowed Muslim Brotherhood leaders and others with Islamic supremacist beliefs and affiliations to travel freely in and out of the United States.

On May 11, 2012, Badawi was scheduled to travel from Halifax, Nova Scotia, to Tampa, Florida, via Newark to speak at a conference of the Islamic Society of North America, another unindicted coconspirator in the 2008 Holy Land Foundation case. CBP officers had already created a dossier requesting that he be denied entry into the United States. However, in an e-mail sent just two days before Badawi's scheduled flight, a DHS officer noted that Badawi had twice sued the government and that his records had been removed from the DHS database, adding that "the DHS Secretary was involved in the matter."[3]

As we'll see later in this chapter, the deletion of my sixty-seven records related to the Institute of Islamic Education case was not the first time important TECS records had been removed by higher-ups in the agency.

In the e-mail, the DHS officer wrote that Badawi had been given a secondary inspection several dozen times but had not been in secondary since September 2010.

The officer said he was passing on his write-up to Canadian officials "regarding possible inadmissibility grounds related to INA 212(a)(3) terrorism charges because of [his] potential inciting, endorsing, and associating with terrorists."

Badawi has "been looked at in the past, but hopefully this collection of twenty supporting open source articles will assist with making an informed admissibility determination," the officer said.

Citing immigration law, the officer said Badawi could also be barred from obtaining asylum in America because he may have participated in the persecution of Islamic women by describing circumstances in which they could be beaten by their husbands.[4]

I'M PUZZLED

A list of questions was prepared for Badawi to answer to determine if he was admissible to the United States.

"Questions should be posed to Badawi," the DHS officer wrote, "to determine the frequency, duration, severity, nature, purpose, and level of contact he had with Muslim Brotherhood officials and individuals associated with, or members of Hamas and organizations listed below and if Badawi knew, or should have known, that the groups and/or individuals were nefarious and/or involved in terrorist activity."

He concluded in a May 10, 2012, e-mail, however, "[It] looks like we won't be able to do anything on Badawi tomorrow but we're requesting the past lawsuits he filed against CBP to see if they were related to him being secondaried all the time, or if they were about his immigration status [admissibility/inadmissibility]."

The officer said that if the lawsuits "were solely related to him being secondaried frequently, that has nothing to do with whether or not he is admissible."

"Once we get a determination on what the lawsuits were regarding, we'll reevaluate if we can take future action against him," he wrote.

Later that day, in a follow-up e-mail, the DHS officer said the NTC watch commander advised that Badawi had sued CBP twice and is one of the several "hands-off" passengers nationwide.

"I'm puzzled," he wrote, "how someone could be a member of the Muslim Brotherhood and unindicted co-conspirator in the Holy Land Foundation trial, be an associate of Yusuf al-Qaradawi, say that the US is staging car bombings in Iraq and that [it] is ok for men to beat their wives, question who was behind the 9/11 attacks, and be afforded the luxury of a visitor visa and de-watchlisted." He added, "It doesn't appear that we'll be successful with denying him entry tomorrow but maybe we could re-evaluate the matter in the future since the decision to de-watchlist him was made 17 months ago."[5]

KEPT IN THE DARK

Nearly two years later, I provided copies of the e-mails to Sen. Charles Grassley, R-IA, chairman of the Senate Homeland Security and Government Operations Committee, and he immediately began seeking answers from DHS about the apparent "hands off" policy.

On February 3, 2014, he wrote a letter to DHS Secretary Jeh Johnson, asking, among other things, why Badawi, who was not named in the letter, was removed from the watchlist in December 2010.[6]

Pointedly, Grassley asked for details regarding the involvement of the then-DHS secretary, Janet Napolitano, in the removal of Badawi from the watchlist. He also asked what "qualifies someone to receive the 'hands off' designation" and whether or not "filing a lawsuit [would] result in being designated 'hands off' and thus avoiding secondary security screenings."

"Who makes the determination that an individual should be considered 'hands off'?" the senator asked.[7]

Grassley requested a response within one month.

More than two months later, on April 10, 2014, the answer arrived, not from Johnson, but from Customs and Border Protection commissioner Gil Kerlikowske.

Kerlikowske pleaded innocent, insisting the agency does not have the discretionary authority to admit an inadmissible alien. "Accordingly," he wrote, "CBP does not have any list or other mechanism which would render an individual free of the grounds of inadmissibility or from any other inspection requirements, including secondary inspections."[8]

According to Kerlikowske, the "process is used only in situations where CBP has determined through a thorough inspection of the person that they are not the subject of the [watchlist] record."[9]

In a classic pass-the-buck maneuver, he also contended that the responsibility for watchlist records rests with the Justice Department: "The Terrorist Watchlist is maintained by the Terrorist Screening Center, which was created by the Attorney General and is administered by the Federal Bureau of Investigations," the CBP chief wrote. "All questions related to the watchlist should therefore be referred to the Department of Justice for response."[10]

To his credit, Kerlikowske did offer to provide the senator with a "more detailed briefing on the particular case cited in your letter, in the appropriate setting."[11]

Clearly not satisfied with the response, Grassley made the e-mails public along with the text of his letter to Johnson.

In May 2014, Grassley's staff held a closed-door meeting with CBP officials, who refused to answer multiple questions about the "hands off" list, according to Grassley spokeswoman Beth Pellett Levine, the *Washington Free Beacon* reported at the time:

> CBP's attempts to explain "the discrepancy" between the internal e-mails released by Grassley. . . and the official denials by CBP leaders were "unpersuasive," according to Levine.

CBP officials further refused to get "into details of the case," making it virtually impossible for the senator's staff to get concrete answers about the controversial list.[12]

In July 2014, the Washington, DC–based government watchdog group Judicial Watch filed a Freedom of Information Act request with DHS for material related to what it called a "terrorist hands off" list. Specifically, Judicial Watch asked for a copy of a DHS inspector general investigation that supposedly addressed allegations about the existence of the list.

After DHS refused to comply, Judicial Watch filed a lawsuit.

Judicial Watch president Tom Fitton said in a statement that the Obama administration's "unlawful secrecy on this 'hands off' list raises concerns about terrorists being allowed into the country. Even when it comes to protecting our borders from known terrorists, the Obama administration places secrecy and politics above national security. Our nation has reached a dangerous pass."[13]

More than a year after Badawi's trip to Tampa, WZTV-TV in Nashville reported concerns raised about the Muslim leader's appearance at the Islamic Center of Murfreesboro in Tennessee.

On October 22, 2013, the station reported that the mosque was to host a November 3 forum called "God's Books." In response, an e-mail had been circulating within the local community warning that Badawi had "connections with radical Islam" and was an unindicted coconspirator in a federal terrorist funding case.

The station said: "It's a claim to date no member of law enforcement has publicly agreed with and we did some checking on Badawi with the U.S. Attorney's Office. A spokesperson there tells FOX17 NEWS there are no alarms raised by any law enforcement agency concerning the Islamic speaker."[14]

Three years after the "hands off" list was revealed, in August 2015, Republican Sens. Jeff Sessions and Ted Cruz provided a long list of seventy-two foreigners who had been involved with or sentenced for terrorist activity who had been granted US entry. The lawmakers asked Attorney General Loretta Lynch and Secretary of State John Kerry to provide details on the immigration history of the individuals and their families that appear on the chart. The senators' list "included terrorists with documented ties to ISIS and other radical Islamic groups . . . including individuals from Yemen, Saudi Arabia, Somalia, and Uzbekistan who have been criminally charged in recent years."[15]

"HARASSMENT"

Back in Atlanta, on July 21, 2010, I was walking through secondary and noticed a well-known imam from Detroit, Ali Suleiman Ali, sitting among the other passengers in the waiting area. Since I already had background information on him, I interviewed him and entered a report into TECS.

By late September 2010, Ali and several other Michigan-area

Muslims had filed a complaint of harassment, intimidation, and religious discrimination against the Border Patrol, FBI, DHS, and the Transportation Security Administration, as well as a number of "unidentified agents" from the same government agencies.

The Michigan chapter of CAIR said it had dozens of reports from constituents claiming Customs and Border Protection agents had pointed guns at them and that they had been detained and handcuffed without charges and questioned about their worship habits.

Since I had interviewed Ali, I was now involved in the case.

On October 1, 2010, a senior adviser for DHS's Office for Civil Rights and Civil Liberties wrote a legal memorandum to Margo Schlanger, an officer for CRCL, concerning the constitutionality of questioning subjects regarding religion.

The senior adviser's memorandum is summarized in the first paragraph:

> You asked me to examine case law regarding the permissible bounds of law-enforcement questioning of individuals regarding their religion, both at the border and within the United States. The query would encompass border inspections as well as consensual and custodial police interrogation, and law on religious profiling would also be relevant. But there is much less law in this area than one would expect. So, notwithstanding the fact that religious questioning and religious profiling implicate First Amendment considerations that questioning or profiling on ethnicity or race do not, there is relatively little to say, other than that courts presume the same limitations on religion-based police activity as on race-cognizant policing.[16]

In an obvious move to create a test case on the "limitations on religion-based police activity as on race-cognizant policing," on March 24, 2011, CAIR's Michigan branch filed a formal complaint with DHS Civil Rights and Civil Liberties on behalf of Muslim Americans who reported similar treatment and questioning related to their religion and religious practices.

In a May 3, 2011, response to the CAIR complaint, Schlanger stated, "Under 6 U.S.C. § 345 and 42 U.S.C. § 2000 ee-1, our complaint process does not provide individuals with legal or procedural rights or remedies. Accordingly, this Office is not able to obtain any legal remedies or damages on your behalf or that of the above complainants."[17]

Despite the fact that the Office of Civil Rights and Civil Liberties could not technically provide any "legal remedies or damages," CRCL still opened an investigation on CAIR's behalf, which was immediately posted on CAIR's website:

> The Michigan chapter of the Council on American-Islamic Relations (CAIR-MI) today welcomed a decision by the U.S. Department of Homeland Security (DHS) Office for Civil Rights and Civil Liberties (CRCL) to launch an investigation into potential civil rights violations and profiling of Muslims by U.S. Customs and Border Protection (CBP) personnel at the United States–Canada border.
>
> On March 24, CAIR-MI filed complaints with both DHS and the Department of Justice (DOJ) seeking civil and potentially criminal investigations into dozens of reports from constituents who reported that CBP agents pointed firearms at them, detained and handcuffed them without predication of crimes or charges, and questioned them about their worship habits.[18]

At the same time—as we discovered later through FOIA—the American Civil Liberties Union was also cooperating closely with DHS CRCL in the CAIR case, again through Schlanger:

> Margo,
>
> I wanted to let you know that retention letters relating to the CBP Religious Questioning Investigation were mailed this afternoon, with CAIR-MI also receiving a copy via e-mail (CAIR letter attached).
>
> The retention memo, which you and Audrey reached agreement on last week, has been put into final along with the request for information.[19]

On the same day, May 4, 2011, Kareem Shora, another DHS CRCL official, sent an internal e-mail advising staff that CAIR was now publicly advertising the March 24, 2011, complaint, along with the May 4, 2011, decision by CRCL to launch an investigation into potential civil rights violations and profiling of Muslims by CBP personnel.

Shora advised:

> Team FYI, I know this topic has come up in several of our round-tables relatively recently and not just in Michigan so wanted to make sure you all saw this since we may be asked about it in upcoming roundtables given that CAIR has publicized our open investigations into the issue. Of course we can confirm, per below, that we have an ongoing investigation and that it is not limited to Michigan but obviously cannot comment beyond that fact.

Someone on the staff then asked:

> Kareem – So just be reactive, or can we pro-actively say we are investigating, but keeping to same level of detail?

Shora responded:

> Might be a good idea to be proactive in events where it's just CRCL, but I would not think it's a good idea to be proactive at events where CBP is present.[20]

In other words, don't tell anyone outside the DHS Civil Rights and Civil Liberties circle what we are actually doing on behalf of CAIR, a known Muslim Brotherhood front group founded by individuals with confirmed links to Hamas and one of the leading Holy Land Foundation unindicted coconspirators.

While the case in Detroit was still in progress, CAIR doubled down in a version of "biting the hand that feeds it" by attacking the DHS's "If You See Something, Say Something" campaign. In an October 2011, letter directed to Schlanger, which we discussed in chapter 7, CAIR, along with other Islamic groups, claimed the campaign elicited "racial and religious profiling" and demanded to know "what policies the DHS uses, to collect, retain, and purge data obtained through the campaign."[21]

The letter indicates that nearly three years after the Holy Land Foundation trial, CAIR was still participating in the Civil Rights and Civil Liberties meetings and had direct involvement in the inner proceedings of a major branch of DHS.

The terms "civil rights," "civil liberties," and "privacy protections" would be heard more and more in the next few years, culminating in the shutdown of major cases, limitations on investigations of individuals with potential links to terrorism, and restrictions on the ability of federal officials to evaluate the social media activities of foreign nationals seeking entry into America.

It took an extraordinary amount of audacity for groups such as CAIR to participate in the US government's counterterrorism efforts at the highest possible levels and then turn around and file lawsuits alleging discrimination, harassment, and intimidation against the very same government agencies.

As preposterous as it seems, it was happening on a regular basis in virtually every agency with a nexus to counterterrorism.

By 2012, it seemed as if the entire federal, state, and local law enforcement community was spending more time meeting with the leaders of American Muslim groups than it was investigating these individuals and their organizations for potential links to terrorism.

It wasn't a big mystery. There were numerous examples of probable cause for such investigations, but virtually nothing was being done. We knew groups such as CAIR, ISNA, and NAIT were linked not only to Hamas, but also to al-Qaeda and many other jihadist groups, as well as to financial crime, visa fraud, money laundering, and trafficking in illegal cargo.

We repeatedly saw images of top officials meeting with the leaders of these organizations, while they reassured Americans they were being kept safe through "engagement and dialogue" and that we were all working together to "counter violent extremism."

For example, on February 8, 2012, FBI director Robert S. Mueller met with the leaders of several American Islamic organizations to discuss the results of a review of "inaccurate and offensive training materials" by subject matter experts chosen from the Army's Combating Terrorism Center at West Point. Among the invited guests were members of ISNA, MPAC, the American-Arab Anti-Discrimination Committee, the Arab American Institute, and the Interfaith Alliance.

A glimpse into the FBI's emerging civil rights and civil liberties–based view of counterterrorism policy can be seen in the March 22, 2012, Guiding Principles Touchstone Document on Training, which includes the following directives:

> FBI training must emphasize the protection of civil rights and civil liberties. Training must clearly distinguish between constitutionally protected statements and activities designed to achieve political, social, or other objectives, and violent extremism, which is characterized by the use, threatened use, or advocacy of use of force or violence (when directed at and likely to incite imminent lawless activity) in violation of federal law to further a movement's social or political ideologies. This distinction includes recognition of the corresponding principle that *mere association with organizations that demonstrate both legitimate (advocacy) and illicit (violent extremism) objectives should not automatically result in a determination that the associated individual is acting in furtherance of the organization's illicit objective(s).* [emphasis added]
>
> Training must emphasize that no investigative or intelligence collection activity may be based solely on race, ethnicity, national origin, or religious affiliation. Specifically, training must focus on behavioral indicators that have a potential nexus to terrorist or criminal activity, while making clear that religious expression, protest activity, and the espousing of political or ideological beliefs are constitutionally protected activities that must not be equated with terrorism or criminality absent other indicia of such offenses.[22]

From the perspective of a law enforcement officer, one of the problems with official guidelines is that we're never told what we *can* base a case on.

Returning now to the CAIR lawsuit against CBP, in a follow-up to the original March 24, 2011, complaint and CRCL's subsequent May 4, 2011, investigation into CAIR's allegations, on April 13, 2012, Ali and several other plaintiffs filed a court injunction against CBP, the FBI, and TSA, alleging:

> The action of targeting and detaining Plaintiffs with a purpose of questioning them about their religious beliefs and practices violates the First Amendment rights of Plaintiffs as guaranteed by the United States Constitution.
>
> The detailed and invasive questioning of Plaintiffs about their religious practices and the Defendants' explicit policy that mandates the above-described treatment constitute an adverse action against Plaintiffs.

The injunction also sought a jury trial and relief that

> bars Defendants from engaging in further unconstitutional practices by questioning Plaintiffs about their religious beliefs and religious practices, and, requires Defendants to remedy the constitutional and statutory violations identified above, including, but not limited to, eliminating any existing policy whereby Plaintiffs, other Muslim Americans, and others similarly situated are subject to religious questioning at ports of entry.[23]

Part of the process included a litigation hold, which made demands for files, notes, memoranda, letters, correspondence, calendars, date books, logs, and draft documents. It also included demands for any relevant documents in government computer systems, laptops, PDAs, smartphones, home and personal computers, archived files, boxes at federal records centers, and digital voice mail.

My own involvement in this part of the process required me to provide two major analysis reports, copies of two TECS records, an incident report, and a spreadsheet of all the information. I was also interviewed on the telephone and asked question such as:

Were you in uniform while you interviewed Mr. Ali?

Was there anyone else in the room with you and Mr. Ali?

Known today as the Cherri case, after the chief plaintiff, it remains unresolved as of March 2016.

BRIEFINGS

On February 28, 2013, I was in Washington, DC, to brief several members of Congress, including some on the House Homeland Security Committee, including chairman Rep. Michael McCaul, R-TX, and Rep. Jeff Duncan, R-SC.

After the general elections of November 2012, the roster in Congress changed dramatically, and many of the committees now had new chairmen and new members. The HHSC was no exception, so I had to start all over in some respects and reintroduce myself to a new group of members as well as to their chief counsels and staff members.

One of things I shared with McCaul and Duncan was that Mohammed Akram al-Adlouni, the mysterious author of the Muslim Brotherhood's Explanatory Memorandum detailing its aims for North America, was not only still alive and well, but was openly raising money for Hamas and the Palestinian cause in Europe and the Far East.

New York Times reporter David K. Shipler described Adlouni as "an author we know little about, [who] writes in the tone of an underling," and dismissed the memorandum itself as an "old document of questionable authority and relevance."[24] These misleading characterizations are still parroted by leaders of US Muslim Brotherhood front groups.

In fact, Adlouni was a key leader in the Muslim Brotherhood network, holding prestigious positions in both the executive office and on the North American Shura Council.[25] On May 5, 2008, Adlouni shared the stage with CAIR executive director Nihad Awad at a conference in Denmark commemorating the sixtieth anniversary of the *nakba*, or "catastrophe," as many Palestinians call the founding of the state of Israel.

Since he was part of the Hamas Network case, Adlouni's name came up on my radar on October 4, 2012, when his organization, known as the Al-Quds International Foundation, was put on the US Department of the Treasury list of charities controlled by Hamas, as designated pursuant to Executive Order 13224.

These topics in February 2013 meetings were typical of the others I have had with members of Congress over the years.

Along with updates on Adlouni, I discussed

- the effect of the "Words Matter" memo on the law-enforcement community (2008);

- the consequences of the DHS inaugural meeting with Muslim leaders (2008);

- the TECS modification project (2009–2010);

- the Muslim Brotherhood–linked individuals chosen for the Combating Violent Extremism Steering Committee (2010);

- background information on Kifah Mustapha (2010), an HLF coconspirator who attended an FBI Citizen's Academy course;

- the deeper meaning of the ISNA-led Ground Zero Press Conference (2010);

- the Muslim Brotherhood front groups' public declaration of America as an Islamophobic country;

- the Assembly of Muslim Jurists of America (2011);

- the CAIR lawsuit in Detroit (2011);

- deletion of the sixty-seven TECS records linked to the Institute for Islamic Education case (2012); and

- the growing disconnect between the FBI and local Fusion Centers (2012).

"WE NEED TO PROTECT YOU"

Two weeks later, on March 13–14, 2013, I had another series of meetings with McCaul, along with his chief counsel, Nick Palarino, and congressional liaison Raymond Orzel.

During that same two-day period, I also met with Duncan and members of his staff, as well as with Reps. Michele Bachmann, Louis Gohmert, and Trent Franks and their staff members.

In the private meeting with McCaul, Orzel and I were huddled around a small round table in the congressman's personal office, looking intently at my computer screen as I walked them through a PowerPoint briefing. Since I was sitting next to McCaul, I could tell that he was extremely concerned about the things I was showing him. As I went through the briefing, we were looking each other eye to eye.

At one point, McCaul said, "We need to protect you, and we need to protect this information!"

He wasn't the first person to say that to me, and he wouldn't be the last.

When we finished our discussion, McCaul looked across the table and said to Orzel, "You want to bring him up?"

Orzel answered, "Yes, sir, let's bring him up."

With that, we all stood up and shook hands.

"Okay, then, let's bring him up," said McCaul.

The plan was to bring me to Washington as an active-duty CBP attaché and work directly with the House Homeland Security Committee to address the national security concerns I had just reviewed. I left the meeting that day thinking what we might be able to accomplish if we had the opportunity to work together.

But I never got the chance to find out. Within days, I heard that coming up to the HHSC was "never going to happen," and that the new plan was to send me over to the inspector general's office and see if I could get some help from them instead.

A month later, the Boston Marathon bombs exploded, and suddenly, all of those meetings with members of Congress were cast in a new light.

I was literally holding the evidence of an intelligence failure in my hands, and as time slowed down, it dawned on me: "This is exactly what I was trying to warn them about."

10

INVISIBLE SHRAPNEL

Three days after two pressure-cooker bombs were detonated at the finish line of the Boston Marathon, killing three people and injuring 264 more, Department of Homeland Security secretary Janet Napolitano was indignant.

At an April 18, 2013, hearing of the House of Representatives' Homeland Security Committee, a perplexed Rep. Jeff Duncan was asking why the Obama administration was about to deport a Saudi national who had been detained by authorities as a "person of interest" in the Boston case.[1] Citing the Department of Homeland Security's slogan, Duncan noted, "We're asking average Americans to help ID and assist law enforcement in identifying who the bomber was—see something, say something. And now we have someone who is being deported due to national security concerns, and I'm assuming that he's got some sort of link to terror or he wouldn't be deported."

The congressman pointed out that the man, twenty-one-year-old Abdul Rahman Ali Alharbi, was at the scene of the attack and possibly could identify the bomber "just like we're asking every other American that was on the scene to provide your pictures, help us identify who may have been acting funny, everybody we're asking that was in Boston, and we've got this guy who was there, we know he was there, he was arrested—or wasn't arrested—was detained in the hospital, covered with blood, he was at the scene, and yet we're going to deport him—"

Napolitano interrupted.

"If I might—I am unaware of anyone who is being deported for national security concerns at all related to Boston," the Homeland Security chief said. "I don't know where that rumor came from . . . "

Duncan interjected: "I'm not saying it's related to Boston, but he is being deported."

The DHS chief continued: "No, I—I—like I said, I—again, I don't even think he was technically a person of interest or a suspect. That was a wash. And I'm unaware of any proceeding there. I will clarify that for you. But I think this is an example of why it is so important to let law enforcement do its job."

The South Carolina Republican insisted, "I want them to do their job, and that's why I said, wouldn't you agree with me that it's negligent for us, as American administration, to deport someone who was reportedly at the scene of the bombing, and we're going to deport him not to be able to question him anymore? Is that not negligence?"

Napolitano's anger was visibly rising.

"I'm not going to answer that question," she said. "It's so full of misstatements and misapprehensions that it's just not worthy of an answer."

Later that day, Chechen brothers Dzhokhar and Tamerlan Tsarnaev were identified as suspects through photographs and a surveillance video. In a massive manhunt the next day, Dzhokhar was arrested and Tamerlan was killed. On April 8, 2015, Dzhokhar was found guilty on thirty charges related to homegrown terrorism and later sentenced to death.

During the two-minute-and-thirty-nine-second exchange with Duncan, Napolitano set off what I call the "third bomb" in the Boston Marathon attack, filled with invisible shrapnel that nevertheless wounded many people, including me.

To this day, a veil of mystery shrouds the young Saudi who was injured near the finish line and hospitalized. Even though no evidence has surfaced that ties him to the Tsarnaev brothers or to the attack, there are still many unanswered questions surrounding the case.

In a Senate Judiciary Committee hearing five days later, on April 23, 2013, Napolitano again declared Alharbi was never a person of interest, but she admitted that he was put on a watchlist while questioned by authorities, then removed from the list "when it was quickly determined he had nothing to do with the bombing."[2]

Ten days after the bombing, TheBlaze founder Glenn Beck held up a piece of paper in front of the camera on the Fox News Channel's *The O'Reilly Factor*, claiming it was proof positive that authorities had designated Alharbi as a terrorist in connection to the Boston bombing and intended to deport him to his home country of Saudi Arabia.[3]

While establishment media was relatively silent, Fox News's Bret Baier addressed the controversy in his video blog post, *The Daily Bret*, holding a copy of the same piece of paper that Beck had shown to the camera:

> Janet Napolitano, the Security of Homeland Security just said today that [Abdul Rahman Ali Alharbi] really was never a person of interest. But out of an abundance of caution and out of diligence according to these U.S. officials, federal authorities at that time, because they wanted to question him, added him to the no fly list. Now, this is key: When anyone inside the U.S. with a U.S. visa is added to the no fly list, the process, the process is started. And I stress process here, to revoke visa. And that's automatically begun according to U.S. officials. The 212 is a national security indication and anyone looking at this would say this is a bad guy. This means they had a lot of stuff on this guy. The U.S. officials we're talking to say this document was simply triggered by them putting him on the no fly list when they went to talk to him.[4]

In March 2014, Alharbi filed a lawsuit against Beck and his media company, claiming assault, libel, and slander, along with defamation and violation of his privacy rights. It should not be overlooked that Alharbi is a foreign national, but he is still being allowed to sue an American citizen through the US justice system.

And now, we come to the heart of the matter.

Whether all of the claims Beck made on his television and radio show about Alharbi will ever be verified remains to be seen, but I know one thing for certain: my boss at the time, Janet Napolitano, was hiding something from the American people.

Put another way, she either was lying or she was grossly misinformed by her staff of advisers.

How do I know this?

The evidence Beck presented on TV was a copy of the "event file" I personally provided to the House Homeland Security Committee, with the obvious presumption that its staffers would protect its contents, as they do any other sensitive information pertaining to national security. How a copy of the file ended up in the hands of Beck and Baier is unknown to me, but it's a significant episode that resurfaces later in my story.

In any case, the file, prepared by my former supervisors at the Customs and Border Protection's National Targeting Center, undermines Napolitano's testimony.

While she was insisting to Congress and the American public that Alharbi was never a "subject of interest" or a "person of interest" and was never set for deportation on "3-B" terrorism charges, the event file on the Saudi national tells a different story.

The file we all saw on TV stated that Alharbi was "linked to the Boston bombing" and, according to Immigration and Customs Enforcement, he was to be deported as an "armed and dangerous terrorist" under section 212(a)(3)(B) of the US code on "security and related grounds" and "terrorist activities." I knew how to look up Alharbi's file because that kind of work had been part of my job when I was at the NTC in 2011–12. I created events for the Tablighi Jamaat Initiative, and I also vetted new events that came in daily from other ports.

More specifically, the reason I looked up his file is that, in law-enforcement parlance, I had a "nexus" to the case. In the hours and days immediately after the bombings, when no one knew who was responsible, every officer in the country with any nexus to the case was doing all he or she could to help find out who did it.

Together, we were trying to put the clues together, not only to help solve the Boston bombing, but also to possibly prevent another attack.

In such situations, officers and investigators don't have the benefit of hindsight. We use every tool and every skill we have, and hope we can connect the dots before something else happens.

I had nexus to the case because the bombing was in Boston, and four years before it happened, I had created TECS records on the Islamic Society of Boston (ISB) as part of a larger report that included 118 other linked records.

In turn, this report was tied directly to the Hamas Network report.

The 118 records in the ISB case were among the 818 records I had "modified" back in 2009–10. So now I was the owner of records that were linked to the Boston bombing but had been diminished in quality, by direct order of DHS top management.

But we still haven't come to the most important point in this story.

During the four-year period, from the time when I first created the ISB report in 2009 to the time of the bombing in 2013, not a single person had queried the records related to the ISB.

Worse still, when federal, state and local law enforcement agencies were all looking for clues about the shadowy Tsarnaev brothers, no one queried TECS for information on the ISB, except for one NTC colleague whom I had called right after the bombing.

With events still in motion, I printed out one of the records and showed it to my colleagues. "Look, this is the mosque attended by the Boston bombing suspects, Dzhokhar and Tamerlan Tsarnaev. Look at the date—May 2009—almost four years ago!"

Everybody said the same thing: "Wow, Haney!"

As it turned out, I was the only one in our whole agency who had entered records linked to the ISB, and there they stood, still archived in the system, shining like a beacon in the middle of the ocean.

A news story published ten days after the bombing may help explain why the records were ignored.

In an interview with *USA Today*, Yusufi Vali, the ISB imam, insisted his mosque did not spread radical ideology and could not be blamed for the acts of a few worshipers, referring to Dzhokhar and Tamerlan Tsarnaev.

Then, he made a remarkably revealing statement.

"If there were really any worry about us being extreme," he said, according to *USA Today*, "U.S. law enforcement agencies such as the FBI and Departments of Justice and Homeland Security would not partner with the Muslim American Society and the Boston mosque."

According to Vali, by 2013, the FBI, DHS, and DOJ had already been partnering with the Muslim American Society and ISB in outreach programs for at least four years.

The American law enforcement community wasn't investigating the ISB or its network of affiliated individuals and organizations.

Far from it.

It was engaging in "outreach," despite the fact that the ISB has well-documented links to Hamas, al-Qaeda, and numerous individuals tied to violence and terrorism, which has been known, at the very least, since 9/11.

For years, federal officers such as I, along with credible counterterrorism specialists in the civilian world, have repeatedly tried to make this information available to political officials and members of the law enforcement community, but with very little success.

This major intelligence failure—culminating with the fact that no one queried TECS records on the ISB after the bombing—is without question the most crucial part of the Boston Marathon story.

What's more, the Obama administration later chose the Islamic Society of Boston to be one of three "model communities" in its vaunted Countering Violent Extremism program rollout.

The other two cities in the program were Los Angeles and Minneapolis–St. Paul. The original plan was to test-drive the CVE program in these three "'model communities," then to have leaders from each area come to the White House to participate in the heavily promoted 2015 CVE Summit.

However, in the days just before the summit was scheduled, February 18, 2015, leaders of all three "model communities" held press conferences and renounced the program, expressing "grave concerns" and charging it "is rooted in the flawed 'radicalization theory'" which "claims that there is a fixed trajectory to radicalization with indicators that, if detected early on, can be interrupted through intervention. Examples of indicators used in this theory as signs of radicalization include growing beards, increasing involvement in social activism and community issues, and wearing traditional Islamic clothing."[5]

POSITIVE MATCH

In the meantime, the Alharbi saga provides irrefutable evidence that the political authorities charged with protecting our national security are conflicted not only by domestic influences but also by longtime foreign alliances.

As NTC officers were creating an event file on Abdul Rahman Ali Alharbi early in the morning of April 16, the Saudi national was also being designated a "Bravo 10," the highest designated threat to national security.

Further, contrary to the insistence of DHS Secretary Napolitano and her colleagues in ICE, the NTC event file showed that the State Department liaison in Riyadh, Saudi Arabia, had been notified by the afternoon of April 16 that Alharbi was to be deported on 3-B, or terrorism-related, charges.

After inspecting his apartment from about 9 p.m. until nearly midnight on April 15, FBI field agents reported their findings to their superiors, who then coordinated with the FBI's Terrorist Screening Center, where officials and analysts at the highest level agreed that the man detained by law enforcement officers at the Boston Marathon finish line should be designated as a potentially armed and dangerous individual.

Operating in close coordination with this internal stream of activity, the Terrorist Screening Center maintains the US government's consolidated terrorist watchlist of those known or reasonably suspected of being involved in terrorist activity. In turn, these officials and analysts cooperate and share information with the NTC, where the events are created and vetted for any additional secret-level, derogatory information.

In the Alharbi case, all of this was done in the hours immediately after the bombing, and by 6 a.m. on April 16, 2013, the next day, a picture had emerged.

But other, still-unknown forces and influences suddenly entered the process, and by the time Napolitano testified on the afternoon of April 18, the picture had changed: Napolitano basically was telling the nation, and the world, that we in the law enforcement community didn't really know what we were doing and that we should all just move on.

There was nothing to see here.

Some of us saw something and said something, but she denied we had even spoken.

Meanwhile, reports of closed-door meetings with President Obama, Secretary of State John Kerry, and Saudi Arabia's highest officials suggested the Alharbi case was an urgent state-level matter.

Unexpectedly, Kerry's April 17 meeting with Saudi Arabian foreign minister Saud Al Faisal was abruptly closed to media.

On the day of the House hearing, April 18, 2013, Obama had another unscheduled meeting with Saudi foreign minister Prince Saud at the White House.

On April 19, 2013, Reps. Michael T. McCaul, Jeff Duncan, Peter King, and Candice Miller sent a signed letter to Napolitano asking for a classified briefing on DHS information and actions related to the case, noting that despite her testimony, "media reports have continued to raise concerns about this individual and adjustments that may have been made to his immigration status, including possible visa revocation and terrorist watch-listing, in the days following the bombing."[6]

To the best of my knowledge, this request was never granted.

Back at the NTC, Alharbi's event file was updated. Fewer than twenty-four hours after the initial notification of deportation, the order was rescinded.

Another important but largely overlooked fact is that Alharbi was "out of status," according to the terms of his F-1 student visa, and was deportable on that basis alone.

Meanwhile, along with Secretary Napolitano, an ICE official claimed that Alharbi had never been in custody and that reports by Glenn Beck's TheBlaze news website that the DHS had opened an event on him and planned to deport him on 212 3(B) charges were "categorically false." In fact, said the official, TheBlaze's "alleged source has no idea what they are talking about."[7]

The simple fact, however, is that NTC officers create events only when they are asked to provide them.

Such a request may come from an officer at a port who is interviewing someone in secondary or from an analyst who is seeking additional information on a case, or, as in the Alharbi case, from another branch of the government.

For the Alharbi record to be created, the officers who questioned the Saudi national in the hospital, then inspected his apartment and belongings, would have to determine whether or not some kind of law enforcement action was warranted. Then, after all of the evidence was reviewed, in cooperation with the National Counterterrorism Center, a request to create an event would be sent to the NTC. At that point, the NTC officers would begin collating the information, both classified and nonclassified, into a standard template format, called a targeting framework, or a TF event.

In other words, they would start "filling in the blanks" until they compiled as much relevant information as possible.

After this, the same group of CIA, FBI, JTTF, NCTC, NTC, State Department, or executive branch officials and analysts who originally requested the event would review the information and make a final decision, which in this case was: deport him.

For Alharbi, the process was set in motion and the consulate liaison at the US embassy in Riyadh, Saudi Arabia, was notified that one of their citizens was about to be deported from the United States.

But just twenty-four hours later, someone at NTC was instructed to send an e-mail to the State Department, rescinding the visa revocation request and pending deportation.

What happened in the twenty-four-hour period between Monday evening, when the deportation order was made, and Tuesday evening, when it was rescinded?

About three weeks later, this strange case became even more mysterious.

On May 8, 2013, a record was entered into the system indicating that Alharbi's F-1 student visa was no longer valid. The instruction to frontline CBP officers was to notify NTC-ICE immediately if he tried to enter the United States.

What is going on here? I thought as I examined the record.

Alharbi presumably was not deported, but this new record indicated that he was no longer in the United States.

Three weeks after the bombing the Saudi national, who was never a person of interest, never a subject of interest, and never scheduled for deportation (according to Napolitano), and who was really someone else (according to ICE), was gone.

ON CAPITOL HILL

By this point in my career, I was becoming familiar with the consequences of saying something after I had seen something. Now my colleague, congressional liaison Raymond Orzel, was about to learn the same lesson.

Within fifteen minutes of the end of Napolitano's April 18, 2013, testimony, Rep. Louis Gohmert's chief of staff, Connie Hair, called me. "You've got to go get the records and fax them to Ray," she said, "because they're going to fire him."

Orzel was caught with an M50 pointed at him. If he couldn't produce the evidence, he would have been discredited right then and there.

After all, Napolitano had just made her infamous declaration, which I call "the Three Nos": no person of interest, no subject of interest, no deportation.

It was my day off, but I got dressed and went to a secure location near the airport and printed off copies of the files.

At about 4:45 p.m., I faxed the files to the secure number at the House Homeland Security Committee offices in the Ford Building.

With Orzel on the phone to confirm each page as it arrived, all I could hear him say was, "Thank God, Philip, thank God."

As soon as I knew he had everything, I shredded my copies and went back home.

While I was driving home, Orzel presented the documents to the committee, confirming that Napolitano had either just lied, or at the very least grossly misstated the facts of the case.

And now they had the evidence.

Within the next few days, someone, presumably from within the committee, provided copies of the documents to Beck at TheBlaze and Baier at Fox News.

Within a month, Orzel was pulled off the committee and reassigned to a cubicle in the corner of the ICE building. In less than three months, DHS Internal Affairs was targeting me in an investigation of who leaked the Alharbi information to the two newsmen.

BECK LAWSUIT

For Glenn Beck, saying something resulted in a civil lawsuit filed on March 28, 2014, by Alharbi in federal court in Massachusetts, against him, TheBlaze Inc., Mercury Radio Arts, Inc., and Premiere Radio Networks Inc., alleging assault, libel, and slander:

> Plaintiff Abdulrahman Alharbi alleged that Defendant Glenn Beck repeatedly and falsely identified Mr. Alharbi as an active participant in the 2013 Boston Marathon bombing, repeatedly questioned the motives of federal officials in failing to pursue or detain Mr. Alharbi, and repeatedly and falsely accused Mr. Alharbi of being a criminal who had funded the attacks.[8]

On a side note, allowing a foreign national from an Islamic country to sue an American citizen for slander sets a dangerous precedent with respect to First Amendment rights of free expression.

According to Islamic law, slander, or *ghiba*, is considered a capital offense. In Islam, slander is much more complex than the standard *Webster's Dictionary* definition, which is to make a false, libelous remark about someone.

In Islam, you can slander someone even when you are telling the truth about him. Or, as written in the Hadith, the sayings of Muhammad, "If what you say of him is true, you have slandered him, and if what you say of him is not true, you have reviled him."

Also, from an Islamic perspective, actions such as the targeting of Muslim communities by law enforcement officers to find violent jihadists is seen as a form of persecution, also known as *fitna*, meaning opposition or oppression. Causing any kind of fitna within the Islamic community is also seen as a capital offense.

The lawsuit claimed that Beck had made repeated false statements about Alharbi on Beck's radio show. Alharbi charged that the statements had damaged his reputation and subjected him to public messages, via the Web, calling him a murderer, child killer, and terrorist.

On broadcasts following the bombing, Beck said Alharbi was an al-Qaeda "control agent" or moneyman who recruited the Tsarnaev brothers to carry out the bombing.[9] He also contended that Alharbi was designated as a 212 3(B) subject after being interviewed and having his apartment searched, but a retired Immigration and Naturalization Service (INS) special agent, Bob Trent, told Beck in a TheBlaze television interview that the 3(B) designation is applied only to foreign nationals before entering the country.[10]

To date, no evidence has surfaced that would link Alharbi to the Boston bombing plot. Nor is it certain exactly when the 212 3(B) designation was given to Alharbi.

Was he already on the law enforcement radar before the Boston Marathon attack? But with that designation, he should have either never been allowed to enter the country in the first place, or been deported and barred from ever reentering the country again.

His proximity to one of the worst terrorist attacks on American soil would warrant the suspicion of any reasonable law enforcement officer or public official.

Somewhere amid the fog of denials and disinformation, there are still some facts about the Alharbi case that remain inescapable.

First, according to the terms of his F-1 student visa, he was out of status and could have been deported on that basis alone.

Second, he was scheduled to be deported the day after the bombings, apparently under the radar, in all probability because of the complicated relationship between the United States and its oil-rich Middle East ally.

In Saudi Arabia, the Alharbi family is as prominent and wealthy as the bin Laden family. At the same time, more than ten individuals from the Alharbi clan have been linked to al-Qaeda, with as many as five members imprisoned at the US facility in Guantánamo Bay, Cuba. It's significant to note that on the day of the 9/11 attacks, the Bush administration precipitously airlifted from the United States to Saudi Arabia high-ranking Saudis, including members of Osama bin Laden's family, even as US airways were shut down. All this, while fifteen of the nineteen hijackers who carried out the 9/11 attacks came from the Islamic kingdom.[11]

Third, Alharbi actually was designated a 3(B). Afterward, decisions may have been made to change or revoke the designation, but that does not change the fact that he was designated as a 3(B).

Even if it was only for five minutes, it still happened.

If there were good reasons for the decisions that were made, it would have been simple enough for Napolitano to explain it to Congress in a closed-door session. If that had been done in a reasonable and professional manner, none of the law-enforcement sensitive information about Alharbi would have ever been made public.

But when DHS and ICE officials made their false claims in public, it became the solemn duty and obligation of individuals like me to fulfill our oath to protect our country from threats both foreign and domestic, and to do our utmost to notify someone in a position of authority.

Consider if we had simply chosen to say nothing and something even worse had happened. Would history have accepted our reasons for not coming forward and doing all we could to help protect our country?

Meanwhile, Beck appealed to federal Judge Patti B. Saris to dismiss the defamation case. But in December 2014, she allowed it to move forward, rejecting defense arguments that Alharbi was a "limited purpose" or "involuntary" public figure who failed to show that Beck acted with "actual malice": "Choosing to attend a sporting event as one of thousands of spectators is not the kind of conduct that a reasonable person would expect to result in publicity," Saris wrote.[12]

In June 2015, the judge allowed Alharbi to amend his defamation lawsuit by adding a count for unjust enrichment.[13]

The case is now in the discovery phase. According to legal editor Steven J. J. Weisman of *Talkers* magazine, "Beck's attorneys are seeking information from the Boston Police Department, the Massachusetts State Police and 10 federal agencies, including the FBI, the CIA, and the Department of Homeland Security."[14]

ISLAMIC SOCIETY OF BOSTON

Whether or not Alharbi was involved in the Boston plot, the fact remains that law enforcement officials had access to information showing that dozens of individuals associated with the Islamic Society of Boston—whose Cambridge, Massachusetts, mosque was attended by the Tsarnaev brothers—have ties to terrorism.

Remarkably, the ISB later became the center of the administration's policy of Countering Violent Extremism, held up as "a model community" at the February 18, 2015, White House Summit on Countering Violent Extremism.

But the ISB was founded by Hamas and Hezbollah supporter Abdurahman Alamoudi, who in 2004 was sentenced to twenty-three years in prison on terrorism-related charges. ISB's Cambridge mosque is run by the Muslim American Society, which federal prosecutors say is a front for the Muslim Brotherhood. Its roster of worshippers includes the infamous "Lady al Qaeda," Aafia Siddiqui, who was arrested in Afghanistan in 2008 while allegedly planning a chemical attack in New York City.

Yusuf Qaradawi, the spiritual leader of the Muslim Brotherhood, was a founding trustee of the ISB.

Imam Abdullah Faaruuq, who often spoke on behalf of the Cambridge mosque, cited "Lady al Qaeda" Siddiqui in his criticism of the antiterrorism USA PATRIOT Act, which was passed in response to 9/11 under the George W. Bush administration. "After they're done with [Siddiqui], they are going to come to your door if they feel like it," he said in a video obtained by the counterterrorism nonprofit Americans for Peace and Tolerance.[15]

When Siddiqui was arrested in Afghanistan, she was in possession of a cyanide canister. In detention, she grabbed a rifle and, in the tussle, shot at military officers and FBI agents. She was convicted in New York in 2010 and sentenced to eighty-six years in prison.

Another worshipper at the Cambridge mosque was Tarek Mehanna, who was sentenced in 2012 to seventeen years in prison for conspiring to aid al-Qaeda in an attack on a Boston-area mall.

Americans for Peace and Tolerance found writings by Syed Qutb, the former leader of the Muslim Brotherhood in Egypt regarded by al-Qaeda as its spiritual father, at the Cambridge mosque's library in 2003.

The top propagandist for ISIS, Ahmad Abousamra, also was a regular worshipper at the Cambridge mosque, according to the FBI. Paul Sperry reported in the *New York Post* September 2014 that the FBI suspected Abousamra was operating ISIS's sophisticated media wing promoting the group's beheadings and other atrocities through videos posted on the Internet.[16]

The trustee of the Islamic Society of Boston, the North American Islamic Trust, was also designated as an unindicted coconspirator in the Holy Land Foundation case. NAIT holds title to more than three hundred mosques and has helped finance more than five hundred

Islamic centers in America. NAIT's properties include the Chattanooga, Tennessee, mosque attended by Mohammad Youssef Abdulazeez, who killed four Marines at a recruiting center in July 2015, and the Islamic Community Center of Phoenix, where worshippers included two ISIS terrorists who attacked the Garland, Texas, "Draw Muhammad" event in May 2015 and planned to shoot up the Super Bowl.

TROJAN HORSE

Less than one month after the Boston bombing, CAIR submitted a report to McCaul's House Homeland Security Committee as a supplement to a May 9, 2013, committee hearing, titled "The Boston Bombings: A First Look." The report contended that "[v]iolent extremism is not limited to any one ethnicity, political ideology or religion" and said that al-Qaeda's "ideology is a combination of extreme political and fringe religious views that exist outside mainstream Islamic beliefs and practices."[17]

Al-Qaeda's ideology may be many things, but it is not *a fringe religious view that exists outside mainstream Islamic beliefs and practices*. Like the core teachings of the Muslim Brotherhood—the ideological parent of al-Qaeda—it is based on Quranic doctrine and sharia, and Muslims around the world know this is true.

On the evening of June 19, 2013, I had an opportunity to discuss these concerns with House Homeland Security vice-chairman Jeff Duncan. During a sidebar conversation between just the two of us, I showed him evidence of what I called a "Trojan horse" within his committee.

The evidence was a series of five documents, which I laid on a small table in chronological order. One was a copy of the CAIR report to his House committee, another was a report I had compiled on Ali Suleiman Ali—one of the principal plaintiffs in the CAIR lawsuit against CBP in Detroit—and the other three documents were related to the lawsuit.

Why did I refer to the CAIR report as a "Trojan horse"? Because CAIR would not have submitted such a report unless it was solicited and accepted by someone within the House committee.

The next day, June 20, 2013, I gave a PowerPoint presentation to Sen. Tom Coburn's investigative staff. My presentation reiterated what I had just shared with Duncan and touched on many related issues.

My observations about CAIR were of particular interest to Coburn because he had written a February 24, 2009, letter to FBI director Robert Mueller to express his own concerns about the FBI's relationship with the organization.

11

KILL THE MESSENGER

On a sultry afternoon in late July 2013, I stood in front of the Ford House Office Building near the US Capitol with former Defense Department inspector general Joseph E. Schmitz and Republican Rep. Louis Gohmert's chief of staff, Connie Hair. We had just finished a forty-five-minute meeting at the offices of the House Committee on Homeland Security with Charles K. Edwards, the acting inspector general for the Department of Homeland Security, with four or five other staff members from both the House and Senate in attendance.

Standing in the middle of Second Street, in plain sight of the US Capitol and the Rayburn House Office Building, Schmitz looked right at me and tapped his forehead with his right index finger. "Philip," he said, "the things you know, the things you have between your ears, people will kill you for."

As we were riding back to the Rayburn Building a few minutes later, Schmitz also remarked that I had "cases embedded within cases, just in the short briefing you gave to the IG."

Schmitz's ominous warning set off an avalanche of memories, as I recalled the countless times my friends—many with former military and law-enforcement experience—and my colleagues in Customs and Border Protection had told me the same thing. Since as far back as 2006, when this whole ordeal began, their sincere warnings of, "Watch your back, Haney," had become a familiar refrain.

On July 31, 2013, in compliance with Edwards's directive during the briefing, House Homeland Security committee chairman Michael McCaul, R-TX, and Senate Homeland Security Committee and Governmental Affairs ranking member Sen. Tom Coburn, R-OK, submitted a signed letter to Edwards requesting that his office "investigate with particular sensitivity to the whistleblower's work situation and request ongoing updates as facts become known."

Remarkably, on that same day, I was being interviewed in Atlanta by two CBP Internal Affairs contract investigators about my involvement in the Alharbi case.

As I soon discovered, both CBP and the DOJ suspected I was the one who leaked details of a report related to the Boston Marathon bombing that originally came from the National Targeting Center. (See last chapter.)

The affidavit shows they not only asked me why I had accessed Alharbi's event file, but also what websites I browsed, how often I watched Fox News, what my opinion of Glenn Beck was, and my personal e-mail address.

TO THE HIGHEST LEVELS OF GOVERNMENT

On August 15, 2013, I met with Office of Inspector General Special Agent Davis (not his real name) in his downtown Atlanta office to review the case and talk about what to expect. During our meeting, I also showed him the PowerPoint briefing that I had presented to Edwards in Washington, DC.

We met in the Atlanta branch office, because as IG Edwards had plainly stated to everyone in the room, the working plan was to transfer the case down to the IG branch office in Atlanta, my home port, so that I would be available, if needed, during the investigation.

However, just a few days after meeting with Davis, I received a phone call from another OIG special agent, whom I'll call Agent Michaels, who said that the IG investigation was being transferred back up to Washington, DC.

I asked him why.

"The investigation was requested by members of the House and Senate, and it will go to the highest levels of the government," he explained.

When I finally met Michaels for the first time on November 13, 2013, I gave him the PowerPoint presentation that I had given to Edwards and Davis, and also provided copies of all the files and documents I had that were related to the investigation.

Then, in another twist of fate, Edwards resigned in disgrace in December 2012 from his IG position after it was discovered that he had been allowing DHS officials—the very targets of his investigations—to review and edit his final reports.

Looking back, I have often wondered why Edwards took my case in the first place. By June 2013, if not earlier, he knew he was under investigation himself.

But I am thankful that he did. Of nearly all the public officials I encountered during this long ordeal, he was among the most straightforward and efficient. Though many things have been said about him, he gave me, an unknown CBP officer from Atlanta, the chance to state my case. I will never forget how alarmed and serious he was during that forty-five-minute briefing in the Ford Building, when he told the people in the room how he wanted them to proceed with the case.

It was just three months after the Boston Marathon bombing, and some of the most incriminating information I presented that day was directly related to the attack.

Just before the meeting, one of my legal advisers cautioned me that I needed to capture Edwards's attention within the first two or three minutes of the briefing, and that if it went on for much more than thirty minutes, people would start to lose focus.

As it turned out, I didn't need to worry about capturing anyone's attention.

It wasn't two minutes into the presentation before Edwards, nearly yelling, said, "This is really a problem!"

For a few moments, everyone was quiet, and then he said it again.

I continued walking through the PowerPoint slides, and just a minute or two later, Edwards interjected once again. This time, as he pointed his index finger toward me, he announced to the entire room: "Mr. Haney, we need to protect you, and we need to protect this information!"

Four months earlier, House Homeland Security Chairman McCaul had told me exactly the same thing as we were huddled around a computer screen in his office.

From whom did I need protection? Were they talking about enraged jihadists from the Middle East? I suspect it was from somewhere much closer to home. In any case, I decided it was best not to take any chances.

THE STATE OF OUR UNION

On Monday, January 27, 2014, I videoed my entire story, from start to finish, in the office of the chairman of the House Judiciary Committee. It took seven hours to cover everything, and Reps. Louie Gohmert and Steve King of Iowa took turns being with me during that time, pointing at a big-screen TV and asking questions along the way.

The following day, I gave a one-hour briefing to four members of Iowa Sen. Charles Grassley's research and investigation staff, including Jim Donahue, Jason Foster, and Tristan Leavitt.

By early that afternoon, it had started snowing down in Atlanta, shutting down the airport. I was scheduled to return to Atlanta that afternoon—in fact, I was supposed to qualify on the shooting range the next morning—but now I was stuck in Washington.

It also happened to be the day President Obama was scheduled to give his State of the Union address before both houses of Congress.

Since I was now stranded in DC, Representative Gohmert asked if I would like to spend the rest of the day with him.

Before the evening was over, I ended up attending a private gathering at Ruth's Chris Steak House in downtown Washington with Sen. Ted Cruz, Fox News Channel's Sean Hannity, former House Speaker Newt Gingrich, talk-radio host and author Mark Levin, *Duck Dynasty*'s

Willie J. Robertson and his wife, and about ten or fifteen other guests. Representative Gohmert was there with his wife, Kathy, and his chief of staff, Connie Hair.

As we talked about the state of our union and the coming November midterm elections, Hannity stood and proposed a toast to America.

Then, Newt Gingrich followed suit, proposing a toast to the principles of the Constitution.

I paused for a few moments, then decided to stand and recite my favorite passage from Abraham Lincoln's December 1, 1862, message to Congress: "The dogmas of the quiet past, are inadequate to the stormy present. The occasion is piled high with difficulty, and we must rise—with the occasion. As our case is new, so we must think anew, and act anew. We must disenthrall ourselves, and then we shall save our country."

A week or two later, a photograph from the evening was posted on the TMZ website.[1] By the time I reported for duty that day, it had captured the attention of my colleagues.

"Haney, was that really you in the TMZ picture?"

"That's not *really* you, is it?"

"It was Photoshopped, right?"

Meanwhile, since our first in-person meeting on November 13, 2013, OIG Special Agent Michaels and I had been talking on the phone and exchanging text messages. He had asked me on December 9 for additional information, so I knew he was working the case. He also called a couple of times near the end of December to ask who else I might want him to interview.

On January 29, 2014, the snow in Atlanta had cleared up and the airport was open again. While I was waiting at Reagan National for my flight back home, I decided to text Michaels: "Are you free sometime tomorrow?" I wanted to see whether it would be possible to brief the incoming inspector general, whenever he was finally appointed and confirmed.

He responded, "I'm tied up today; but, no . . . you do not need to try to brief the incoming IG."

The exchange troubled me. Why wouldn't the incoming IG want to be briefed on my case? After all, I thought this investigation was requested by both the House and the Senate, and that it was going to go "to the highest levels of the government."

At that moment, it started to dawn on me that the IG investigation was becoming yet another long ordeal—a whole new complicated process with a whole set of new rules and a whole new cast of characters.

ENTERING DIALOGUE

At this point in the story, it's helpful to recall major events in the rest of the world that had a direct bearing on my motivation to remain engaged in this long battle with DHS and the administration.

On February 13, 2014, deputy spokesperson for the US State Department Marie Harf declared at a press conference that the United States "does not rank the Muslim Brotherhood as a terrorist group."

"This is in the context of the U.S.'s attempts to enter dialogue with all parties of the political process in Egypt," she said.[2]

There was that word again, "dialogue."

Later in the year, the administration would go even further in its support of the Muslim Brotherhood. On December 1, 2014, the White House rejected a "We the People" petition to declare the Muslim Brotherhood organization a terrorist group. The petition garnered more than two hundred thousand signatures, far beyond the one-hundred-thousand-signature threshold needed for a response. The White House stated:

> We have not seen credible evidence that the Muslim Brotherhood has renounced its decades-long commitment to non-violence.
>
> The United States does not condone political violence of any kind and we continue to press actors of all viewpoints to peacefully engage in the political process. The United States is committed to thwarting terrorist groups that pose a threat to U.S. interests and those of our partners.[3]

In the middle of the official White House statement was another of the administration's favorite buzzwords: "engage."

Joined together, "engagement and dialogue" form the basis of America's current counterterrorism foreign policy. In fact, "engagement and dialogue" is synonymous with the administration's domestic counterterrorism policy, Countering Violent Extremism.

On a side note, apparently, "pressing actors of all viewpoints" included the administration's decision to cut off foreign aid to the Egyptian military government to encourage the military to reconcile with the Muslim Brotherhood and perhaps be more inclusive towards them in the new government.[4]

TEACHING TRICKS OF THE TRADE

In early 2014, I was told I would be allowed to go on a six-month TDY assignment to the Federal Law Enforcement Training Center (FLETC), in Glynco, Georgia.

I had put in for it a couple of months earlier but really didn't expect to be approved. I was doubtful partly because the February 5, 2013, Letter of Council from the Islamic Institute of Education investigation was probably still in my personnel file. Technically, federal personnel aren't supposed to be promoted, change jobs, or go on any TDY assignments if they are involved in any kind of active investigation. Also, the IG investigation was still going on. Even though it was supposed to be on my behalf and not against me, it was nonetheless an active investigation.

Another reason why I had doubts that I would be approved was that candidates for consideration as FLETC instructors must be among the best of the best in CBP. Since FLETC instructors are the first contact that most new recruits have with the agency, we are vetted not only by our home port to make sure we met the selection criteria, but also by FLETC personnel who are in charge of the training program.

A thumbs-down by either team, and you don't make the cut.

As adversarial as my relationship with the CBP chain of command had been for the last few years, I didn't think they would approve my request.

But to FLETC I was going, and on February 18, 2014, I reported for duty along with about twenty other CBP officers from around the country. As we went through the two-week Instructor Certification course, many of us became friends.

FLETC turned out to be among the most enjoyable assignments of my entire CBP career. I loved interacting with the new students, teaching them the little tricks of the trade and sharing war stories. Many of the new recruits were military veterans, and they had some harrowing war stories themselves.

FLETC instructors are not allowed to socialize with the students, especially outside of class, but often, during breaks, I would just sit quietly in the back and listen to them talk, and, boy, did I get an earful.

On February 25, 2014, during a break between classes, I called Michaels.

He answered and told me that the investigation had been completed, but he couldn't release it to me, because it still had to be submitted for final review, and parts of it might change.

That sounded odd. "It might change?" I asked.

Who would change it?

At that time, we were still in the interim between when Edwards resigned in late 2013, and when John Roth, former director of the Office of Criminal Investigations at the Food and Drug Administration, took over on March 10, 2014.

VOICE FOR MUSLIMS

Coincidentally, on the same day, a press release announced that on March 12, eight major national American Muslim organizations would hold a news conference at the National Press Club in Washington, DC, to announce the formation of the US Council of Muslim Organizations (USCMO), an umbrella group that would "serve as a representative voice for Muslims as that faith community seeks to enhance its positive impact on society."[5]

The eight organizations were Mosque Cares (of Imam W. Deen

Mohammed), Muslim American Society, American Muslims for Palestine, Council on American-Islamic Relations, Islamic Circle of North America, Muslim Legal Fund of America, Muslim Alliance in North America, and the Muslim Ummah of North America.

It was most of the same cast of characters that I had been researching as far back as 2006, only this time they were forming a new coalition.

In a statement prior to the planned launch, the new coalition's secretary general, Oussama Jammal, declared that a "national council unifying Muslims in the United States has long been a dream of our community. The goal of the US Council of Muslim Organizations," he continued, "is to help strengthen relationships among the member organizations in order to better serve members of the Muslim community and all Americans. A detailed census will allow the larger Muslim community to better participate in our nation's political process."[6]

I recognized Jammal's name immediately. For years, he had been a close affiliate and business partner of Kifah Mustapha, another Holy Land Foundation unindicted coconspirator.

Together, they lead the Mosque Foundation,[7] better known as the Bridgeview Mosque, in Chicago, which has ties to numerous other Muslim Brotherhood–linked individuals and organizations involved in the Holy Land Foundation trial. The entire Bridgeview Mosque network was also included in my 2006 Hamas report.

Just four days later, on March 14, 2014, the State Department's Marie Harf met with foreign journalists and confirmed, once again, that the United States was in direct communication with the Muslim Brotherhood in Egypt, while denying that this outreach represented support for the organization:

QUESTION: So do you think that these contacts have any effect on the United States relations with Egypt? And are these just mere contacts or support? Because this is very important for the Egyptian public opinion. Thanks.

MS. HARF: Well, they're contacts, and let's just—I'll put it in a little context here. We think it's important to have contacts with all the parties in Egypt, because all the parties in Egypt ultimately are going to need to be a part of Egypt's future, and that we want to help them be a part of that future and move Egypt out of the situation it's in today. So we think this is important to do. Do we always agree, do they always agree with what we're saying? Of course not. But we believe it's important to have the dialogue.[8]

It was a revealing moment like this when I saw why I was constantly in so much trouble with the administration.

If the administration was openly and covertly supporting the Muslim Brotherhood both here and overseas, then they certainly didn't need a CBP officer in Atlanta entering derogatory information into TECS about the very same individuals and organizations they were supporting.

Meanwhile, on March 26, 2014, the House Homeland Security Committee released a report on the Boston Marathon bombings that identified four areas for continued improvement, along with recommendations. The committee hoped to:

- Expand cooperation between federal and local law enforcement;

- Refine the policy surrounding the use of travel records and the screening of international travelers;

- Increase information sharing with regard to various terror/travel watch lists at the federal level; and

- Develop more sophisticated efforts to mitigate terrorist threats.[9]

All good goals, to be sure, but they were virtually identical to the recommendations made after the Umar Farouk Abdulmutallab "underwear bombing" attempt on Christmas Day 2013, and to some of the conclusions in *The 9/11 Commission Report*.[10]

THE MUSLIM BROTHERHOOD AND BENGHAZI

Another major event that ties directly into my reasons for becoming a whistle-blower is the Benghazi attack of September 11, 2012.

On April 22, 2014, the Citizens' Commission on Benghazi, which includes retired military and CIA officers, released an interim report, *How America Switched Sides in the War on Terror,* pointing out that the rebel forces were dominated by the Libyan Muslim Brotherhood and al-Qaeda.

The following day, in London, Secretary of State Hillary Clinton announced US government support for the Brotherhood-led Libyan Transitional National Council in its revolt against Libyan dictator Moammar Gadhafi.

The report said the White House and senior congressional members "deliberately and knowingly pursued a policy that provided material support to terrorist organizations in order to topple a ruler who had been working closely with the West actively to suppress al-Qa'eda. The result in Libya, across much of North Africa, and beyond has been utter chaos, disruption of Libya's oil industry, the spread of dangerous weapons (including surface-to-air missiles), and the empowerment of jihadist organizations like al-Qa'eda and the Muslim Brotherhood."[11]

It further tied the Muslim Brotherhood to the Benghazi attack, which resulted in the death of US ambassador Christopher Stevens and three other Americans:

> During their visit to Tripoli, the UAE officials discovered that half of the $1 billion worth of weapons it had financed for the rebels had, in fact, been diverted by Mustafa Abdul Jalil, the Muslim Brotherhood head of the Libyan TNC, and sold to Qaddafi. . . .
>
> The key significance of this episode is the demonstration of a military chain-of-command relationship between the Libyan Muslim Brotherhood leadership of the TNC and the al-Qa'eda-affiliated militia (Ansar al-Shariah) that has been named responsible for the attack on the U.S. mission in Benghazi.[12]

Also in April 2014, declassified documents obtained by the Clarion Project provided evidence that the Office of the Director of National Intelligence (ODNI) misled members of Congress in 2012 about its involvement with Muslim Brotherhood–linked entities: "On July 11, 2012, ODNI told Rep. Michele Bachmann that it had not engaged in outreach to Muslim Brotherhood entities such as the Islamic Society of North America." But the files show that "Director James Clapper met an ISNA leader just one month earlier."[13]

Further, the documents show that messages within the Office of the Director of National Intelligence expressed concerns about ISNA's and other groups' Brotherhood links.

The Clarion Project noted that on June 12, 2012, a ninety-minute "Roundtable Discussion" took place at National Intelligence's head-quarters in McLean, Virginia, in which Clapper met with an ISNA representative. Also present were National Counterterrorism Center director Matthew Olson and Alexander Joel, ODNI civil liberties protection officer.

Just keeping track of all these astonishing developments could have been a full-time job in itself, but I was still on TDY as an instructor at FLETC, still under investigation by CBP Internal Affairs about the Boston Marathon bombing, and still waiting for a final response to the IG investigation.

JUSTICE DEPARTMENT CALLING

Then, from out of the blue, I received an e-mail from Special Agent Shaw (not her real name), a CBP Internal Affairs investigator, on April 22, 2014, saying, "The Office of Internal Affairs is requesting to inter-view you."

She wrote:

The interview is voluntary and relates to the Boston bombing.

Are you available Thursday, April 24, 2014 at 2:30 pm to meet with me?

Please feel free to call me for additional information.

I called Shaw and told her I wasn't saying yes or no, but I had never heard of a "voluntary interview." I added that I would need to have more information before I answered her request.

"Fine," she said. "Just let me know when you decide what you'll do."

Immediately I called my lawyer, Joe Schmitz, and, on his advice, I deferred agreeing to the voluntary interview and chose instead to wait until Shaw contacted me again.

More than a year later, I learned that a voluntary interview can be conducted only in cases involving criminal charges and that a lawyer may be present. On the other hand, interviews involving administrative charges are never voluntary—you must appear when summoned—neither can a lawyer be present.

In other words, the proposed voluntary interview on April 24, 2014, would have included a discussion about pending criminal charges. Had I simply agreed to the request, I may have walked right into a legal trap.

In the meantime, I decided to reach out to Nick Palarino, House Homeland Security chairman Michael McCaul's chief counsel.

On April 24, 2014, I sent him a memo expressing concerns based on the Senate report on alleged misconduct by former acting inspector general Charles Edwards.[14] By this time I already knew, according to Inspector Michaels, that the investigation was finished, but no one from the IG's office had contacted me.

I wrote to Palarino:

After reading the entire Senate report on the IG, I am very concerned that the report on my investigation, which has been under review for at least two months, will be edited and/or altered in favor of DHS.

Moreover, we still have no idea what the original report on my case said.

There are several points in the new Senate report that established precedent for my case, should it be edited.

I've done all I was asked to do, putting my career and welfare in jeopardy, while I continue waiting for the case to be resolved.

Finally, I have been contacted by CBP Internal Affairs . . . once again . . . re the Boston [Bombing] case, for a "voluntary" interview.

I'm standing by for help from the Homeland Security Committee, to finally resolve this case, which is 8-years old and counting.

I never received a response from Palarino.

Things were quiet for about three more weeks, until 10:42 a.m. on May 15, 2014, when I received another call on my cell phone from Special Agent Shaw, who asked me if I had a lawyer, and if so, to give her contact information.

Six days later, on May 21, 2014, the hammer hit the anvil.

This time, it was my lawyer, Joe Schmitz, who received a phone call, but it wasn't from Shaw.

The call came from Richard Evans, a lawyer within the Department of Justice's Office of Public Integrity.

Evans said that I was the subject of an ongoing Department of Justice investigation regarding the Boston bombing. No formal indictment had been issued, he said, but under consideration was the offer of a "Pre-Indictment Proffer Letter," a legal procedure that allows a defendant to plea bargain or avoid charges by cooperating with the investigation.

The case, he said, was based on alleged violation of 18 USC 1030(a) (3), misuse of a government computer. Charges of violation of privacy also could be included.

As I learned later, proffer agreements proposed by DOJ prosecutors often provide the witness or defendant with very little protection.

Schmitz also told me that the DOJ lawyer said he didn't know I was a whistle-blower or that I had already been investigated by CBP regarding the Boston bombing on July 31, 2013. He told me he reminded Evans about the Whistleblower Protection Act, which describes "whistleblowing" as "making a disclosure evidencing illegal or improper government activities." It says further that the "protections of the WPA apply to most federal executive branch employees and become applicable where a 'personnel action' is taken 'because of' a 'protected disclosure' made by a 'covered employee.'"[15]

As soon as the initial shock wore off, I asked, "Who gave the DOJ my name?"

As we'll see in the next chapter, it took more than a year, but I eventually found out the answer to that question.

Two days later, on May 23, 2014, there finally was some movement in the inspector general investigation. Staff members from the offices of Sens. Tom Coburn and Charles Grassley, and House members Michael McCaul and Louis Gohmert, were briefed on the results of the investigation by IG personnel from 9 a.m. to 11:20 a.m. in the Ford Building.

It's a good thing I wasn't expecting too much, because I wasn't disappointed.

My contacts in the meeting told me that I still wouldn't be allowed to have a copy, and as with the "hands off" case, the meeting generated more questions than answers.

Judicial Watch stepped in later that summer and filed a FOIA request on my behalf.

Through the summer of 2014, the "hands off" case generated about twenty-five stories in the media, including a May 21, 2014, Breitbart News article citing McCaul's disclosure that the case had been under investigation by the new DHS inspector general, John Roth, for about three months.

McCaul said Roth is "pretty decent" and "well respected," unlike his predecessor.

The article also cited Sen. Charles Grassley telling Brian Kilmeade on Fox News Radio on May 5 that not every whistle-blower that comes to his office may have a legitimate case, but the individual who presented the evidence to Grassley had provided enough information to investigate the issue further.[16]

Thank you, Senator Grassley.

Meanwhile, back in my office at FLETC, when I read McCaul's criticism of Edwards, I couldn't help but wonder why he decided to send me over to the Office of the Inspector General in the first place, rather than just bringing me up to Washington as a CBP attaché, as we had agreed in our March 2014 meeting.

In the same Breitbart article, Rep. Louie Gohmert, who read Grassley's letter to DHS Secretary Johnson on the House floor two weeks earlier, said he was "thrilled" the Iowa Republican was looking to "get to the bottom of this."

"For an internal e-mail to indicate that Secretary Napolitano had a hands off list that included people with terrorist ties should be an affront to anyone who cares about security in this country and explains a lot why things like Boston could happen even after we're supposed to know what we're doing," Gohmert said.[17]

WHISTLE-BLOWER PROTECTION

Remarkably, DHS Secretary Johnson sent out an internal memo on May 20, 2014, encouraging whistle-blowers to cooperate with John Roth, our newly confirmed inspector general:

> As you may know, John Roth recently took office as the Department of Homeland Security's (DHS) new Inspector General. I welcome him to the Department and look forward to his leadership and insight. I believe that the Inspector General serves an important role in helping the Department prevent and detect fraud, waste, mismanagement, and abuse.
>
> . . . This memorandum is a reminder that I expect all DHS employees to cooperate fully with the Inspector General and his staff in its work and should provide prompt access to requested materials and information.[18]

On June 17, 2014, Roth distributed an official follow-up memo on DHS stationery, expressing how concerned he and DHS were about protecting whistle-blowers:

> One of the ways we do this is through investigations, audits, and inspections. Some of our best work has been the result of conscientious and dedicated DHS public servants who have provided us information that has resulted in saving DHS millions of dollars, or stopped ethically

questionable activity. We very much appreciate your assistance.

You can remain anonymous, although we are able to more fully investigate your claim if you identify yourself. The *Inspector General Act* and the *Whistleblower Protection Act* give the Inspector General powerful legal tools both to protect your identity and to ensure that you are not retaliated against for reporting allegations. I take my obligation to protect whistleblowers very seriously. We have had hundreds of individuals report matters to us, and we have an outstanding track record in ensuring that your identity is protected.

Part of our program involves the Office of Inspector General Whistleblower Protection Ombudsman. The Ombudsman ensures Department employees and contract personnel are aware of the role and importance of whistleblowers in improving the effectiveness and efficiency of the Department's operations and educates them on their legal rights and protections against retaliation. We also alert Department officials and managers to the possible repercussions of retaliation against those who make protected disclosures.

Wow, two encouraging memos within a month, one from Secretary Johnson and one from Inspector General Roth!

It all sounded good, so I decided to take them up their offer and call the IG's office in Washington to ask about the status of my case.

After introducing myself to the phone receptionist and explaining the purpose of my call, she told me they were not authorized to give me a copy of the investigation.

Instead, I would have to submit a Freedom of Information Act request for it.

"I'm an active-duty CPB officer. I just got the memo from John Roth, our new IG, assuring us of his desire to cooperate with whistleblowers," I said. "And now you're telling me you have no provision to provide me with a copy of the report?"

She replied, "Yes, I understand, but that is the procedure."

I said: "Do you realize how surreal that sounds? May I talk with your supervisor, please?"

In a few moments, the supervisor came on the line, and ultimately she also informed me that to see the report, I would have to file a FOIA request.

So, that's just what we did.

Judicial Watch filed a FOIA request on my behalf in midsummer of 2014, and more than a year later, on July 15, 2015, we received the first cache of documents related to the case. Another cache arrived in September 2015, and two more came in November 2015.

Valuable information was buried within these FOIA documents. As we'll discuss in the final chapter, some of the memos and e-mails would have a direct bearing on events surrounding the December 2, 2015, attack in San Bernardino.

HITTING THE WALL

My TDY assignment at FLETC came to an end August 8, 2014, so I prepared to return to Atlanta.

While I was away, my wife, Francesca, had become very sick, so after I returned home, I took emergency family leave for a couple of weeks to take care of her.

Then, after being away for almost seven months, I returned to work at the port. In two or three days, I was settled back into the daily routine, and things seemed pretty normal until Sunday, September 21, 2014.

That day, as I walked into the Federal Inspection Station, one of the supervisors on the floor caught my attention and said, "Haney, you need to go straight back to the chief's office."

This can't be good, I thought.

It was right at the shift change, so I had to wait for a few minutes in the chief's office until they called for me.

I got a few looks, but no one said anything, until someone called and told me, "Haney, report to the conference room by Yellow Secondary."

When I walked into the conference room, two management personnel and a union representative were already there waiting for me. We didn't sit down or exchange pleasantries. Instead, one of the two management personnel said, "Haney, we need your gun, now."

"Okay, do you want me to drop the magazine first, and how do you want me to hand it to you?"

I dropped the magazine and handed the gun to him, pointed sideways between us. He also asked for the other two magazines in my belt.

Next, they told me my access to all the systems had been suspended and that I would be put on a "modified duty" schedule and reassigned to a supervisor in the Cargo Office, which is in an offsite building, about a mile from the airport.

They added that I was under investigation, but said that was all they really knew about it.

I was asked to sign a few forms that said my authority to carry a government-issued firearm was temporarily rescinded, due to a pending investigation, and that I would be notified upon completion of the case. The forms also advised me that any failure to follow the reporting instructions could result in possible disciplinary actions.

After we finished, they offered to let me take annual leave for the rest of the day, which I did.

As I left the airport to drive home, I notified my law firm and called my contacts in Congress.

What is this investigation about? I wondered.

I already knew I was under investigation by CBP Internal Affairs for allegedly leaking information about the Boston Marathon bombing. I also knew that the DOJ was investigating me for the same thing, except their case included possible criminal charges.

What I didn't know—and still don't know to this day—was whether the actions that had just been taken, which included taking away my service weapon, were related to either case, or both, or yet a third investigation.

A NEW APPROACH

When I got home, my wife was gone, so I waited there alone until she returned. Later, she told me that as soon as she pulled into the driveway and saw my pickup truck, she knew something was wrong.

We sat down in the living room, and I told her what had just happened at work.

On the outside, she seemed to take the news well, but on the inside, it was a different story.

Earlier, I mentioned that my wife had been very sick while I was on TDY at FLETC. What I didn't mention before is that she is also handicapped.

After a few minutes, the impact of what I told her became too much for her delicate system to absorb. She went into trauma-induced shock, and before the evening was over, we were in the emergency room at Emory University Hospital in Atlanta.

She was admitted and stayed in the hospital for three days. While I sat with her, we talked about what to do next, and we decided together that I would apply for Emergency Family Leave and start using up the 550 hours of sick leave that I had saved up over the years.

We also decided that I would put in the paperwork to retire as soon as possible, which would be on my sixty-second birthday in July 2015.

At that moment, I took a new tactical approach. From here on, my focus would be to help her get better and to survive until I could retire.

The only question at this point would be, "Will I get shot out of the sky, or have to bail out; will I crash-land, or will I actually make it all the way home, and come in for a soft landing?"

After she was released from Emory, we packed up a few things and left Atlanta for several weeks.

While we were away, I stopped in Washington and met with Representative Gohmert and his chief of staff, Connie Hair, on September 30, 2014.

We met as friends. Gohmert encouraged my wife and me not to give up, and to see it all through, at least until I was able to retire.

During that week, I met with my lawyer with the Brownell Firm, at the firm's Washington, DC, office. Brownell had been my legal counsel for more than a year already, but this was the first time any of us had met face-to-face.

The meeting was cordial but very complicated. By this time, in late 2014, there were so many moving parts to my case that I wouldn't blame anyone for being overwhelmed by its complexity.

First, there was no communication from my own agency. My status as a whistle-blower depended on who you talked to. Congress said I was a whistle-blower, but my own agency ignored the question, and my law firm insisted it wasn't in their purview.

Second, the DHS inspector general who had originally taken my case had resigned in disgrace, while the IG's office told me I had to FOIA my own investigation. Moreover, the OIG investigator had told me I "didn't need to brief the new IG."

Third, along with the IG report, Congress was trying to get to the bottom of several of my other allegations, but they ran into a wall everywhere they turned.

This was the most difficult part of the whole ten-year ordeal.

My status was unclear—was I a whistle-blower or a criminal? No one was talking, and my career—and life, for that matter—hung in the balance.

A month later, the Brownell Firm assigned a criminal defense lawyer and former federal prosecutor to my case, and on November 20, 2014, we had our first hour-long conversation on the phone.

During our conversation, my lawyer said, according to my contemporaneous notes:

> Don't give anything to anyone anymore. The people in Congress are not your friends; they will take what you give them, but won't do anything to help you—they won't be there when you need them.
>
> If you chose to disregard my advice, I will have to reconsider whether or not I will represent you.
>
> I don't know whether or not you're really a whistleblower.

On December 9, 2014, my lawyer informed me by e-mail that he had received a call from Bill Pittard, an attorney at the House of Representatives, General Counsel's Office, to let him know that

Department of Justice investigators Charles Walsh and Ray Hulser wanted to interview Connie Hair. They knew I had provided information to her and others on the Hill and that Congress believed me to be a whistle-blower. The prosecutors also confirmed that they were investigating allegations that I had misused a government computer, using it to provide information to the media.

Pittard said he did not think Hair would agree to an interview and that if DOJ served her or anyone else on the Hill a subpoena, they would resist under the Speech and Debate Clause.

Nevertheless, the DOJ served subpoenas to the staff of members of Congress.

This complicated things even further, because now that the DOJ had inserted itself into the case, I could no longer talk to anyone on the Hill who might be somehow involved in the investigation.

Otherwise, it could be seen as collusion or obstruction of justice.

Now, I was even more alone.

Meanwhile, things didn't go well with my criminal defense attorney either.

On December 18, 2014, he told me in an e-mail that he had resigned:

> I am writing to confirm our previous conversation [on December 16, 2014].
>
> Due to irreconcilable differences, I cannot continue to represent you.
>
> I also told you that you are a target of a Federal criminal investigation. I advise you to seek new counsel and to cooperate fully with this attorney.
>
> I wish you the best of luck going forward.

Fired by my own attorney.

Before it was finally over, Brownell also withdrew as my counsel, and the federal employee insurance company that provided my liability insurance also terminated any further coverage of the case.

Much of the conflict between my legal team and me had to do with the murkiness of whistle-blower status.

On January 13, 2015, the Brownell Firm tried to explain it to me as follows:

> Please note that we have not (and do not) comment on the legal sufficiency of your prior whistleblower disclosures.
>
> This is an exceedingly complex and factually-intensive area of law that is most effectively addressed in response to allegations of wrongdoing that, to date, have not been formally charged.
>
> While we understand that you are a self-designated whistleblower, we do not speculate at this time as to whether your assertions are correct, or entitle you to any protections under the law.

I must have read over those words at least twenty times, but to this day, I still don't know what they mean.

I guess that must be what amounts to "irreconcilable differences."

This whole complex story goes back to April 18, 2013, when DHS Secretary Napolitano insisted during public testimony before Congress that the Saudi national, Alharbi, was never in custody and never a subject of interest in the Boston bombing case. If all this was really true, then why were CBP Internal Affairs and the DOJ both investigating me?

Perhaps we'll know the real answer one day, but in the meantime, this is what killing the messenger with invisible shrapnel looks like.

12

UPHOLDING MY OATH

During the last two months of 2014, and into the first couple of months of 2015, I was on Emergency Family Leave about half of the time.

In some ways, it was the most normal time in my CBP career: I worked from 7:30 to 3:30, avoided the Atlanta traffic, for the most part, and had weekends off.

But night and day the specter of uncertainty loomed.

Would I get an e-mail from CBP Internal Affairs for another "voluntary interview," a subpoena from the DOJ to appear for another deposition, or maybe a call from the FBI, or even a knock at the front door?

And, I still wasn't able to talk to my contacts in Congress, because the Department of Justice case was still in progress.

It was assumed that my calls and e-mails were being monitored—they were—and my friends and colleagues were hesitant to talk to me. They believed me and felt I was doing the right thing, but with most people there was an element of uncertainty in every conversation.

There were notable exceptions, however.

Several of my active-duty colleagues never wavered in their support, including my former FLETC instructor Anthony (Tony) Rahaim, who was a constant source of encouragement and good advice.

In particular, I'm thankful to Ronnie Matheson, my first-line supervisor in the Cargo Office, who made the last nine months of my "modified duty" much more pleasant than it might have been.

There were also several others from my time as a TDY instructor at FLETC and from the Port of Atlanta who consistently offered support and encouragement.

GRAND JURY

In early February 2015, I came up to Washington to discuss some post-retirement business opportunities and stayed in the home of my friend and fellow counterterrorism specialist Stephen Coughlin.

That evening, Stephen and I rendezvoused at a local restaurant with Patrick Poole, an investigative reporter on terrorism and national security.

After we ordered and got settled in, they said they had some news for me. "The DOJ has convened a grand jury and is seeking to indict you on criminal charges," they told me.

In law enforcement, we call this a "comma, pause for effect" moment.

Both said they didn't know much more than that, but I had a fairly good idea that those charges would be the ones that the DOJ lawyer had cited to Joe Schmitz on May 21, 2014: 18 US Code §1030(a)(3), which is "fraud and related activity in connection with computers."

More specifically, the code threatens punishment to:

> Whoever . . . intentionally, without authorization to access any nonpublic computer of a department or agency of the United States, accesses such a computer of that department or agency that is exclusively for the use of the Government of the United States or, in the case of a computer not exclusively for such use, is used by or for the Government of the United States and such conduct affects that use by or for the Government of the United States . . .[1]

To anyone who reads this and says, "What the heck is that supposed to mean?" I agree completely. It has to be one of the most subjective and vague statutes ever written, a "catchall clause."

The key point of statute 1030(a)(3) is the phrase "without

authorization," which means that it never applied to my situation in the first place. I certainly was authorized to access a government computer. I had been doing it in my service with the Passenger Analysis Unit, the Investigative Review Unit, the Advanced Targeting Unit, the National Targeting Center, FLETC, and on the primary and secondary lines for more than ten years.

As a well-known subject matter expert within CBP, I had also received multiple cash awards, commendation letters, FBI and JTTF recognition, and numerous offers from my colleagues in sister agencies to help them with terrorism-related cases.

Yet, this would be the charge they would hang their whole investigation on, along with a possible Privacy Rights Violation, which I wouldn't find out about until a few months later.

So, I caught my breath, again, and kept moving forward.

Then came another period of quiet, which lasted for a little more than two months, until Memorial Day, May 25, 2015.

ATTENDANCE REQUIRED
That morning, I reported for duty at the Cargo Office and found the following e-mail waiting in my in-box:

> CBP Office of Internal Affairs is requiring your attendance for a subject interview on Wednesday, May 27, 2015 at 9:00 am.
>
> It is possible the interview may require two days.
>
> If so, we will resume our interview on Thursday, May 28, 2015 at 9:00 am as well.
>
> You will be interviewed in an administrative investigation and you are entitled to union representation.
>
> Please understand that this is a compelled interview and you are not to disclose it to anyone unless they have an official need to know.
>
> On Wednesday, please report to the office of APD [author's redaction].
>
> Please feel free to contact me or SA Murphy [pseudonym] with any questions.

I contacted my union representative, Steve Francis (not his real name), right away. He came over to the Cargo Office an hour or two later, and we talked it over.

We agreed that I would write a memo summarizing the major points of the case, along with a list of our unanswered questions and concerns.

The plan was to present the memo to Special Agents Shaw and Murphy, and to hopefully have a few of the questions answered before we started the "compelled interview."

Here are the four questions that were included in the memo:

1. Is the purpose of the interview this morning related to the ongoing CBP investigation [which began July 31, 2013]?

2. Is that CBP Internal Affairs investigation related to the DOJ case?

3. This interview is defined as "Administrative," while the DOJ case is defined as "Criminal." In light of this, do I have any specific legal rights (i.e., Fifth Amendment rights) that need to be considered before we proceed with today's interview?

4. What role does Part 792 of the Whistleblower Protection Act play in the proceedings this morning?

The morning of May 27, 2015, arrived, and Officer Francis and I reported to the APD's office.

After exchanging a few pleasantries and settling into our places, Officer Francis announced that he would like to read the questions in our memo into the record. Both of the special agents agreed, so Officer Francis went ahead and began reading.

But before he even got halfway through the second question—which was whether or not the CBP Internal Affairs case was linked to the DOJ case—Agent Shaw interrupted.

"Let's just cut to the chase," she said. "I'm the one who turned your name in to DOJ. Yes, the two cases are related, but the DOJ case has been dropped."

It was another "comma, pause for effect" moment.

However, we had to continue with the compelled interview, so neither Francis nor I had time to fully absorb what Shaw had just said. So we carried on.

That first day was tough. The questions were coming fast, one after the other, for eight hours straight, except for a quick, late pause for lunch.

By the end of the day, my head was spinning. I felt like a boxer who was backed into the corner, just trying to keep my hands up and keep from getting hit.

By now, it had become obvious that the point of the interview was to get me admit—once and for all—that I was the one who leaked the information on Alharbi to Glenn Beck and/or to Fox News.

But no matter how many different ways they kept asking me the same question, it couldn't change the simple fact that I was not the one who leaked it.

"DO THIS"

That night, I was restless, tossing and turning in bed.

Then, just as I was about to finally fall asleep, I suddenly knew exactly what I needed to do; that is, how to go from being on the defensive and backed into a corner to getting back into the fight.

In my heart, my mind, I heard, *Do this, and you will disarm them.*

First, come to terms quickly with your accusers; otherwise, you will never get out until you pay every last cent of your sentence.

Second, tell them exactly what happened, from start to finish, and the truth of what you tell them will set you free.

When you go in tomorrow morning, offer them an agreement and have them put it in the record.

Tell them you would like to expedite the whole process—not circumvent it, but expedite it—by recounting exactly how you became involved in this case.

If you do that, you will disarm the situation.

So, that is exactly what I did.

Before we went in the next morning, I met with Officer Francis and told him I was going to make them an offer, on the record, to tell them everything that happened in the Boston case from start to finish, and how I got pulled into the middle of it all.

He said, a little hesitantly, "Well, okay."

And with that, in we went.

I told them immediately that I would like to make them an offer, first without the recorder, to see if they would agree. Then, if they agreed, I would repeat the exact same offer, only this time it would become part of the record.

I also added that it would be a win-win for them. For one, if they already had a working premise of what really happened, then what I was about to tell them would just confirm their premise. For another, maybe some of what I was about to tell them would be new information.

Either way, it would help them resolve the case.

After a slight pause, they agreed to my offer.

They turned on the tape recorder, and I stood up and gave them a moment-by-moment account of how I accessed the information in the system just a few hours after the bombings, then watched the hearings three days later as Secretary Napolitano give her infamous "three nos" to vice-chairman Duncan.

I continued on, from the moment I got the call that congressional liason Orzel was about to be fired from the House Homeland Security Committee to when I sent the information to a secure fax in the committee office, to the moment a week later, when I saw Glenn Beck showing some of the same information on TV.

As I sat down, Agent Shaw excused herself and went into the restroom adjacent to our meeting room. When she came back a few moments later, she was dabbing her eyes with a tissue.

After she sat down again, she paused for a few more moments, then looked at me. "Mr. Haney," she said, "you have really touched my heart, deeply, and my estimation of you has gone up immeasurably."

We took a short break, then came back and resumed the interview.

In those few moments, something had changed. Before, the atmosphere had been overtly adversarial, but now it was more cordial, almost like four cops working on a case together, which, technically, it was.

I said *almost*, because I was still the one in the middle of the case.

The best way to put it was that the situation had been disarmed.

Yes, the questioning was tough, and we still weren't finished by the end of the second day, but the mood was entirely different than it was the day before.

The third day, May 29, 2015, started off with some drama, and it was all my fault.

At some point early that morning, I was struck by some of the questions the special agents had been asking about people I had spoken with on the phone or corresponded with via e-mail.

All of a sudden, I realized that many of these phone calls and e-mails were from months, if not years, before the Boston Marathon attack.

"Why are they asking me about phone calls and e-mails from way before the bombing?" I asked myself out loud.

I called Officer Francis and said I thought I had found a fatal flaw in the entire procedure. We talked it over just a few minutes before the meeting was to start; then he went in and notified the special agents about my concerns and asked for a brief delay.

After that, we met with the union president to discuss my premise, but in the end, he just said, "The investigators can do anything they want to do."

I didn't have a lawyer to consult with, but since lawyers are not allowed to participate in administrative interviews, it wasn't an issue.

Meanwhile, the special agents were waiting for us, and after about an hour's delay, we got started again.

Finally, by mid-afternoon, all the questions had been asked, and Officer Francis and I were allowed to review a printout of the affidavit. After we had made a few minor changes and signed the approved final draft, we were suddenly finished.

I stood and shook hands one last time with Special Agents Shaw and Murphy, looked them both straight in their eyes, and said goodbye.

By the way, near the end of the third day, I found out that one of the possible criminal charges or administrative actions in the CBP and DOJ investigations was based on an alleged violation of the Saudi national Alharbi's privacy rights, which includes "a person's rights to be free from intrusion into aspects of their life, such as their living space, belongings, and physical body, including a person's right to be free from unreasonable searches by the police or government agents."[2]

Once again, Alharbi remains a foreign national, not an American citizen.

GREAT CALM

It wasn't until the moment it was finally over and we were walking out of the meeting for the last time that I began to realize more fully what had actually happened in the last three days.

One of the first things I realized is that the government is fully capable of moving at high speed if it wishes. Less than two months after the bombing, I was already under investigation.

At least the first month of that time would have been spent initiating the case, securing the contractors, developing the questions for the first affidavit, and arranging the first appointment to interview me in Atlanta.

I also realized that at some point after July 31, 2013—the first Internal Affairs interview and affidavit in Atlanta—CBP became so convinced they had found probable cause to indict me on criminal charges that they sent the case over to the DOJ.

I first heard about the DOJ's involvement in the case on May 21, 2014. During the following year, the DOJ convened a grand jury, subpoenaed members of Congress, and brought at least two lawyers into the case.

But in the end, as I finally was told on May 27, 2014, the DOJ had no choice but to drop the case; the grand jury could find no probable cause.

At the same moment, I also realized that since I was only two months from retirement, it was very unlikely the case would wind its way up through the chain of command or that any subsequent adverse action would be taken.

On May 29, 2014, at approximately 3:30 p.m., it was all over, except for the paperwork.

I also realized that since the DOJ had dropped the charges, I could also start calling my contacts in Congress.

HALLELUJAH

It was as if choruses of hallelujah were echoing across Washington and the country when my friends and colleagues started hearing the news.

Everyone breathed a big sigh of joyful relief. Unconsciously, they were also showing me how concerned they had been all along. Now that it was really over, they could express more freely how they felt.

In a nutshell, a lot of my friends had been worried about me, but when DOJ dropped the criminal charges, and the administrative ordeal was finally over—all within those three days in May—they realized that not only was I telling the truth the whole time, but that in this case, at least, the truth had prevailed.

The truth really did set me free.

During the entire ten-year ordeal, I didn't exaggerate, take away or add anything to the facts of the case, but simply told the story exactly as it happened.

Ultimately, it elevated my credibility within the agency, with my non–law enforcement colleagues, and on Capitol Hill.

Meanwhile, even though I finally had some clarity, my life didn't slow down.

Congress still considered me to be a whistle-blower. On June 2, 2015, I came to Washington for about the fortieth time since early 2012 and met with the chief counsels for Sens. Ted Cruz and Charles Grassley, and Rep. Darrell Issa, R-CA.

The main theme of the conversation was possible abuse or violations of due process, specifically regarding accessing my phone records and e-mails well before the date of the Boston bombing. We also discussed whether I should file a complaint with the Office of Special Counsel and whether I might have a basis to reach out to the Council of the Inspectors General on Integrity and Efficiency, which handle matters dealing with the potentially inappropriate conduct of inspectors general and their offices.

At the moment, these questions remain unresolved, but they will hopefully be addressed in the days to come. Whatever does finally happen, it won't be just for my benefit but also for others who may find themselves in a similar situation.

In one last parting shot, on June 8, 2015, the CBP Personnel Security Division, Office of Internal Affairs, administratively suspended my secret clearance.

The form I signed included the following statements:

> Until further advised by this office, Mr. Haney cannot have access to any classified information or systems.
>
> The suspension of the security clearance will remain in effect until further notice from this office.
>
> This suspension extends to any temporary assignment, special project, task force, training course, etc., for which clearance is required and/or certification of the employee's clearance to outside agencies/ facilities, etc.
>
> This suspension does not constitute an adverse action.

At least it wasn't an "adverse action." Otherwise, I might have really been upset!

Four days later, on June 12, 2015, virtually everyone in CBP received an e-mail notification that we had been the victims of a malicious cyber intrusion carried out against the US government, which resulted in the theft of our background investigation records—including the very records they used to get my now-suspended secret clearance.

We also learned that our Social Security numbers, dates of birth, residencies, educational and employment histories, personal foreign travel histories, immediate families, business and personal acquaintances details, and other information used to conduct and adjudicate our background clearances were also obtained in the breach.

Now, thanks to the American taxpayer, we all have the option of free credit and identity monitoring services for an indeterminate time.

What agency was responsible for maintaining the security of our personal information?

The Department of Homeland Security's own Office of Personnel Management.

RETIREMENT

During the entire month of July, I took the opportunity to say good-bye in person to as many of my friends and colleagues at the port as I could.

For those who read this that are still in active duty, thank you for your service, and for your support and friendship during the ten most difficult, but most rewarding, years of my life.

You are part of this remarkable story, which is now becoming part of the history of our agency and of our great country.

On July 31, 2015, I officially retired from Customs and Border Protection. On the same day, I drove up to Washington to start my new postretirement as a consultant in national security and counterterrorism. (Some of those business meetings I mentioned earlier were very productive.)

On August 12, 2015, Judicial Watch released a cache of FOIA documents, including the result of a Defense Intelligence Agency report on the Benghazi attack.

The report was originally submitted in August 2012, just one month before the attack on our diplomatic compound occurred.

Among the damning revelations in the DIA report, we learned that the administration was secretly transporting weapons from Benghazi to Syria in small ships that landed at several minor ports along the coast of Syria. We also learned that these weapons were being supplied to groups in Syria who were fighting Bashar al-Assad, including Salafist groups such as Jabhat al-Nusra, the Muslim Brotherhood, and al-Qaeda of Iraq, which were the major driving force of the opposition.

Finally, we learned that "if the situation unravels there is the possibility of establishing a declared or undeclared Salafist principality in eastern Syria."[3]

In simple terms, the administration was arming Muslim Brotherhood and other Salafi jihadist groups in Syria and encouraging them to hold eastern Syria as a buffer against any further westward expansion by Shia forces from Iraq and Iran.

All this while publicly maintaining that the Benghazi attack was caused by a video and that the Muslim Brotherhood was an "umbrella term for a variety of movements, in the case of Egypt, a very heterogeneous group, largely secular, which has eschewed violence and has decried Al-Qaeda as a perversion of Islam," which has "pursued social ends, a betterment of the political order in Egypt . . . In other countries, there are also chapters or franchises of the Muslim Brotherhood, but there is no overarching agenda, particularly in pursuit of violence, at least internationally."[4]

As I sat at my computer, reading the DIA report, it hit me harder than ever before: as a CBP officer, I targeted the Muslim Brotherhood for nearly ten years, trying to warn DHS management and members of Congress that it was a dangerous movement, while the administration was supporting the Brotherhood at home and arming them in the Middle East.

That, my friends, is why I became a whistle-blower.

My oath would not allow me to stay silent.

Then came the shootings in San Bernardino on December 2, 2015.

Within hours, details of the shooters' identities started coming out. A little later, the names of the mosques that Syed Farook had attended also became public.

As I followed the case, I saw the name Darul Uloom al-Islamiya San Bernardino appear in a local news story.

I sat straight up in my chair and yelled at the computer screen, "That's my case!"

It was the Tablighi Jamaat Initiative and the subsequent case with the sixty-seven records that were deleted in September 2012.

I immediately texted one of my colleagues and told him that Tashfeen Malik was a boy's name and that it probably originated in the southern Arabian Peninsula. As we soon found out, Tashfeen was born in Pakistan but grew up in Saudi Arabia.

The Darul Uloom mosque that Syed Farook attended was part of the same network of mosques and schools on which the IIE case had focused.

Where would we be today if these two cases, and others like them, had been allowed to continue?

The search for an honest response to that question, and the willingness to be a part of the solution, is what has brought me to this moment.

FINAL THOUGHTS

As I consistently maintained throughout my entire career with CBP, terrorist networks are always made up of individuals and their affiliated organizations.

As specialists such as I tracked the activities of these individuals and their affiliated organizations, we added them to our database and then made law enforcement–based decisions derived from the articulable facts we had gathered.

That is following the trail, also known as connecting the dots, and that is successful counterterrorism. It was also the original founding purpose of DHS, and it remains the reason why I take my oath to protect our country so seriously.

As a DHS officer, I solemnly swore, "so help me God," that I would "support and defend the Constitution of the United States against all enemies, foreign and domestic."

I'm retired, but my oath is still on active duty. I remain obligated to go wherever my oath will require. For that reason, and for the sake of my family and friends, I'm in this until the end.

I do have hope. After all, we're Americans; we have faced dark periods and difficulties many times before.

This is still a fixable problem. We have the capability, the desire and the tools to do it, if only we are allowed to.

My call to our political leaders is this: Take the handcuffs off of law enforcement and military, and let us do our job.

Since my retirement, many of my colleagues who are still on active duty have cheered me on, saying, "Thank God, someone is finally standing up for us!"

It is for them—along with my family and friends—that I must continue.

Finally, I must continue so that I might honor the sacrifice of our Founding Fathers and their intent to form a government built on principles that would best ensure the "Safety and Happiness" of the people:

> Whenever any Form of Government becomes destructive of these ends, it is the Right of the People to alter or to abolish it, and to institute new Government, laying its foundation on such principles and organizing its powers in such form, as to them shall seem most likely to effect their Safety and Happiness. Prudence, indeed, will dictate that Governments long established should not be changed for light and transient causes; and accordingly all experience hath shewn, that mankind are more disposed to suffer, while evils are sufferable, than to right themselves by abolishing the forms to which they are accustomed. But when a long train of abuses and usurpations, pursuing invariably the same Object evinces a design to reduce them under absolute Despotism, it is their right, it is their duty, to throw off such Government, and to provide new Guards for their future security.[5]

In venatus veritas
(In relentless pursuit of the truth)

APPENDIX

Department of Homeland Security founding member certificate signed by the first secretary, Tom Ridge.

Be it known that

Philip B Haney

is a Founding Member of the Department of Homeland Security, dedicated to preventing terrorist attacks within the United States, reducing America's vulnerability to terrorism, and minimizing the damage from potential attacks and natural disasters.

Tom Ridge, Secretary

Tom Ridge

Washington, D.C., March 1, 2003

Employment offer to Philip Haney for conversion from agricultural officer to Customs and Border Protection officer.

U.S. Department of Homeland Security
Minneapolis Hiring Center
1 Federal Drive, Room 400
Fort Snelling, MN 55111

U.S. Customs and Border Protection

June 25, 2007

Mr. Philip B. Haney
2100 Branch View Drive
Marietta, GA 30062 1901

Dear Mr. Haney:

Congratulations! We are pleased to inform you of a **conditional offer of employment** for the position of Customs & Border Protection Officer, GS 1895-11, with the U.S. Department of Homeland Security, Customs and Border Protection, in Atlanta, GA. Salary, which will include the applicable locality pay, will be $59,883. Please note that the grade level and location of this **conditional offer** have been determined by the selecting official and are not negotiable.

We are making this **conditional offer** of employment based on a projection of hiring needs, the existence of a vacant funded position, the absence of any hiring restrictions, and any other controlling factors. This **conditional offer** is also contingent upon successful completion of all pre-employment requirements as listed below.

We want to emphasize this is a **conditional offer** of employment and should not be relied upon by you in making any decisions at your current place of employment. We hope that you will successfully complete the pre-employment process and that we will be able to provide you with a firm offer at a later date. The speed with which you move through this process depends in large part upon you. It is very important that you promptly respond to scheduling and information requests.

The pre-employment requirements and other necessary documents you must successfully complete prior to receiving a firm offer of employment are indicated below with an "X". Additionally, we are providing a checklist to assist you in completing all required forms.

____ Background Investigation – **You MUST complete the SF-85 online.** We request that you go to the following OPM-IS website: www.opm.gov/e-qip to enter the Electronic Questionnaires for Investigations Processing (e-QIP) Gateway. Please note that e-QIP is not compatible with Macintosh computers. Also, it is recommended you download Adobe Acrobat Reader 7.0 to avoid printing problems. Once you have entered the e-QIP website, please read the "Quick Reference Guide for the Applicant," before you get started. Once you finish reading the quick reference guide, go to the e-QIP Applicant Site and follow the prompts. Please refer to the enclosed e-Qip Checklist for additional information.

____ Modified BI Agreement

CBP supervisor recognition of Philip Haney's service and devotion and request for higher commendation from DHS.

United States Department of Homeland Security
Customs and Border Protection
9076 Binnacle Way
Orlando, Florida 32827

August 14, 2007

James M. Chaparro
Deputy Assistant Secretary
United States Department of Homeland Security
Office of Intelligence & Analysis
Washington, D.C. 20528

Reference: CBP Officer Philip B. Haney and CBP Officer ▓▓▓▓▓▓

Dear Mr. Chaparro,

It was a pleasure to meet you on August 9, 2007 at the Summer Hard Problem Program (SHARP) dinner in Orlando, Florida. I enjoyed the conversation we had and I would like to provide you some information regarding the two Customs and Border Protection Officers (CBPO) that we discussed at the dinner.

I would like to recognize CBPO Philip B. Haney and CBPC ▓▓▓▓▓▓ from the Atlanta, Georgia Passenger Analysis Unit who have gone above the call of duty to analyze, sort, and prepare intelligence reports and databases relating to Islamic terrorist groups and threats against the United States. The intelligence reports have been on topics relating to Global Jihad & Developing Trends. CBPO Haney has also created a database of approximately 185 Islamic Jihadist Groups operating in 81 countries. In addition to other reports, a report titled, <u>Hamas Network in the United States</u> has been created to provide the intelligence community with important information regarding terrorist groups.

The documents they have prepared have been beneficial to local, state, and other federal agencies. We must recognize and keep motivating those that excel and go above the call of duty. Therefore, I feel that the initiative, determination and professionalism of these two officers should be commended.

I will always be grateful to you for the opportunity to recognize these two Customs and Border Protection Officers. I believe this is the right thing to do for their service to the Department of Homeland Security and the United States of America.

Respectfully,

Jose E. Melendez-Perez
Supervisory Customs and Border Protection Officer
Customs and Border Protection
Orlando, Florida

Attachment (1)

The Director's Award is the Federal Law Enforcment Training Center's highest commendation.

Federal Law Enforcement Training Center
U. S. Department of Homeland Security
1131 Chapel Crossing Road
Glynco, Georgia 31524

 Homeland
Security

February 1, 2008

Philip B. Haney
Customs and Border Protection
Atlanta, GA

Re: Director's Award – LET 1 (OTM/TMD)

Dear Mr. Haney:

Congratulations! I am pleased to announce that you have been selected by your classmates as the student who most exemplifies the core values of a Federal law enforcement officer. Therefore, you are the recipient of the Federal Law Enforcement Training Center's "Director's Award" for Customs and Border Protection Integrated Class Number CBPI-807.

A partnership of agency representatives and FLETC staff has determined that the values essential for a law enforcement officer include: Integrity, Fairness, Respect, Honesty, Courage, and Compassion. It is apparent to your classmates that you have distinguished yourself early in your law enforcement career by clearly and consistently demonstrating the above stated core values.

At the recommendation of your fellow students, I am pleased that this award is to be presented to you. It is with confidence that I trust you will continue to demonstrate these same values throughout your law enforcement career.

A copy of this letter will be forwarded to Mr. Art Morgan, Director, United States Customs and Border Protection Academy, Department of Homeland Security, for inclusion in your personnel file. Congratulations.

Sincerely,

Connie L. Patrick
Director

www.fletc.gov

Commendation from the director of the National Targeting Center-Passenger of Philip Haney's expertise in counterterrorism and his outstanding contribution to the NTC-P.

1300 Pennsylvania Avenue NW
Washington, DC 20229

**U.S. Customs and
Border Protection**

JUN 8 2012

Officer Philip B. Haney
U.S. Customs and Border Protection
12379 Sunrise Valley Drive, Suite C
Reston, Virginia 20191

Dear Officer Haney:

On behalf of U.S. Customs and Border Protection (CBP), I commend your outstanding contributions while assigned to the National Targeting Center-Passenger (NTC-P). Your display of dedication and effort in the fight against terrorism has been exemplary.

Your talents and professionalism have contributed to the continued achievements of the NTC-P. You played a key role by providing support to the CBP mission and the NTC-P lead role in defending and protecting our nation's borders. A key component of NTC-P's success is the invaluable people, like you, who perform the work in our important mission. I am confident to know that CBP can rely upon you to provide expertise to combat threats against our nation.

Additionally, your expertise and experience has been invaluable while assigned to the Advanced Targeting Team (ATT). Your research on the Tablighi Jamaat Initiative has assisted in the identification of over 300 persons with possible connections to terrorism. The assistance you have provided in the development of this initiative has been key to the future success of the project. NTC-P looks forward to your continuing support and assistance in the program.

Once again, I thank you for your unfailing commitment to the success of NTC-P's mission. Your professional actions and achievements reflect favorably on you and all of CBP.

Thank you for a job well done!

Sincerely,

Donald Conroy
Director
National Targeting Center-Passenger

US Rep. Michael McCaul, chairman of the House Committee on Homeland Security, and US Sen. Tom Coburn, chairman of the Senate Homeland Security and Governmental Affairs Committee, urge the deputy inspector general to investigate Philip Haney's allegations of DHS misconduct.

Congress of the United States
Washington, DC 20515

July 31, 2013

Dr. Charles K. Edwards
Deputy Inspector General
DHS Office of Inspector General
Washington, D.C. 20528

Dear Dr. Edwards:

We appreciate you attending the briefing on Friday, July 26, 2013 that was presented to Committee staff concerning allegations by a DHS whistleblower. We request you conduct an investigation into the matters discussed, specifically the alteration and/or deletion of TECs records which deal with possible links to terrorism. Additionally, we would like you to investigate the circumstances of the alleged administrative actions against the whistleblower and whether they were appropriate.

We expect your office to investigate with particular sensitivity to the whistleblower's work situation and request ongoing updates as facts become known.

We appreciate you addressing this request in an expeditious manner. If you have any questions, please have your staff contact Dr. R. Nicholas Palarino, Deputy Chief of Staff/Policy, U.S. House of Representatives Committee on Homeland Security at 202-226-8417 and/or Dan Lips, Director of Homeland Security, Senate Homeland Security and Government Affairs Committee at 202-224-4751.

Sincerely,

Michael T. McCaul
Chairman
House Committee on Homeland Security

Tom Coburn
Ranking Member
Senate Homeland Security and Governmental Affairs Committee

Request from US Rep Darrell Issa to the DHS deputy inspector general to complete his investigation into Philip Haney's allegations of DHS misconduct.

DARRELL E. ISSA, CALIFORNIA
CHAIRMAN

JOHN L. MICA, FLORIDA
MICHAEL R. TURNER, OHIO
JOHN J. DUNCAN, JR., TENNESSEE
PATRICK T. McHENRY, NORTH CAROLINA
JIM JORDAN, OHIO
JASON CHAFFETZ, UTAH
TIM WALBERG, MICHIGAN
JAMES LANKFORD, OKLAHOMA
JUSTIN AMASH, MICHIGAN
PAUL A. GOSAR, ARIZONA
PATRICK MEEHAN, PENNSYLVANIA
SCOTT DesJARLAIS, TENNESSEE
TREY GOWDY, SOUTH CAROLINA
BLAKE FARENTHOLD, TEXAS
DOC HASTINGS, WASHINGTON
CYNTHIA M. LUMMIS, WYOMING
ROB WOODALL, GEORGIA
THOMAS MASSIE, KENTUCKY
DOUG COLLINS, GEORGIA
MARK MEADOWS, NORTH CAROLINA
KERRY L. BENTIVOLIO, MICHIGAN
RON DeSANTIS, FLORIDA

LAWRENCE J. BRADY
STAFF DIRECTOR

ONE HUNDRED THIRTEENTH CONGRESS

Congress of the United States
House of Representatives

COMMITTEE ON OVERSIGHT AND GOVERNMENT REFORM

2157 RAYBURN HOUSE OFFICE BUILDING

WASHINGTON, DC 20515-6143

MAJORITY (202) 225-5074
MINORITY (202) 225-5051

http://oversight.house.gov

ELIJAH E. CUMMINGS, MARYLAND
RANKING MINORITY MEMBER

CAROLYN B. MALONEY, NEW YORK
ELEANOR HOLMES NORTON,
DISTRICT OF COLUMBIA
JOHN F. TIERNEY, MASSACHUSETTS
WM. LACY CLAY, MISSOURI
STEPHEN F. LYNCH, MASSACHUSETTS
JIM COOPER, TENNESSEE
GERALD E. CONNOLLY, VIRGINIA
JACKIE SPEIER, CALIFORNIA
MATTHEW A. CARTWRIGHT, PENNSYLVANIA
MARK POCAN, WISCONSIN
L. TAMMY DUCKWORTH, ILLINOIS
ROBIN L. KELLY, ILLINOIS
DANNY K. DAVIS, ILLINOIS
PETER WELCH, VERMONT
TONY CARDENAS, CALIFORNIA
STEVEN A. HORSFORD, NEVADA
MICHELLE LUJAN GRISHAM, NEW MEXICO

November 6, 2013

Mr. Charles K. Edwards
Deputy Inspector General
U.S. Department of Homeland Security
245 Murray Lane SW, Building 410
Washington, D.C. 20528-0305

Dear Mr. Edwards:

As part of the Committee on Oversight and Government Reform's ongoing oversight of the Department of Homeland Security, I am writing regarding your office's investigation into allegations raised by ██████████ a U.S. Customs and Border Protection officer. Officer ██████ has raised potentially serious allegations related to CBP and the Department's handling of information relating to suspected terrorists.   b6, 7C

I urge you to complete this investigation in a thorough and expeditious manner. Additionally, I request that you direct your staff to make arrangements to brief Committee staff on the status of your investigation.

The Committee on Oversight and Government Reform is the principal oversight committee of the House of Representatives and may at "any time" investigate "any matter" as set forth in House Rule X.

If you have any questions about this request, please contact Ashley Callen or Ashok Pinto of the Committee staff at (202) 225-5074. Thank you for your attention to this important matter.

Sincerely,

Darrell Issa
Chairman

Notice of administrative suspension of Philip Haney's Secret Clearance, which did not constitute an "adverse action."

1300 Pennsylvania Avenue NW
Washington, DC 20229

U.S. Customs and
Border Protection

JUN 0 8 2015

TO: Ronnie L. Matheson
Supervisory Customs and Border Protection Officer
Atlanta Hartsfield International Airport
U.S. Customs and Border Protection
Atlanta, GA 30320

FROM: Susan Gulbranson
Assistant Director
Employee Operations Unit
Personnel Security Division
Office of Internal Affairs

SUBJECT: Suspension of Security Clearance

This is to advise you that the Personnel Security Division (PSD) has administratively suspended the Secret Clearance for Philip B. Haney, (xxx-xx-0915), Customs and Border Protection Officer, pending resolution of any internal investigations. *Until further advised by this office, Mr. Haney cannot have access to any classified information or systems.*

You must advise this employee immediately of the above action. Both you and the employee must acknowledge receipt of this notification. The original signed and dated copy of the memorandum should be promptly returned to the Director, Personnel Security Division, at the following address, for permanent record retention:

U. S. Customs and Border Protection
ATTN: Michael Radford
Office of Internal Affairs
90 K Street, NE, Suite 600
Washington, DC 20229-1054

The suspension of the security clearance will remain in effect until further notice from this office. This suspension extends to any temporary assignment, special project, task force, training course, etc., for which a clearance is required and/or certification of the employee's clearance to outside agencies/facilities, etc. This suspension does not constitute an adverse action.

The following documents obtained through the Freedom of Information Act show that it was the DHS Office of Civil Rights and Civil Liberties, along with the State Department, that "moved" the Tablighi Jamaat Initiative "in other directions," as recounted in chapter 1.

All redactions in this document are pursuant to FOIA exemptions (b)(6) and (b)(7)(C). Any additional exemptions used are indicated in the margin near their redaction.

MEMORANDUM OF ACTIVITY

From ▮▮▮▮▮▮▮▮▮▮▮▮▮▮▮▮▮▮ was ▮▮▮▮▮▮▮▮ the NTC▮. ▮▮▮▮▮▮▮▮▮▮▮▮▮ was assigned work on ▮▮▮ ▮▮▮▮ Project (▮▮▮▮ Project)'. ▮▮▮▮▮▮▮▮▮▮▮▮ was already linking **7E** persons in TECS to ▮▮▮▮▮▮▮▮, and had created a Memorandum of Information Received (MOIR)² on ▮▮▮▮▮▮▮ in TECS. ▮▮▮▮▮▮▮▮▮▮▮▮ was only supposed to research and document ▮ finding in the Targeting Framework³. ▮was instructed not to put individuals on the Watchlist, but instead document them for nomination. TECS records were created to identify the nomination while it was being reviewed.

After a meeting between the NTC, DHS Privacy Office and DHS Office for Civil Rights and Civil Liberties, it was determined that individuals could only be "watchlisted" based on an association with a known or suspected terrorist already "watchlisted" in the TSDB – not based on their affiliation with ▮▮▮▮▮▮ (or any ▮▮▮ organization). **7E**

When ▮▮▮ returned to ▮▮▮▮▮▮▮▮▮▮▮▮▮▮▮▮▮▮ continued to do two things. First, ▮ continued to enter subjects into TECS based on their affiliation with ▮▮▮▮▮▮. Second, ▮ continued to enter subjects into TECS under the authority ▮ had been granted while ▮▮▮▮▮▮ **7E** ▮▮, and referenced the NTC event. Since ▮▮▮ left ▮; however, the ▮▮▮▮▮▮ had moved in other directions, and new guidelines had been established. ▮▮▮ was unaware of the new protocols and objectives, and entered numerous records into TECS which were not in compliance. During this time, ▮▮▮ nominated some individuals to the Watchlist, but ▮ nominations were declined because there were ▮▮▮▮▮▮▮▮▮▮▮▮▮ – only links to the ▮▮▮▮ **7E** ▮▮▮▮ organization.

The proper process for a CBP officer to nominate a subject to the Watchlist requires the officer to submit the nomination to his supervisor (GS-13 or above). After reviewing the nomination, the supervisor can forward it to the NTC, or they can refuse to submit it. A CBP supervisor does not have to forward nominations they feel are not worthy of submission. According to ▮▮▮ how to create a TECS record for NTC purposes is a Standardized Operating Procedure.

7E

² A Memorandum of Information Received (MOIR) is a TECS record which documents information an officer found, ▮▮▮▮▮▮

³ Targeting Framework is the case management system for the National Targeting Center

MEMORANDUM OF ACTIVITY

delete TECS records if they were accurate. ▅▅▅▅ also saw nothing wrong with ▅▅▅ linking records to the NTC ▅▅▅▅▅▅▅ Initiative; however, ▅▅▅▅ was later required to remove ▅▅▅▅ references from ▅ TECS entries. [Agent's Note: DHS Office for Civil Rights and Civil Liberties determined that individuals could only be "watchlisted" based on an association with a known or suspected terrorist already "watchlisted" in the TSDB – not based on their affiliation with ▅▅▅▅ (or any ▅▅▅ organization).]   **7E**

▅▅▅▅ stated that ▅▅▅ worked within the rules created in the Automated Targeting System (ATS). Essentially, the Office of Intelligence and Investigative Liaison (IOIL) creates rules in the ATS to identify certain individuals entering the country. These rules can include any number of variables such as ▅▅▅▅▅▅▅▅▅▅▅▅▅▅▅▅▅▅▅▅▅▅▅▅▅▅▅▅▅▅▅   **7E**

When ▅▅▅ created Memorandums of Information Received (MOIRs) linked to the ▅▅▅ ▅▅ Initiative, ▅ used the phrase ▅▅▅▅▅▅▅▅▅▅▅▅▅▅▅▅▅▅▅▅▅▅▅▅▅ ," (Attachment 1) ▅▅▅ said that he found this to be appropriate. [Agent's Note: On February 5, 2013, ▅▅▅ received an office counseling notice for improperly entering ▅▅▅▅▅▅ TECS records related to the ▅▅▅▅ Initiative.]   **7E**

▅▅▅ said that in August 2013, ▅▅▅ provided him information on U.S. citizen ▅▅▅ ▅, who was arrested ▅▅▅▅▅▅ recognized that ▅▅▅ was ▅▅▅▅▅ ▅▅▅▅▅▅▅▅▅▅▅▅▅▅▅▅▅ forwarded the information directly to ▅▅▅ at the NTC for vetting. It was determined that ▅▅▅ was arrested after a search of his residence uncovered bomb making material to be used in a terrorist attack on ▅▅▅▅▅ . ▅▅▅ stated this is an example of the thorough work ▅▅ does. (Attachment 2)

Attachment:

1. Email string between ▅▅▅▅ and ▅▅▅▅ dated September 24, 2012.
2. Documents referencing ▅▅▅▅ provided by ▅▅▅▅ on November 13, 2013.

(b) (6)

I understand Officer [b) (6)] has been entering TECS records with links to [(b) (7)(C), (b) (7)] [E] Please be advised that any records entered by Officer [b) (6)] should not reference the NTC. . There has been a lot of push back from [(b) (5)] and CRCL regarding the [] initiative and since [] is not a designated terrorist organization. Records entered by NTC are required to go through a very specific review process so as in order to comply with [(b) (5)] CRCL and DOS concerns. Again, please have Officer [b) (6)] share [b) (6)] potential targets with the NTC for vetting. Please call me if you have any concerns.

(b) (6)
Assistant Director, Tactical Targeting
National Targeting Center- Passenger
Office of Field Operations
(b) (6), (b) (7)(C)

This document and any attachment(s) may contain restricted, sensitive, and/or law enforcement-sensitive information belonging to the U.S. Government. It is not for release, review, retransmission, dissemination, or use by anyone other than the intended recipient.

From: (b) (6)
Sent: Mon 9/17/2012 12:54 PM
To: (b) (6)
Subject: RE: (b) (7)(C), (b) (7)

(b) (6)

I just became aware that Officer [b) (6)] has input 25 Subject Records and 41 Organization Records since returning to [b) (6)], all with identical remarks:

REMARKS- DATE [] NEW REMARKS [(b) (7)(E)] MORE REMARKS [(b)(7)(E)]
LINKED TO NTC-P [(b)(7)(E), (b)(7)(C)]
(b)(7)(E)

I would like to discuss a way forward, either deleting these records out of TECS or transferring ownership to the NTC.

Give me a call when you have a minute.

Thanks, (b) (6)

(b) (6)
(b) (6), (b) (7)(C)
(b) (6), (b) (7)(C)

NOTES

INTRODUCTION

1. U.S. Department of Homeland Security (hereinafter, DHS), "'If You See Something, Say Something™'" Video: Protect Your Every Day Public Service Announcement (English–30 Seconds)," official website of the Department of Homeland Security, accessed January 15, 2016, http://www.dhs.gov/video/%E2%80%9Cif-you-see-something-say-something%E2%84%A2%E2%80%9D-video-protect-your-every-day-public-service-announceme-1.
2. See DHS, "If You See Something, Say Something," official website of the U.S. Department of Homeland Security, accessed January 15, 2016, http://www.dhs.gov/see-something-say-something.
3. See DHS, "Countering Violent Extremism," official website of the U.S. Department of Homeland Security, accessed January 15, 2016, http://www.dhs.gov/topic/countering-violent-extremism.

CHAPTER 1: FROM JEDDAH TO SAN BERNARDINO

1. Soumya Karlamangla, Paloma Esquivel, and Laura J. Nelson, "Rampage killers led secret life, hiding plans and weapons," Los Angeles Times, December 3, 2015, http://www.latimes.com/local/lanow/la-me-ln-syed-farook-tashfeen-malik-shooters-san-bernardino-20151203-story.html.
2. Stephanie Gosk, Hannah Rappleye, and Tracy Connor, "Mosque Members Say Shooter Syed Farook Seemed 'Peaceful,' Devout," NBC News, December 3, 2015, http://www.nbcnews.com/storyline/san-bernardino-shooting/mosque-members-say-shooter-syed-farook-seemed-peaceful-devout-n473721.
3. United States District Court for the Central District of California, in the matter of *United States of America v. Enrique Marquez Jr.*, par. 23, available online from the *Los Angeles Times* at "Criminal complaint for Enrique Marquez, December 17, 2015, http://documents.latimes.com/criminal-complaint-enrique-marquez/, p. 7.
4. Part 3.C. question 4 (p. 3), on the Department of Homeland Security's U.S. Citizenship and Immigration Service Form I-485, Application to Register Permanent Residence or Adjust Status, http://www.uscis.gov/sites/default/files/files/form/i-485.pdf.

5. Fred Burton and Scott Stewart, "Tablighi Jamaat: An Indirect Line to Terrorism," Stratfor Global Intelligence, January 23, 2008, https://www.stratfor.com/weekly/tablighi_jamaat_indirect_line_terrorism.

CHAPTER 2: FINDING THE TRAIL

1. Eric Pianin and Bill Miller, "Soaring homeland security costs / Bush budget to call for huge expenditures," *SFGate*, December 22, 2001, http://www.sfgate.com/politics/article/Soaring-homeland-security-costs-Bush-budget-to-2836160.php.
2. George W. Bush, *The Department of Homeland Security* (2002), http://www.dhs.gov/sites/default/files/publications/book_0.pdf, 1.
3. Homeland Security Act of 2002, Pub. L. No. 107-296, 116 Stat. 2135 (2002), http://www.dhs.gov/sites/default/files/publications/hr_5005_enr.pdf.
4. "Who Joined DHS," official website of the Department of Homeland Security, accessed January 15, 2016, http://www.dhs.gov/who-joined-dhs.
5. "Creation of the Department of Homeland Security," official website of the Department of Homeland Security, accessed January 15, 2016, http://www.dhs.gov/creation-department-homeland-security.
6. See list of publications on the website of the International Society of Citriculture, http://www.crec.ifas.ufl.edu/societies/ISC/author/israel.shtml, accessed January 15, 2016.
7. See Deborah Meyers, "'One Face at the Border'—Is It Working?" Migration Policy Institute website, July 1, 2005, http://www.migrationpolicy.org/article/one-face-border-it-working/.
8. Ibid.
9. Cf. U.S. Customs and Border Protection, "About CBP," official website of the Department of Homeland Security, accessed January 15, 2016, http://www.cbp.gov/about.
10. "Full Transcript of Bin Ladin's Speech," Information Clearing House, accessed January 15, 2016, http://www.informationclearinghouse.info/article7201.htm.
11. Bradley Graham, "15,000 U.S., troops will leave Iraq next month," *Washington Post*, February 4, 2005, http://www.chron.com/news/nation-world/article/15-000-U-S-troops-will-leave-Iraq-next-month-1931148.php.
12. Stephen Sego, "Afghanistan in 2005," *Encyclopedia Britannica*, accessed January 15, 2016, http://www.britannica.com/place/Afghanistan-Year-In-Review-2005.

CHAPTER 3: SHADOW LINE

1. "Controversial Muslim Group Gets VIP Airport Security Tour," WND, August 18, 2006, http://www.wnd.com/2006/08/37520/.
2. Philip B. Haney, "Green Tide Rising," *FrontPageMag.com*, March 16, 2006, http://archive.frontpagemag.com/readArticle.aspx?ARTID=5200.
3. Ibid.
4. See the Immigration Court correspondence dated November 24, 2004, at http://www.investigativeproject.org/documents/case_docs/830.pdf.

5. See Abdel Jabbar Hamdan v. Alberto Gonzales et al., CV 05-5144-TJH (central dist. Cal. 2006), judgment, at http://www.investigativeproject.org/documents/case_docs/831.pdf.
6. See U.S. Immigration and Customs Enforcement, "Former High-Ranking Official for Holy Land Foundation Ordered Removed from the United States," news release, February 8, 2005, http://www.investigativeproject.org/documents/case_docs/829.pdf.
7. See their official website at http://www.islamicity.org/, accessed January 18, 2016.
8. See Pamela Geller, "Jihad in South Africa: "Kill One Jew or Christian and Get Reward of Jannah," Pamela Geller's website, December 10, 2014, http://pamelageller.com/2014/12/kill-one-jew-or-christian.html/#sthash.twIviE8x.dpuf.

CHAPTER 4: WORDS MATTER

1. See Department of Homeland Security, "Maximum Age for Appointment to the Department of Homeland Security Customs and Border Protection Officer Positions," May 17, 2008, http://www.dhs.gov/xlibrary/assets/foia/chco_maximum%20age%20for%20appointment_md%20252-08.pdf.
2. Ibid., 2.
3. Federal Bureau of Investigation, *Counterterrorism Analytical Lexicon* (undated), http://cryptome.org/fbi-ct-lexicon.pdf.
4. Ibid., 3, 5, 6.
5. Ibid., 8.
6. U.S. Department of Homeland Security, Office for Civil Rights and Civil Liberties, "Terminology to Define the Terrorists: Recommendations from American Muslims," January 2008, http://www.dhs.gov/xlibrary/assets/crcl_terminology_paper_final_3_10_08.pdf.
7. "Words that Work and Words that Don't: A Guide for Counterterrorism Communication," March 14, 2008, http://www.investigativeproject.org/documents/misc/127.pdf, 1.
8. Office of the Under Secretary for Public Diplomacy and Public Affairs, "Changing the Nature and Scope of Public Diplomacy," November 1, 2007, U.S. Department of State Archive, http://2001-2009.state.gov/r/update/94615.htm.
9. See "Center for Strategic Counterterrorism Communications" on the website of the U.S. Department of State, accessed January 18, 2016, http://www.state.gov/r/cscc/.
10. Ibid.
11. The White House, Office of the Press Secretary, "Fact Sheet: National Strategy for Counterterrorism," news release, June 29, 2011, https://www.whitehouse.gov/the-press-office/2011/06/29/fact-sheet-national-strategy-counterterrorism.
12. U.S. Department of State, Office of the Spokesperson, "Appointment of Rashad Hussain as United States Special Envoy and Coordinator for Strategic Counterterrorism Communications," media note, February 18, 2015, http://m.state.gov/md237585.htm.
13. Judicial Watch, "Obama Islam Envoy A Lying Terrorist Defender," *Corruption Chronicles* (blog), February 22, 2010, http://www.judicialwatch.org/blog/2010/02/obama-islam-envoy-lying-terrorist-defender/.

14. Office of the Spokesperson, "Appointment of Rashad Hussain as United States Special Envoy."
15. "Words that Work and Words that Don't," 1.
16. Ibid.
17. Ibid., 2.
18. Ibid., 3.
19. "CAIR's origins," accessed January 18, 2016, https://www.investigativeproject.org/documents/misc/109.pdf.
20. Ibid.
21. FBI, "No Cash for Terror: Convictions Returned in Holy Land Case," FBI: Stories, November 25, 2008, https://www.fbi.gov/news/stories/2008/november/hlf112508.
22. Laila Al-Arian, "Verdict Against Holy Land Charity Could Have a Chilling Effect on the Muslim Community," *AlterNet*, November 25, 2008, http://www.alternet.org/story/108740/verdict_against_holy_land_charity_could_have_a_chilling_effect_on_the_muslim_community.
23. Ahmad ibn Naguib al-Misri, Reliance of the Traveller, revised edition, ed. and trans. by Nuh Ha Mim Keller (Beltsville, Md., Amana Publications, 1991), http://shariahthethreat.org/wp-content/uploads/2011/04/reliance_of_the_traveller.pdf.
24. See Center for Security Policy, *Shariah: The Threat to America: An Exercise in Competitive Analysis: Report of Team B II* (Washington, DC: Center for Security Policy, 2010), https://www.centerforsecuritypolicy.org/upload/wysiwyg/article%20pdfs/Shariah%20-%20The%20Threat%20to%20America%20%28Team%20B%20Report%29%20Web%20Version%2009302010.pdf, Appendix II: "An Explanatory Memorandum on the General Strategic Goal for the Group in North America," 295, 281–82. See also pp. 310–11, 313.

CHAPTER 5: INTEL SCRUB

1. Bruce Phillips, "The War Against Hamas: Why Does It Matter?" WND, January 17, 2009, http://www.wnd.com/2009/01/86313/.
2. See "Salah Sultan" in *Global Muslim Brotherhood Daily Watch*, accessed January 18, 2016, http://www.globalmbwatch.com/salah-sultan/.
3. Islamic Society of Boston home page, February 4, 2005, https://web.archive.org/web/20051016061129/http://www.isboston.org/v3.1/viewitem.asp?MenuID=&DocID=2965.
4. Elisha Fieldstadt, "Egyptian-American Mohamed Soltan Released from Egypt Jail After 2 Years: Family," NBC News, May 30, 2015, http://www.nbcnews.com/news/world/u-s-egyptian-mohamed-soltan-released-egypt-jail-family-n367076.
5. See http://www.lawandsoftware.com/ina/INA-237-sec1227.html; http://www.lawandsoftware.com/ina/INA-212-sec1182.html#a_3.
6. United States Department of Justice, "Attorney General Eric Holder on Department of Justice's Outreach and Enforcement Efforts to Protect American Muslims," June 4, 2009, http://www.justice.gov/opa/speech/attorney-general-eric-holder-department-justice-s-outreach-and-enforcement-efforts.

7. Loretta Sanchez et al., letter to Eric Holder, July 24, 2009, http://www.investigativeproject. org/documents/misc/282.pdf.

8. Ibid., p. 3.

9. Investigative Project on Terrorism "FBI Replaces Brotherhood-Tainted Liaison with Brotherhood-Tainted Liaison," IPT News, June 25, 2009, http://www.investigativeproject. org/1074/fbi-replaces-brotherhood-tainted-liaison-with#.

10. See "Secret: North American Islamic Trust (NAIT)," accessed January 18, 2016, http:// www.investigativeproject.org/documents/misc/151.pdf.

11. Abdul Hakeem Malik, *Quranic Prism: Subject Index of the Holy Quran* (Islamic Research Fundation Global, 2002). A description of the book can be see on the Goodreads website, at http://www.goodreads.com/book/show/255014.Quranic_Prism.

12. "Embattled Muslim aide to leave Pentagon job," WND, February 11, 2008, http://www. wnd.com/2008/02/56110/#L4Um1EkchpRoo7CF.99.

13. Steven Emerson (Fox News), "Expert on Radical Islam Fired from Pentagon," Investigative Project on Terrorism, January 11, 2008, http://www.investigativeproject.org/584/expert-on-radical-islam-fired-from-pentagon.

14. Chris Irvine, "Detroit terror attack: suspect president of university Islamic society," *Telegraph* (UK), December 29, 2009, http://www.telegraph.co.uk/news/uknews/ terrorism-in-the-uk/6902785/Detroit-terror-attack-suspect-president-of-university-Islamic-society.html.

15. See "'A Failure to Connect the Dots,'" *Wall Street Journal*, upd. January 8, 2012, http:// www.wsj.com/articles/SB10001424052748704130904574644852758778552.

CHAPTER 6: A NEW RELATIONSHIP

1. See Todd Holzman, "Obama Seeks 'New Beginning' With Muslim World," NPR, http:// www.npr.org/templates/story/story.php?storyId=104891406.

2. §212(a)(3)(B)(iv)(VI)(dd) is part of the Immigration and Nationality Act code related to terrorism charges.

3. Secretary of State Hillary Rodham Clinton, State Department Special Order, 2004, http://www.nytimes.com/packages/pdf/world/clinton_statedeptorder_ramadanhabib. pdf.

4. See Center for Security Policy, "Who's Who in the American Muslim Brotherhood," on the website of *Shariah: The Threat to America*, accessed January 18, 2016, http:// shariahthethreat.org/a-short-course-1-what-is-shariah/a-short-course-17-who's-who-in-the-american-muslim-brotherhood-msa-isna/.

5. See http://www.judicialwatch.org/files/documents/2010/dhs-napolitano-jan-meeting-docs-3.pdf.

6. Ibid.

7. See Office of the Press Secretary, "Readout of Secretary Napolitano's Meeting with Faith-Based and Community Leaders," news release, January 28, 2010, http://www.dhs.gov/ news/2010/01/28/readout-secretary-napolitanos-meeting-faith-based-and-community-leaders.

8. Richard Pollock, "Napolitano Meets with Muslim Brotherhood Leaders," PJ Media, February 17, 2010, https://pjmedia.com/blog/napolitano-meets-with-muslim-brotherhood-leaders-pjm-exclusive/.

9. DHS-CRCL Community Stakeholder Meeting Agenda, January 28, 2010, http://www.judicialwatch.org/files/documents/2010/dhs-napolitano-jan-meeting-docs-excerpt-3.pdf.

10. Ari Melber and Safia Samee Ali, "Exclusive: Homeland Security passed on plan to vet visa applicants' social media," MSNBC, December 17, 2015, http://www.msnbc.com/msnbc/exclusive-homeland-security-rejected-plan-vet-visa-applicants-social-media.

11. Homeland Security Advisory Council, *Countering Violent Extremism (CVE) Working Group* (Spring 2010), 2, http://www.dhs.gov/xlibrary/assets/hsac_cve_working_group_recommendations.pdf.

12. Ibid., 15.

13. See U.S. Citizenship and Immigration Services, "Terrorism-Related Inadmissibility Grounds (TRIG)," uscig.gov, upd. October 1, 2014, http://www.uscis.gov/laws/terrorism-related-inadmissability-grounds/terrorism-related-inadmissibility-grounds-trig.

14. For all references to 8 U.S.C. 1182, see the appropriate section in: 8. U.S.C., United States Code, 2014 ed., Title 8: Aliens and Nationality, chap. 12, Immigration and Nationality, subchap, 2: Immigration, pt. 2: Admission Qualifications for Aliens; Travel Control of Citizens and Aliens, sec. 1182: Inadmissible aliens, from the U.S. Government Publishing Office, https://www.gpo.gov/fdsys/pkg/USCODE-2014-title8/html/USCODE-2014-title8-chap12-subchapII-partII-sec1182.htm.

15. Jeh Charles Johnson and John Kerry, "Exercise of Authority Under Section 212(d)(3) (B)(i) of the Immigration and Nationality Act," a notice by the Homeland Security Department and the State Department, February 5, 2014, *Federal Register*, https://www.federalregister.gov/articles/2014/02/05/2014-02357/exercise-of-authority-under-section-212d3bi-of-the-immigration-and-nationality-act.

16. Adam Kredo, "Controversial DHS Adviser Let Go Amid Allegations of Cover Up," *Washington Free Beacon*, September 15, 2014, http://freebeacon.com/issues/controversial-dhs-adviser-let-go-amid-allegations-of-cover-up/.

17. Ibid.

18. Margo Schlanger, letter to complainant, May 3, 2011, https://www.aclu.org/files/borderquestioning/ACLU_BQ_000034.pdf.

19. The *Washington Times*, "U.S. sponsors Islamic convention," *Washington Times*, August 27, 2007, http://www.washingtontimes.com/news/2007/aug/27/us-sponsors-islamic-convention/.

20. "Muslim Brotherhood Supreme Guide: 'The U.S. Is Now Experiencing the Beginning of Its End'; Improvement and Change in the Muslim World 'Can Only Be Attained Through Jihad and Sacrifice,'" MEMRI special dispatch no. 3274, October 6, 2010, http://capro.info/Cults_and_Isms/Islam/PDFs/Muslim_Brotherhood_Supreme_Guide-Muhammad%20Badie.pdf.

CHAPTER 7: THE GREAT PURGE

1. Lucy Madison, "Attorney General Eric Holder: Threat of Homegrown Terrorism 'Keeps Me Up at Night,'" CBS News, December 21, 2010, http://www.cbsnews.com/news/attorney-general-eric-holder-threat-of-homegrown-terrorism-keeps-me-up-at-night/.

2. Paul Richter and Peter Nicholas, "U.S. open to a role for Islamists in new Egypt government," *Los Angeles Times*, January 31, 2011, http://articles.latimes.com/2011/jan/31/world/la-fg-us-egypt-20110201.

3. Josh Gerstein, "DNI Clapper retreats from 'secular' claim on Muslim Brotherhood," *Under the Radar* (blog), February 10, 2011, http://www.politico.com/blogs/under-the-radar/2011/02/dni-clapper-retreats-from-secular-claim-on-muslim-brotherhood-033259#ixzz3xi9TR65v.

4. Muslim Brotherhood Fact Sheet, StandWithUs website, accessed January 19, 2016, https://www.standwithus.com/news/article.asp?id=1757.

5. Dan Murphy, "Egypt revolution unfinished, Qaradawi tells Tahrir masses," *Christian Science Monitor*, February 18, 2011, http://www.csmonitor.com/World/Middle-East/2011/0218/Egypt-revolution-unfinished-Qaradawi-tells-Tahrir-masses.

6. "Two million Egyptians in Tahrir Square many chant To Jerusalem we are heading, Martyrs in the millions," posted February 9, 2011, https://www.youtube.com/watch?v=ENKn5lDtLvE.

7. Rachel Hirshfeld, "Muslim Cleric: Jerusalem to be Capital of Egypt Under Mursi Rule," *Arutz Sheva* Israel National News, June 9, 2012, http://www.israelnationalnews.com/News/News.aspx/156692#.VrzRFMfYVre.

8. Ibid.

9. Global Muslim Brotherhood Daily Report, "Muslim Brotherhood leader of Tunisia calls for an end to Israel," Spero News, May 19, 2011, http://www.speroforum.com/a/54102/Muslim-Brotherhood-leader-of-Tunisia-calls-for-an-end-to-Israel#.Vp56UiorKUl.

10. "Muslim Brotherhood Supreme Guide: 'The U.S. Is Now Experiencing the Beginning of Its End'; Improvement and Change in the Muslim World 'Can Only Be Attained Through Jihad and Sacrifice,'" MEMRI special dispatch no. 3274, October 6, 2010, p. 2, http://capro.info/Cults_and_Isms/Islam/PDFs/Muslim_Brotherhood_Supreme_Guide-Muhammad%20Badie.pdf.

11. Owen Bennett Jones, "Salafist groups find footing in Egypt after revolution," BBC News, April 7, 2011, http://www.bbc.com/news/world-middle-east-12985619.

12. Bill Gertz, "Anti-Terror Trainers Blocked," *Inside the Ring*, October 6, 2011, http://www.gertzfile.com/gertzfile/ring100611.html.

13. Michael Winter, "FBI halts training lecture critical of Muslims," *On Deadline* (blog), September 15, 2011, http://content.usatoday.com/communities/ondeadline/post/2011/09/fbi-drops-anti-islam-lecture-from-agents-training/1#.Vp6K4CorKUl.

14. Mariam Eltoweissy, "MPAC Co-Signs Letter to FBI Demanding Reformation in Flawed, Anti-Muslim Training," Muslim Public Affairs Council website, October 5, 2011, http://www.mpac.org/programs/government-relations/mpac-co-signs-letter-to-fbi-demanding-reformation-in-flawed-anti-muslim-training.php.

15. See "Countering Violent Extremism (CVE) Training Guidance & Best Practices," provided by U.S. Department of Homeland Security, Office for Civil Rights and Civil Liberties, October 2011, http://www.dhs.gov/xlibrary/assets/cve-training-guidance.pdf.

16. Office for Civil Rights and Civil Liberties, "Countering Violent Extremism Training: Do's and Don'ts," p. 1, http://www.training.fema.gov/emiweb/docs/shared/cve%20 do%20and%20dont.pdf.

17. Alejandro J. Beutel, Building Bridges to Strengthen America: Forging an Effective Counterterrorism Enterprise between Muslim Americans and Law Enforcement, unabridged version (Washington, DC: Muslim Public Affairs Council), http://www. mpac.org/assets/docs/publications/building-bridges/MPAC-Building-Bridges-- Complete_Unabridged_Paper.pdf, 6 (table of contents). The referenced sections are on pages 16–17 and 34–43 of the paper.

18. Ibid., 17, 68n141.

19. Office for Civil Rights and Civil Liberties, "Countering Violent Extremism Training," p. 1, Goals B., C.

20. Ibid., p. 1, Goal D.

21. Ibid., p. 2, Goal F.

22. AlMaghrib Institute et al., letter to the Honorable John Brennan, October 19, 2011, pp. 1, 5.

23. Ibid., 3.

24. Ibid., 5.

25. Ibid.

26. Ryan J. Reilly, "DOJ Official: Holder 'Firmly Committed' To Eliminating Anti-Muslim Training," Talking Points Memo, October 19, 2011, http://talkingpointsmemo.com/ muckraker/doj-official-holder-firmly-committed-to-eliminating-anti-muslim-training.

27. Ibid.

28. The American-Arab Anti-Discrimination Committee et al., letter to Margo Schlanger, October 2011, https://www.cair.com/images/pdf/Letter-to-DHS-CRCL-re-See-Something-Say-Something.pdf.

29. Department of Homeland Security, If You See Something, Say Something, "About the Campaign," official website of the U.S. Department of Homeland Security, accessed January 20, 2016, http://www.dhs.gov/see-something-say-something/about-campaign.

30. United Nations Human Rights Council (HRC), Resolution 16/18, "Combating intolerance, negative stereotyping and stigmatization of, and discrimination, incitement to violence and violence against, persons based on religion or belief," April 12, 2011, http://www.refworld.org/docid/4db960f92.html.

31. Pakistan Penal Code (Act XLV of 1860), http://www.lawsofpakistan.com/wp-content/ uploads/2012/03/Pakistan-Penal-Code.pdf. See, for example, 295C.

32. "Secretary Clinton's Remarks at the OIC Meeting on Combating Religious Intolerance," July 15, 2011, HumanRights.gov, http://www.humanrights.gov/secretary-clintons-remarks-at-the-oic-meeting-on-combating-religious-intolerance.html.

33. "OIC coming back with another attempt to stamp out free speech," National Secular Society, February 21, 2013, http://www.secularism.org.uk/news/2013/02/oic-coming-back-with-another-attempt-to-stamp-out-free-speech.

34. Rabat Plan of Action on the prohibition of advocacy of national, racial or religious hatred that constitutes incitement to discrimination, hostility or violence, adopted October 5, 2012, http://www.ohchr.org/Documents/Issues/Opinion/SeminarRabat/Rabat_draft_outcome.pdf, p. 10.

CHAPTER 8: PRIMARY ACCESS

1. See Erica Ritz, "House Members Demand Answers on Depth of U.S. Involvement with the Muslim Brotherhood," TheBlaze, June 15, 2012, http://www.theblaze.com/stories/2012/06/15/house-members-demand-answers-on-depth-of-u-s-involvement-with-the-muslim-brotherhood/.

2. Dana Milbank, "Dana Milbank: Modern-day McCarthyism," *Washington Post*, August 8, 2012, https://www.washingtonpost.com/opinions/dana-milbank-modern-day-mccarthyism/2012/08/08/0c6090fc-e1a5-11e1-98e7-89d659f9c106_story.html.

3. Ed O'Keefe, "John Boehner: Accusations against Huma Abedin 'pretty dangerous,'" *Washington Post*, July 19, 2012, https://www.washingtonpost.com/blogs/2chambers/post/john-boehner-accusations-against-huma-abedin-pretty-dangerous/2012/07/19/gJQAeDT6vW_blog.html.

4. Alex Seitz-Wald, "Keith Ellison slams Bachmann's 'galling' witch hunt," *Salon*, August 4, 2012, http://www.salon.com/2012/08/04/keith_ellison_slams_bachmanns_galling_witch_hunt/.

5. O'Keefe, "John Boehner."

6. PRNewswire-USNewswire, "CAIR 'Grateful' Constitution Limits Michele Bachmann's McCarthyism," PR Newswire, July 19, 2012, http://www.prnewswire.com/news-releases/cair-grateful-constitution-limits-michele-bachmanns-mccarthyism-163069136.html.

7. Jake Sherman, "Republicans line up to rip Bachmann," Politico, July 19, 2012, http://www.politico.com/story/2012/07/republicans-lining-up-to-rip-bachmann-078741.

8. Breitbart News, "EXCLUSIVE—FAIL: Muslim Group Calls on Romney to Denounce Bachmann, But No One Cares," Breitbart, August 6, 2012, http://www.breitbart.com/big-government/2012/08/06/mpac%20fail/.

9. See the website of the Investigative Project on Terrorism to view a summary of Mohamed Akram's "An Explanatory Memorandum on the General Strategic Goal for the Brotherhood in North America," May 19, 1991, http://www.investigativeproject.org/document/20-an-explanatory-memorandum-on-the-general. The site also provides a link to the full document in its original language.

10. See "Adjudicative Guidelines for Determining Eligibility for Access to Classified Information" (approved by the president March 24, 1997), on the website of FAS, http://fas.org/sgp/spb/class.htm, Guideline B.

11. Ibid., Guideline A.

12. See P. David Gaubatz and Paul Sperry, *Muslim Mafia: Inside the Secret Underworld That's Conspiring to Islamize America* (Los Angeles: WND Books, 2009), 12, 180.

13. Joe Kaufman, "Has CAIR Violated Its Non-Profit Tax Status?" FrontPageMagazine. com, May 19, 2008, reprinted at MilitantIslamMonitor.org, May 20, 2008, http://www. militantislammonitor.org/article/id/3460.

14. Jana Winter, "Some Muslims Attending Capitol Hill Prayer Group Have Terror Ties, Probe Reveals," Fox News, November 11, 2010, http://www.foxnews.com/ politics/2010/11/11/congressional-muslim-prayer-group-terror-ties.html.

15. Catherine Herridge, "Al Qaeda Leader Dined at the Pentagon Just Months After 9/11," Fox News, October 20, 2010, http://www.foxnews.com/us/2010/10/20/al-qaeda-terror-leader-dined-pentagon-months.html.

16. All references in this chapter to *Rose El-Youssef* are gleaned from Ahmad Shawqi, "Six brothers and a man in the White House," *Rose El-Youssef* magazine, December 22, 2012, http://www.rosa-magazine.com/News/3444/%D8%B1%D8%AC%D9% 84%D9%886-%D8%A5%D8%AE%D9%88%D8%A7%D9%86-%D9%81%D9%89- %D8%A7%D9%84%D8%A8%D9%8A%D8%AA-%D8%A7%D9%84%D8%A3%D 8%A8%D9%8A%D8%B6 (as translated from original); and from the English translation of this same article, titled "A man and 6 of the Brotherhood in the White House!" on the website of the Investigative Project on Terrorism, at http://www.investigativeproject. org/3868/a-man-and-6-of-the-brotherhood-in-the-white-house.

17. Adam Kredo, "Controversial DHS Adviser Let Go Amid Allegations of Cover Up," *Washington Free Beacon,* September 15, 2014, http://freebeacon.com/issues/controversial-dhs-adviser-let-go-amid-allegations-of-cover-up/.

18. Art Moore, WND Exclusive, "Congressman: Muslim Obama adviser leaked secret reports to media," WND, October 28, 2011, http://www.wnd.com/2011/10/361253/.

19. Andrew C. McCarthy, "Did Obama appointee access confidential database in effort to smear Perry as an 'Islamophobe'?" *The Corner* (blog), October 27, 2011, http://www. nationalreview.com/corner/281523/did-obama-appointee-access-confidential-database-effort-smear-perry-islamophobe-andrew.

20. Ibid.

21. Shawqi, "Six brothers and a man in the White House" / "A man and 6 of the Brotherhood in the White House!"

22. Aaron Klein, "Obama Adviser Speaks Alongside Defender of WTC Bombers," WND July 5, 2011, http://www.wnd.com/2011/07/319021/.

23. "Text: Obama's Speech to the Muslim World," June 4, 2009, CBS News, http://www. cbsnews.com/news/text-obamas-speech-to-the-muslim-world/; emphasis added.

24. AL-MA'IDAH (The Table Spread), http://quran.com/5/30-36.

25. Andrew Kirell, "GOP Rep. Gohmert: Obama Admin Has 'A Bunch of Muslim Brotherhood Members Giving Them Advice,'" *Mediaite* (blog), November 29, 2012, http://www.mediaite.com/online/gop-rep-gohmert-obama-admin-has-a-bunch-of-muslim-brotherhood-members-giving-them-advice/.

26. Mohamed Akram, "An Explanatory Memorandum on the General Strategic Goal for the Brotherhood in North America," May 19, 1991, on the website of the Investigative Project on Terrorism, http://www.investigativeproject.org/document/20-an-explanatory-memorandum-on-the-general.

CHAPTER 9: HANDS OFF

1. Adam Kredo, "DHS Secretly Allowed Suspects with Terror Ties Into Country," Washington Free Beacon, May 12, 2014, http://freebeacon.com/national-security/dhs-secretly-allowed-suspects-with-terror-ties-into-country/.

2. See "IIIT Hospitality Suite," on the website of the International Institute of Islamic Thought, accessed January 20, 2016, http://www.iiit.org/NewsEvents/News/tabid/62/articleType/ArticleView/articleId/317/IIIT-Hospitality-Suite.aspx.

3. Adam Kredo, "DHS Secretly Allowed Suspects with Terror Ties into Country," *The Counter Jihad Report* (blog), May 13, 2014, http://counterjihadreport.com/tag/dhs-hands-off-list/.

4. May 2012 e-mail chain between U.S. Immigration and Customs Enforcement (ICE) and U.S. Customs and Border Protection (CBP) as revealed by Sen. Charles Grassley in a letter to the Honorable Jeh Johnson, secretary of the Department of Homeland Security, February 3, 2014, http://www.grassley.senate.gov/sites/default/files/judiciary/upload/CBP%2C%2002-03-14%2C%20CEG%20to%20DHS%20%28border%20admissions%29%20%282%29.pdf.

5. "DHS Emails Reveal U.S. May Have Terrorist 'Hands Off' List," *Corruption Chronicles* (Judicial Watch blog), May 9, 2014, https://www.judicialwatch.org/blog/2014/05/dhs-emails-reveal-u-s-may-terrorist-hands-list/.

6. May 2012 e-mail chain between U.S. Immigration and Customs Enforcement (ICE) and U.S. Customs and Border Protection (CBP).

7. "Grassley Inquires About Terrorist 'Hands Off' list; CBP Promises to Brief," May 6, 2014, news release, website of Chuck Grassley, http://www.grassley.senate.gov/news/news-releases/grassley-inquires-about-terrorist-%E2%80%9Chands-off%E2%80%9D-list-cbp-promises-brief.

8. R. Gil Kerlikowske, letter to the Hon. Charles E. Grassley, April 10, 2014, http://www.judicialwatch.org/wp-content/uploads/2014/05/CBP-04-11-14-CBP-to-CEG-border-admissions-1.pdf, p. 1.

9. Ibid., 2.

10. Ibid.

11. Ibid.

12. Adam Kredo, "DHS Stonewalls Congress on 'Hands Off' Permitting Those with Terror Ties into U.S.," *Washington Free Beacon*, May 28, 2014, http://freebeacon.com/national-security/dhs-stonewalls-congress-on-hands-off-permitting-those-with-terror-ties-into-u-s/.

13. Kerry Picket, "Watchdog Sues DHS for Terrorist 'Hands Off' List," *Daily Caller*, April 1, 2015, http://dailycaller.com/2015/04/01/watchdog-sues-dhs-for-terrorist-hands-off-list/.

14. gmbwatch, "US Muslim Brotherhood Leader Scheduled to Speak at Tennessee Mosque," *Global Muslim Brotherhood Daily Watch*, October 24, 2013, http://www.globalmbwatch.com/2013/10/24/muslim-brotherhood-leader-scheduled-speak-tennessee-mosque/.

15. "Chart Lists Terrorists in U.S. Due to Lax Immigration Policies," *Corruption Chronicles*, August 18, 2015, http://www.judicialwatch.org/blog/2015/08/chart-lists-terrorists-in-u-s-due-to-lax-immigration-policies/.

16. [Redacted], Senior Advisor, Office for Civil Rights and Civil Liberties, to Margo Schlanger, memorandum, October 1, 2010, available online at https://www.aclu.org/files/borderquestioning/ACLU_BQ_000001.pdf.

17. Edwin Mora, "CAIR Says Gov't Asked Muslim Americans How Often They Prayed," cnsnews.com, April 24, 2012, http://www.cnsnews.com/news/article/cair-says-govt-asked-muslim-americans-how-often-they-prayed.

18. PRNewswire/USNewswire, "DHS to Probe CAIR-MI Complaints on Border Questioning of Muslims," PR Newswire, May 4, 2011, http://www.prnewswire.com/news-releases/dhs-to-probe-cair-mi-complaints-on-border-questioning-of-muslims-121282324.html.

19. [Redacted], e-mail to Margo Schlanger, May 3, 2011, captured at https://www.aclu.org/files/borderquestioning/ACLU_BQ_000412.pdf.

20. See the e-mail chain from and to Kareem Shora, May 4, 2011, at https://www.aclu.org/files/borderquestioning/ACLU_BQ_000277.pdf.

21. The American-Arab Anti-Discrimination Committee et al., letter to Margo Schlanger, October 2011, https://www.cair.com/images/pdf/Letter-to-DHS-CRCL-re-See-Something-Say-Something.pdf.

22. The FBI Academy, "The FBI's Guiding Principles: Touchstone Document on Training 2012," FBI website, accessed January 21, 2016, https://www.fbi.gov/about-us/training/the-fbis-guiding-principles. Emphasis added.

23. Cherri v. Mueller, Complaint and Jury Demand, in the United States District Court Eastern District of Michigan, Southern Division, pp. 9, 12, online at http://www.investigativeproject.org/documents/case_docs/2014.pdf.

24. Patrick Poole, "Pulitzer Prize Winner Hawks 'Protocols of the Elders of the Anti-Islam Movement' in the *New Yorker*," PJ Media, May 13, 2015, https://pjmedia.com/blog/pulitzer-prize-winners-journalistic-malpractice-over-the-u-s-muslim-brotherhood.

25. Kyle Shideler, "Mohammad Akram and Explanatory Memo Still Matter," *Counter Jihad Report*, May 18, 2015, http://counterjihadreport.com/tag/al-quds-international-foundation/.

CHAPTER 10: INVISIBLE SHRAPNEL

1. To hear the following conversation, see "Janet Napolitano Deportation of 'Person of Interest': 'Not Worthy of an Answer,'" YouTube video, 2:39, from an exchange between Jeff Duncan and Napolitano on April 18, 2013, posted by "LIVEFREE ORDIE," April 18, 2013, https://www.youtube.com/watch?v=MWOLfdeCJsc&feature=youtu.be.

2. Erica Ritz, "Janet Napolitano's Major Admission: Saudi Student Was Put on Watchlist," TheBlaze, April 23, 2013, http://www.theblaze.com/stories/2013/04/23/janet-napolitanos-major-admission-saudi-student-was-put-on-watch-list/.

3. See the video at Fox News, "Glenn Beck on the Boston Marathon bombing," Fox News, April 25, 2013, http://www.foxnews.com/transcript/2013/04/26/glenn-beck-boston-marathon-bombing/.

4. Wilson, "How is Fox News' Bret Baier covering the Saudi national story?" Glenn Beck website, April 24, 2013, http://www.glennbeck.com/2013/04/24/how-is-fox-news-bret-baier-covering-the-saudi-national-story/.

5. See Pamela Geller, "Co-Conspirators Muslim Student Associations (MSAs) Against 'Countering Violent Extremism' Measures," Pamela Geller blog, February 22, 2015, http://pamelageller.com/2015/02/co-conspirators-muslim-student-associations-msas-against-countering-violent-extremism-measures.html/.

6. See Erica Ritz, "Exclusive: Key Congressmen Request Classified Briefing on Saudi 'Person of Interest' in Boston Bombing," TheBlaze, April 21, 2013, http://www.theblaze.com/stories/2013/04/21/key-congressmen-requests-classified-briefing-on-saudi-person-of-interest-in-boston-bombing/.

7. Tiffany Gabbay, "ICE Official Calls TheBlaze Source's Claim on Deportation 'Categorically False'—But Says They Do Have Different Saudi in Custody," TheBlaze, April 18, 2013, http://www.theblaze.com/stories/2013/04/18/ice-official-responds-to-blaze-report-categorically-false/.

8. See "Alharbi v. TheBlaze, Inc. et al," at Justia Dockets & Filings, accessed January 21, 2016, https://dockets.justia.com/docket/massachusetts/madce/1:2014cv11550/159562.

9. Terrence McCoy, "Glenn Beck sued for defamation after calling victim of Boston Marathon bombings the 'money man' behind attack," Washington Post, April 1, 2014, https://www.washingtonpost.com/news/morning-mix/wp/2014/04/01/glenn-beck-sued-for-defamation-after-calling-victim-of-boston-marathon-bombings-the-money-man-behind-attack.

10. See "Bob Trent – TheBlazeTV – The Glenn Beck Program – 2013.04.24" YouTube video, 7:35, in which former special Agent Bob Trent explains what the 212 3 (B) note on the event file means and what it takes to change it, posted by Jared Law, April 25, 2013, https://www.youtube.com/watch?v=V-CuoUZjOC4.

11. Walid Shoebat, "Innocent" Saudi Has Ties To Several Al-Qaeda Terrorists," Shoebat.com, April 17, 2013, http://shoebat.com/2013/04/17/innocent-saudi-has-ties-to-several-al-qaeda-terrorists/.

12. Christine Stuart, "Glenn Beck Defamation Case Is Going Strong," Courthouse News Service, December 4, 2014, http://www.courthousenews.com/2014/12/04/glenn-beck-defamation-case-is-going-strong.htm.

13. See "ALHARBI v. BECK," at Leagle, accessed January 21, 2016, http://www.leagle.com/decision/In%20FDCO%2020150507B76/ALHARBI%20v.%20BECK.

14. Steven J. J. Weisman, "Glenn Beck Defamation Lawsuit Update," Talkers magazine, June 18, 2015, http://www.talkers.com/2015/06/18/glenn-beck-defamation-lawsuit-update/.

15. Mark Tapson, "AAFIA SIDDIQUI: REPAYING OPPORTUNITY WITH TERROR," FrontPage Mag, April 29, 2013, http://www.frontpagemag.com/fpm/187583/aafia-siddiqui-repaying-opportunity-terror-mark-tapson.

16. Paul Sperry, "Boston bombers' mosque tied to ISIS," *New York Post*, September 7, 2014, http://nypost.com/2014/09/07/jihadi-behind-beheading-videos-linked-to-notorious-us-mosque/.

17. Robert S. McCaw, "Written Statement of the Council on American-Islamic Relations on the Boston Bombings: A First Look: Submitted to the United States House Committee on Homeland Security May 9, 2013," http://www.cair.com/images/governmentaffairs/Boston-Bombings-A-First-Look.pdf, 2, 4.

CHAPTER 11: KILL THE MESSENGER

1. See TMZ staff, "Willie Robertson: SUCK IT OBAMA! I'M A WAY BETTER TIPPER!" TMZ, February 11, 2014, http://www.tmz.com/2014/02/11/duck-dynasty-star-willie-robertson-sean-hannity-ted-cruz-steak-dinner-conservative/.

2. Bahaa El Tawel, "US addresses embassy staff member's detention," *Cairo Post*, February 13, 2014, http://thecairopost.youm7.com/news/88523/news/us-addresses-embassy-staff-members-detention.

3. Sam Taylor, "White House Shoots Down Petition to Declare Muslim Brotherhood a Terrorist Organization," *Washington Free Beacon*, December 1, 2014, http://freebeacon.com/national-security/white-house-shoots-down-petition-to-declare-muslim-brotherhood-a-terrorist-organization/.

4. Lally Weymouth, "Rare interview with Egyptian Gen. Abdel Fatah al-Sissi," Washington Post, August 3, 2013, https://www.washingtonpost.com/world/middle_east/rare-interview-with-egyptian-gen-abdel-fatah-al-sissi/2013/08/03/a77eb37c-fbc4-11e2-a369-d1954abcb7e3_story.html.

5. "U.S. Muslim Groups to Launch New Council with Political Census," news release, PR Newswire, March 10, 2014, http://www.prnewswire.com/news-releases/us-muslim-groups-to-launch-new-council-with-political-census-249291411.html.

6. Ibid.

7. See "The Mosque Foundation," the Clarion Project, November 3, 2013, http://www.clarionproject.org/analysis/mosque-foundation.

8. Raymond Ibrahim, "U.S. Admits Contact with Terrorist Brotherhood to 'Support People of Egypt,'" RaymondIbrahim.com, March 15, 2014, http://www.raymondibrahim.com/2014/03/15/obama-admin-supports-egyptian-people-by-supporting-brotherhood-terrorists/.

9. The Homeland Security Committee, "Homeland Security Committee Releases Report on Boston Marathon Bombings," Homeland Security Committee website, March 26, 2014, https://homeland.house.gov/press/homeland-security-committee-releases-report-boston-marathon-bombings/.

10. See Thomas H. Keen et al., *The 9/11 Commission Report*, http://www.9-11commission.gov/report/911Report.pdf.

11. Citizens' Commission On Benghazi, *How America Switched Sides in the War on Terror* (April 22, 2014), 4, http://www.aim.org/benghazi/wp-content/uploads/2014/04/CCB-Interim-Report-4-22-2014.pdf

12. Ibid., 5.

13. Ryan Mauro, "National Intel Misled Congress About Brotherhood Contacts," the Clarion Project, April 23, 2014, http://www.clarionproject.org/analysis/national-intel-misled-congress-about-brotherhood-contacts.

14. See United States Senate Subcommittee on Financial and Contracting Oversight, Committee on Homeland Security and Governmental Affairs, Investigation into Allegations of Misconduct by the Former Acting and Deputy Inspector General of the Department of Homeland Security (April 24, 2014), at http://www.ronjohnson. senate.gov/public/_cache/files/4f916bda-8373-4ac8-b2cd-4d0ba115e279/fco-report-investigation-into-allegations-of-misconduct-by-the-former-acting-and-deputy-inspector-general-of-the-department-of-homeland.pdf.

15. L. Paige Whitaker, "The Whistleblower Protection Act: An Overview," March 12, 2007, summary, http://fas.org/sgp/crs/natsec/RL33918.pdf.

16. Kerry Picket, "DHS 'Hands Off Terrorist List' Investigation in Hands of Inspector General," Breitbart, May 21, 2014, http://www.breitbart.com/national-security/2014/05/21/dhs-hands-off-terrorist-list-matter-in-hands-of-ig/.

17. Ibid.

18. Jeh Johnson, memorandum to all DHS employees, May 20, 2014, https://www.oig.dhs. gov/assets/PDFs/OIG_John_Sign_Coop_052014.pdf.

CHAPTER 12: UPHOLDING MY OATH

1. See "18 U.S. Code § 1030 – Fraud and related activity in connection with computers," on the website of Cornell University's Legal Information Institute, accessed January 22, 2016, https://www.law.cornell.edu/uscode/text/18/1030.

2. See "Violation of Privacy Laws," LegalMatch website, accessed January 22, 2016, http:// www.legalmatch.com/law-library/article/violation-of-privacy-lawyers.html.

3. See Robert Barsocchini, "DIA Docs: West Wants a 'Salafist Principality in Eastern Syria'?" Washington's Blog, May 23, 2015, http://www.washingtonsblog.com/2015/05/dia-docs-west-wants-a-salafist-principality-in-eastern-syria.html; and http://www.judicialwatch. org/wp-content/uploads/2015/05/Pg.-291-Pgs.-287-293-JW-v-DOD-and-State-14-812-DOD-Release-2015-04-10-final-version11.pdf, point 8C.

4. "Obama's Intel Chief: Muslim Brotherhood Non-Violent, 'Secular' Group," Fox Nation, February 11, 2011, http://nation.foxnews.com/culture/2011/02/10/obamas-intel-chief-muslim-brotherhood-non-violent-secular-group.

5. United States Declaration of Independence.

ABOUT THE AUTHORS

PHILIP HANEY studied Arabic culture and language while working as a scientist in the Middle East before he was hired as a founding member of the Department of Homeland Security in 2003. After becoming an armed Customs and Border Protection officer, he served two tours of duty at the National Targeting Center near Washington, DC, where he quickly was promoted to its Advanced Targeting Team. For more than forty years, he specialized in Islamic theology and the strategy and tactics of the global Islamic movement. He retired honorably in July 2015.

ART MOORE is a news editor for online news giant WND. With a background in radio, newspaper, and magazine reporting, he joined WND shortly after 9/11. He has reported extensively on counterterrorism issues since then.

INDEX

CPSIA information can be obtained
at www.ICGtesting.com
Printed in the USA
BVHW030035210221
600719BV00003B/18